*Soft*
*Boundaries*

# SOFT BOUNDARIES

## Re-Visioning the Arts and Aesthetics in American Education

### CLAIRE DETELS

Ralph A. Smith, Advisory Editor

**BERGIN & GARVEY**
Westport, Connecticut • London

**Library of Congress Cataloging-in-Publication Data**

Detels, Claire Janice, 1953–
    Soft boundaries : re-visioning the arts and aesthetics in American
education / Claire Detels.
        p.    cm.
    Includes bibliographical references and index.
    ISBN 0–89789–666–1 (alk. paper)
    1. Arts—Study and teaching—United States.   2. Aesthetics—Study
and teaching—United States.   3. Education—United States—
Curricula.   I. Title.
LB1591.5.U6D48        1999
700'.71—dc21            99–14844

British Library Cataloguing in Publication Data is available.

Library of Congress Catalog Card Number: 99–14844
ISBN: 0–89789–666–1

First published in 1999

Bergin & Garvey, 88 Post Road West, Westport, CT 06881
An imprint of Greenwood Publishing Group, Inc.
www.greenwood.com

Printed in the United States of America

The paper used in this book complies with the
Permanent Paper Standard issued by the National
Information Standards Organization (Z39.48–1984).

10 9 8 7 6 5 4 3 2 1

It is therefore one of the most important tasks of culture to subject human beings to form even in their purely physical lives, and to make them aesthetic as far as ever the realm of Beauty can extend, since the moral condition can be developed only from the aesthetic, not from the physical condition.

—Friedrich Schiller,
*Letters on the Aesthetic Education of Man* (1799)

# Contents

# Preface

The roots of this book go back to two crucial influences I encountered in 1991. The most important influence was my experience at the 1991 NEH Summer Institute on Philosophy and the Histories of the Arts at San Francisco State University. There I shared a very stimulating five weeks with almost forty other academics: mainly philosophers specializing in aesthetics, with a few arts historians (including myself in music) along for the occasionally bumpy ride. What I discovered that summer—in addition to learning a great deal from Director Arthur Danto and others at the institute—was how strongly different disciplinary backgrounds and training affect one's perception, not only of what the answers are to questions about the arts but also what the questions should be. The experience of trying as a music historian to communicate meaningfully about the arts with analytic philosophers for those five weeks left an indelible impression on me. If we historians and philosophers had so much trouble communicating with each other, how could we possibly communicate with the public? I began to investigate ways in which specialization in the arts and aesthetics had led to academic autism: the loss of the ability and even the desire to communicate outside of one's speciality. Those investigations eventually led to this book.

My other main influence in 1991 was reading Susan McClary's groundbreaking work of feminist musicology *Feminine Endings: Music, Gender, and Sexuality* (published the same year). McClary's writing about gender in music and, more generally, the cultural connections of musical styles kept me reading all night, something a musicology monograph had never done before; and it introduced me to major works and concepts in feminist theory that have influenced the ideas in this book greatly. In fact, the concept of "soft boundaries" came to me first as a paradigm for a feminist approach to musical aesthetics, designed to support and spread the new gender-conscious analysis that McClary and others were doing.

McClary's work has since turned out to be a major influence on the discipline of musicology, to musicology's benefit. What impressed me most, however, was the fully interdisciplinary character of McClary's thinking and research. Many of the chapters in the book had appeared previously in interdisciplinary journals and were accordingly aimed at a broader audience than just music specialists, but with no apparent loss in intellectual depth. On the contrary, she raised very profound questions about the meaning and evolution of musical styles. I found McClary's approach to be a breath of fresh air compared to the narrower focus of traditional musicological research. It suggested to me that serious thinking about the arts need not remain isolated in an academic ghetto marked with a sign reading specialists only. That metaphorical sign was restricting communication about and participation in a necessary human experience, leaving the public inadequate access to any but the simplest, most popular musical styles. I began to think about why that isolation had occurred, how it manifested itself at each educational level from kindergarten through graduate school, and how it might be alleviated.

An additional influence on my thinking about specialization at this time was philosopher Bruce Wilshire's book *The Moral Collapse of the University* (1990), which explores psychological motivations for the exclusivity of academic disciplines and their specialists. In Wilshire's view, some of the energy and excitement that specialists feel about their disciplines comes from their fulfillment of primitive identity needs for affirmation by other insiders and, at the same time, their exclusion of outsiders. This process of "mimetic engulfment," to use Wilshire's colorful term, has the unfortunate result of (1) encouraging specialists to communicate mainly with each other, and (2) discouraging students and the general public from learning how to think and act more philosophically—the exact opposite of what philosophy teachers presumably want. Applying Wilshire's ideas to the arts and aesthetics, it seemed that the specialists there were also engaged at least to some extent in discouraging widespread understanding and appreciation of the arts and aesthetic experience rather than encouraging it. The fault was not with the individual teachers but with the exclusionary structure of the curriculum in the arts and aesthetics. The hard boundaries of the disciplines were keeping most people out and encouraging the few specialists who were inside the disciplinary boundaries to think and write about their subjects in exclusionary ways. It was a vicious cycle that could only be broken by challenging the underlying assumption that hard-boundaried specialization is the only route to increased knowledge and understanding. I began to think of softer more permeable boundaries as preferable to hard boundaries, and I began writing this book.

I received invaluable advice and encouragement in writing this book from many people in and out of the university system. I wish to particularly thank NEH Institute Directors Arthur Danto, Anita Silvers, Jerrold Levinson, Noel Carroll; faculty members and lecturers Kwame Anthony Appiah, Sally Banes, Norman Bryson, David Carrier, Whitney Davis, Lydia Goehr, Goran Hermeren, Dale Jamieson, Peter Kivy, Joseph Margolis, Julius Moravsik, Anthony Savile,

Leo Treitler, Kendall Walton, and Richard Wollheim; and the other participants of the Institute on Philosophy and the Histories of the Arts for the influence they had on the formation of my ideas. I also thank Frank Scheide for his help in creating and teaching our interdisciplinary Introduction to the Arts and Aesthetics at the University of Arkansas in Fayetteville; and to arts faculty members Marilyn Nelson, Cyrus Sutherland, Pat Romanov, Tina Redd, Ethel Goodstein, Ken Stout, and Terry Brusstar for their help with the course. Thanks are also due to University of Arkansas colleagues Gerald Sloan, David Saladino, Lori Holyfield, and Sandra Edwards for their suggestions on individual chapters and Larry Burlew and Richard Lee for their suggestions on the overall organization and flow of the book. In addition, I've profited from discussions with colleagues at the University of Arkansas Teaching and Faculty Support Center and with present and former public schoolteachers Betty Butcher, Marianne Wilson, Paula Van Hoose, Nancy Umiker, and Millie Peters. Presentations of parts of this material at meetings of the American Society for Aesthetics and the College Society of Music resulted in further valuable input from philosophers Hilde Hein, Jeffrey Geller, Douglas Dempster, Jerrold Levinson, Flo Leibowitz, and Renée Lorraine; and from educators Ralph Smith and David A. Williams. I particularly thank Jennifer Judkins, Mary Reichling, Wayne Bowman, Paul Woodford, and Angela La Porte for their comments on late drafts of the manuscript.

I've also received crucial support and insights from family members who are knowledgeable in different aspects of the arts and aesthetics. My aunt Mimi Detels is a docent at the Los Angeles County Museum, my tour guide for all Los Angeles arts events, and the patient reader of an early draft of this manuscript. My sister Polly Detels is a singer and historian who taught me to love Barbra Streisand, Peter, Paul, and Mary, and Gabriel Fauré in that order, and who gave me my lifelong love of vocal accompanying. My brother-in-law Charles Embry is a fine poet, gardener, and movie enthusiast, in addition to his day job teaching political science; our discussions about Plato and education have been very stimulating and influential to the ideas in this book. I also thank my father, Paul Detels, whose legal career trained him to be able to memorize and supply the names of obscure artists of all disciplines and times whenever the situation calls for such erudition (and sometimes when it doesn't); and my mother, Bette Detels, who has become an award-winning photographer since her retirement from social work and whose fascination with all the arts has inspired my own. Last but not least, I thank my husband, Lewis Chamness, a counselor and a great lover of poetry and philosophy, for his steady insistence that whatever ideas I'm thinking about are brilliant and that whatever I've just written is the best thing I've ever done. Without Lewis, this book would be impossible, and life would be no fun.

# Introduction

This book is an expression of my concern for the neglect of the arts and aesthetics within American education. By "the arts" I mean creative human expressions in sensually perceivable media such as music, painting, sculpture, film, poetry, and drama, among others. By "aesthetics" I mean intellectual inquiry into perception in the arts and other sensory experiences or, more simply, the practice of making sense of sensory experience.[1]

Love of the arts in general and of music in particular has been an essential part of my life. Experiencing and thinking about the arts is the main basis with which I have tried to understand who I am as a human being and what it means to be alive. Studying the history of the arts has taught me how people of other times and places have thought, felt, and lived; how ideas and ways of living differ from one culture to the next; and what we human beings have learned and failed to learn about getting along with each other. More than any other field of study, the arts have taught me about relationships among people and nations.

Unfortunately I can't say that I owe this understanding to our educational system. Indeed there is very little opportunity for experiencing or studying the arts in American education. In K–12 and college-level education, the arts are represented as single-disciplinary practices, unconnected with each other and with the core curriculum and oriented more to the training of specialists than to the education of general students and the public. The closest we get to an integrated study of the arts is in the field of aesthetics. Unfortunately, aesthetics is taught only at the college level as a subdiscipline of philosophy, and generally involves specialized philosophical debate over the meaning of concepts in a manner too far removed from ordinary experience for general students and the public to understand.

The poor representation of the arts and aesthetics in American education is a sign of our highly materialistic times, an era when the idea that whatever can't be quantified—especially in monetary terms—isn't important has pretty much overtaken our lives. Because the arts and aesthetic experience are not easily quantified or translated into monetary gain, their uses are not readily appreciated and not easily incorporated into contemporary educational standards and tests. Subjects that are more easily quantified—such as competency at math and reading—receive the most attention in K–12 and college-level education, while the arts and aesthetics are mainly left to chance.

For decades now, the overly materialistic character of American education has been criticized by a wide range of educational experts, including Jerome Bruner, Howard Gardner, Neil Postman, Harry Broudy, Robert Coles, and Charles Fowler. Neil Postman has been particularly eloquent about the soullessness of American education in his recent *End of Education: Redefining the Value of School* (1995); Postman says that economic utility, science, and technology have acted as false gods for American educators, politicians, and the public, while values for individual and societal growth and harmony traditionally studied in the arts and humanities have been sorely neglected. Even Bill Clinton, "the education president," has justified education mainly on pragmatic grounds, as training for the more technologically-skilled jobs of the future.[2]

Yet, while the critiques of Postman and others have been widely read, they have had little effect on our educational system because they have failed to address a crucial underlying reason for the marginalization of the humanities (including the arts and aesthetics). That reason is the fragmented, single-disciplinary structure of our educational curricula and institutions. This structure treats the humanities as separate disciplines of study like any other (except that they're far less lucrative), rather than as what they are or, at least, should be: the main source for the understanding of values and meaning in our lives. Of all the humanities, the arts and aesthetics have been particularly hurt by this fragmented structure. They have come to be represented in our educational system as a long list of separate, highly technical subjects taught by and for specialists, instead of the means through which all students may come to terms with artistic creativity and sensory experience individually and communally.

According to my analysis, the current state of affairs in education results from a paradigm—that is, a structural model of how to think and act—according to which hard, strict boundaries between concepts and disciplines are automatically preferred to the practice of seeing and seeking relationships among them. The paradigm of hard boundaries is a materialistic one, leading to a higher valuation of whatever can be strictly defined and quantified, or—to use the philosophical term—reified; and a corresponding lower valuation of whatever cannot be so easily defined.

In education, the paradigm of hard boundaries goes back to the scientific revolution in Western thought and the corollary rise of the academic specialist in place of the more traditional Renaissance scholar, whose knowledge was assumed to extend through all major fields of study.

As I will explain further in chapter 1, the hard-boundaried paradigm has led to great advances of knowledge in the area of the sciences, but its results in the humanities have been more damaging than productive, leading to the development of separate disciplines, methodologies, terminologies, and journals, and a corollary loss of communication with outside disciplines and the general public. In the case of the arts and aesthetics, hard boundaries have not only led to separate disciplines, they have also resulted in separate subdisciplines of intellectual study and studio practice within each arts discipline, a marginalization of the arts and aesthetics within the broader areas of philosophy, history, and the humanities, and, worst of all, an enormous gap between the specialists of the separate arts disciplines and the general public. Recently, this gap between academic arts specialists and the public has become so large that the public has for the most part stopped paying attention to the specialists, instead developing and patronizing only the most approachable arts of popular culture. At the same time, the arts of popular, culture are unwisely ignored by academic specialists, whose analytical skills could be invaluable in helping the public understand and, where necessary, resist their powerful influence.

The gap between arts specialists and the public is a growing concern as we move into the twenty-first century, an age of "virtual reality." In the coming century, students who receive little or no education in the arts and aesthetics will have increasing trouble understanding the power and influence of the new sensually-immersive technologies of virtual reality over their minds and lives. The ultimate danger is that without such education we will lose the ability to think about our sensory experiences; that, in effect, they will "think" us.

In order to address the isolation and fragmentation of the arts and aesthetics in American education, I believe we need a new approach to thinking and learning about the arts: an approach that will create practitioners and educators who can communicate and interact with the general public about the meaning and power of artistic imagery and other sensory experiences in the contemporary world and the past, as well as being able to maintain old traditions and create new ones. The need is so great and so distant from current practice that it requires a change of paradigm, from the hard boundaries of contemporary education to soft boundaries—between disciplines of the arts, between subdisciplines of history, theory, and practice within the separate art disciplines, and between the arts and other disciplines of the humanities and sciences. The fact that the old paradigm of hard boundaries is a historical model that is no longer beneficial must be recognized, and the new paradigm—soft boundaries—must be understood and spread to practice. This is an ambitious venture.

Fortunately, recognition of the drawbacks of the hard-boundaried paradigm may already be under way. Insights from poststructural theory about the constructed nature of reality and the contingent nature of what once seemed to be clearly definable truths have affected research in many academic disciplines. Thomas Kühn's much cited *Structure of Scientific Revolutions* (1970) has influenced scholars in the humanities, social sciences, and the natural sciences to produce challenging postmodern approaches to many traditional disciplines, as in postmodern anthropology and biology and poststructural and feminist literary theory, art criticism, and more recently, musicology. The term "paradigm" has been used so often in this challenging work that it has become subject to criticism as jargon. "Buddy, Can You a Paradigm?" was the title of a recent *New York Times* review of one of these works.

There has also been much discussion of the need for curricular reform in the arts, as recognition of their marginalization in our current academic system has risen. Most notably, when the initial 1990 version of the Goals 2000: Educate America Act was released with no provision for arts education (outside of the literary forms covered in English and reading classes), arts educators were forced to consider how and why the arts had become so marginalized and what to do about it. In 1994, a consortium of arts educators from music, dance, drama, and the visual arts released a set of National Standards for Arts Education which were then incorporated into the Goals 2000 program passed by Congress in 1995. Unfortunately, since the hard-boundaried paradigm was still operative, these educators were not able to create the kind of unified program in arts education that might have resulted in long-term improvement; rather, they created separate standards for teaching music, dance, drama and visual arts—even though teachers in each of these disciplines are in most cases not present on a school faculty. Thus, the resulting standards cannot be implemented in many cases; there are literally no teachers to teach them. Real improvement will require a more soft-boundaried approach to instruction, allowing for interdisciplinary instruction in the arts and interdisciplinary integration of the arts and aesthetics into the general curriculum as well as the availability of specialized study. (This will be discussed further in chapter 8, "Towards Integrative, Interdisciplinary Education in the Arts and Aesthetics.")

My idea of soft boundaries involves interdisciplinarity, but it is different from the concept of interdisciplinarity as it's often practiced, with traditionally trained scholars team-teaching or doing brief research projects involving a discipline outside their specialty. It is also different from "no boundaries": a land of no disciplines, no standards and, worse yet, of Rush Limbaugh ties. Soft boundaries is, rather, a paradigm for valuing and encouraging thought and communication across the boundaries of disciplines and concepts, yet without disregarding the value of boundaries, judgments, and specialization in furthering knowledge. With soft boundaries, we may continue to use specialization in the arts and aesthetics to further knowledge and skills in separate disciplines without reifying those boundaries in a way that deters inquiry and development of interdisciplinary knowledge and skills. Soft boundaries will allow for the continuing development of specialists while also providing nonspecialists the opportunity to learn more fully about the arts of the past and present and to develop the artistic and aesthetic competence necessary for understanding the more complex sensually immersive technologies of the twenty-first century.

The biggest problem I have faced in writing this book was figuring out how to bring all the soft-boundary issues I wanted to address together into one fairly coherent whole. Some of the issues dealt with aesthetics, some with historical canons of the arts, some with interdisciplinary arts education, and some with music in particular. The problem was how to bridge the gap between these usually separate issues and bring them into one book. The biggest gap was the one between my ideas on music and those on the arts and aesthetics in general. After much sorting and resorting of chapters, I decided to make a kind of sandwich, with music mainly in the middle and the arts and aesthetics in general in the outer sections. Thus Part I, "The Boundaries of the Arts and Aesthetics," gives a broad picture of the hard boundaries of the arts and aesthetics, followed by an examination of boundaries within the single discipline of music in Part II. Part III returns to the broad picture with recommendations for interdisciplinary, integrative reforms, first in music and then in the arts and aesthetics in general—reforms that may help prepare us to better understand the sensually immersive technologies of the twenty-first century as well as the arts of our own time. The special emphasis on music in this organization is present for two reasons: (1) music is my specialty, so I am most knowledgeable about its conceptual and disciplinary structures, and (2) music is the art with the strongest representation in K–12 education and, thus, the art with the greatest effect on the educational system as a whole. While it might seem more logical to start with the musical microcosm and move from there to the larger picture, I didn't want to discourage nonspecialists with details on the functioning of music departments before painting the big picture. Rather, I wanted to give all readers, including music specialists, a sense of the fuller context of our educational problems before getting into the messy details.

Another gap I have attempted to bridge is that between aesthetic education and education in the arts. Aesthetic and artistic education overlap, but they are not the same thing: education in the arts is learning about history, theory, and practice of the arts, while aesthetic education is learning about our intellectual, emotional, and sensory experience of the arts and other sensory stimuli. Originally the emphasis in aesthetics was on cognitive (mental) judgments of beauty, but avant-garde developments in the arts of the nineteenth and twentieth centuries have led to an expansion of the concept of aesthetic judgment to include experiences of sublimity (i.e., awe of the monumental) and ugliness.

American education in aesthetics and the arts is segmented into college-level aesthetics—taught mainly as an elective in philosophy departments—and classes in the history, theory, and practice of individual art forms—taught mainly to arts majors in separate departments of the arts. (As in K–12 education, literary arts receive the best coverage due to their inclusion within general language arts study.) Although aesthetic knowledge is relevant to all art forms (as well as to other disciplines in the humanities and sciences), the training of arts specialists in aesthetics varies from some emphasis in the literary and visual arts to little or no emphasis in the performing arts of music, drama, and dance. As a result, there is almost no contact and communication between philosophers of the arts and historians, theorists, and practitioners of the performing arts disciplines (and very little contact in the literary and visual arts).

The gap between aesthetics and the individual arts disciplines is part of the problem of hard boundaries this book addresses, so I had to try to bridge the gap—to soften the boundaries—between them. The approach I recommend in this book is, simply stated, to join arts education and aesthetic education at all levels for courses offered to nonspecialists, while maintaining separate higher-level training for specialists (majors) at college- and graduate-level studies. Under this approach, aesthetic experience, concepts, and questions will act as a foundation for education in the arts at all levels and may also be used to enrich scientific and historical inquiry into nature and history. Without aesthetic understanding, after all, nature is without beauty and meaning; and without the arts, history and the other social sciences become a dull recitation of facts and theories. Teaching about other cultures of the past and present must include examination of their arts and their aesthetic values in comparison with our own. If we are to use our human capabilities to their fullest, we must learn to be artistically aware and creative. It is not realistic or right for the schools to attend only to our logical and verbal skills, because thinking, feeling adults must be able to do more than add and spell.[3]

The final gap I have faced in writing this book is that between feminist theory and other forms of scholarship. As mentioned in the Preface, "soft boundaries" came to me first as an explicitly feminist concept for understanding music. Two of the chapters of this book (5 and 6), were initially published with the term "feminist" in their titles and were directed primarily to exploring the implications of feminist theory for music. However, as I became more and more familiar with other theoretical approaches and with the full implications of soft boundaries, I decided that leaving it as an explicitly feminist paradigm would defeat my purpose of trying to, yes, soften the boundaries among scholarly communities and the public as much as possible. The book I initially considered writing—"Soft Boundaries: A Feminist Approach to Education in the Arts and Aesthetics"—would have been a book categorized and marketed under the heading of feminist studies, whereas I wanted the reach to be broader than that. I did not and do not wish to hide the influence that feminist theory has had on my thinking and on the softening of boundaries in many academic areas. As it happens, though, feminist theory harmonizes so well with new ideas from post-structural theory, cognitive learning theory, and other recent theoretical approaches of the postmodern era, that it is sometimes hard to say what ideas have emerged from where.

Of course, there are differences among these approaches, but getting into the definition of those differences in the context of this book would have changed my focus from improving education towards precisely the technical issues that I think have most alienated those outside the disciplines of the arts and aesthetics. So, in short, I decided to leave the term "feminist" out of my title and to concentrate instead on making the ideas here clear to the widest possible community. My writing may as a result err on the simplistic side, but I would rather that than to limit my audience to a few specialists. The idea, as my favorite sweatshirt proudly proclaims, is to "Eschew Obfuscation."

On the other hand, I have drawn one fairly hard boundary in this book by primarily addressing it to American education. While some of the material may be relevant to educational systems outside the United States, I decided it was a big enough challenge to analyze American education in the arts and aesthetics without trying to generalize for other systems as well. Also, I believe there are particular factors in American culture and education that set it apart and make it predictive of events to come elsewhere in the world. For example, the problem of teaching students to function in a global culture has come to American education in a uniquely challenging way, and what we do with it will influence education all over the world. Historically Americans have been rather insular, learning only one language and thinking of culture—when we think of it—as European in origin. In the late twentieth century, our influences and contacts have become much more global, involving growing relationships with Asian, African, and South American countries. Learning in the arts and aesthetics can and should play an important role in a globally directed education. Appreciating the aesthetic values and arts of another culture is probably the best introduction to understanding and cooperating with people of other cultures. Achieving such understanding and cooperation among people of diverse cultural backgrounds may now be our most important challenge as a society. Neglecting to provide sufficient aesthetic and artistic opportunities for cross-cultural understanding in our educational system may be tantamount to leaving racism—from which this country has suffered greatly—unchallenged.[4]

Another unique factor in American education is that the United States has been the leading country in the development of late-industrial, consumer capitalism. At this stage, the American economy no longer runs only on the manufacturing of products for commercial gain, but also on manufacturing the illusion of need for these products through the multibillion-dollar industry of advertising. The way the advertising industry manufactures need is essentially artistic: through the manipulation of visual and other sensual imagery in an attractive or otherwise interesting manner. Of course, the reason they do it is for increasing sales and profits, regardless of the value or need for the products advertised.

Thus, through advertising, artistic imagery is playing a central influence in our daily choices and in our overall economy, at a time we are receiving little or no instruction in understanding the power of that influence. While the arts have often been subject to monetary concerns and influences, they have never been as subject to commercialism as they are in American advertising. It is as if advertising and the arts were bound in an unholy marriage, in which the arts, like almost everything in our culture, are only allowed to serve monetary gain.

Given the central role of advertising in our economy, the stakes for creating an artistically, aesthetically competent public in late-industrial America have become very high. We have reached a point where the ability to make sense of sensory experience—the essence of aesthetic competence—has become essential to leading a rich and thoughtful life. We have become consumers of artistic imagery and sensory experience in everything that we do, every thought that we have, every decision we make. Technological advances have led to prominent, powerful use of sensually immersive imagery and media to influence us in every aspect of our lives. As we stand at the beginning of the twenty-first century, virtual reality is around the corner, and without aesthetic competence, we will very likely drown in it. With a softer-boundaried approach, however, we may begin to provide the artistic and aesthetic education that students and the general public need in order to understand and productively engage with the complex sensory experiences of the future.

# Part I

# The Boundaries of the Arts
# and Aesthetics

The chapters in this section identify and discuss the problems created by the hard boundaries between the disciplines of the arts and aesthetics, especially in their separation of historical inquiry—conducted within the individual disciplines of the arts—and philosophical inquiry—conducted within the philosophical subdiscipline of aesthetics. Chapter 1, "Hard Times, Hard Boundaries," explores the roots of our hard disciplinary boundaries and the ways they have hurt American education in the arts and aesthetics; it also proposes a new paradigm of soft boundaries. Chapter 2, "History, Philosophy, and the Canons of the Arts," questions the hard-boundaried separation of history and philosophy in the study of the arts and explores the failure of historians and historical canons—currently the main approach to academic teaching of the arts—to come to terms with philosophical questions about meaning in the arts. Chapter 3, "Uses of History in Some Recent Aesthetic Writings," examines the corollary failure of philosophers in aesthetics to come to terms with the actualities of art history and practice in their definitions of concepts. I will return to the broad interdisciplinary concerns of Part I with some concrete suggestions for change in Part III, chapter 8, "Towards Integrative, Interdisciplinary Education in the Arts and Aesthetics."

# 1

# Hard Times, Hard Boundaries

Since the scientific and industrial revolutions, life in the West has been characterized by increasing specialization: a tendency toward ever-higher standards of competence for ever-narrower goals. Ernest Gellner has define this phenomenon as "single-purpose, instrumental/rational activity," in which individuals define and pursue specialized goals with far greater efficiency and uniformity than is possible in the "multipurposed" behavior of less technologically advanced societies.[5] In industry, specialization has brought us the production line and a constant growth of technology and new consumer products. In academics, specialization has brought us a proliferation of knowledge in every imaginable area of human thought, leading to ever-increasing specialization as disciplines and subdisciplines expand beyond the ability of individual scholars to understand them.

## THE EFFECT OF SPECIALIZATION ON EDUCATION IN THE HUMANITIES

Specialization has taken root in academics in part because the needs for and benefits of academic specialization are so obvious. With specialization, the knowledge and skills in a discipline seem to be constantly growing, as new generations of specialists and specializations arise. In his *History of Knowledge* (1991), Charles Van Doren explains the historical development of academic specialization:

The Aristotelian ideal of the educated person, "critical" in all or almost all branches of knowledge, survived for centuries as the aim of a liberal education. . . . [But t]he twen-

An earlier version of this chapter appeared in the Spring 1999 issue of *Philosophy of Music Education Review* under the title "Hard Boundaries and the Marginalization of the Arts in American Education."

tieth century has seen radical change in this traditional scheme of education. The failure of the Renaissance to produce successful "Renaissance men" did not go unnoticed. If such men as Leonardo, Pico, Bacon, and many others almost as famous could not succeed in their presumed dream of knowing all there was to know about everything, then lesser men should not presume to try. The alternative became self-evident: achieve expertise in one field while others attained expertise in theirs. Much easier to accomplish, this course led to a more comfortable academic community. Now an authority in one field need compete only with experts in his field.[6]

Before the twentieth century, the traditional liberal arts education was one in which the humanities—literature, languages, philosophy, and the arts—were the major focus of learning: the way in which young students were introduced to the cultural heritage, values, and communication skills of their society. With the rise of specialization in higher education in the nineteenth century, however, the humanities became separate from the natural sciences and social sciences, and separate departments within each of these areas were created to define and control knowledge in their respective disciplines. Along with the rise of separate academic disciplines and departments, the college curriculum changed from one in which all students had a humanities-based liberal arts curriculum to a specialized experience in which students picked a major and did a large part of their course work in that discipline.[7] Humanities disciplines were initially the most popular majors, but they gradually lost students to the sciences and, with the expansion of the American land-grant university into practical education, to majors in agriculture, mining, engineering, and business. By the mid-twentieth century the concept of the "liberal arts education" was losing power to the individual disciplines, which in turn exercised more and more control over the faculty who taught and trained within them, including influence over their credentialling, the publication of their work, the awarding of research grants and honors, and the tenure and promotion process. Prestige and power also came to vary widely from one discipline to the next, with faculty in the sciences generally receiving higher pay and lighter teaching loads than those in the humanities.

While academic specialization has served a crucial role in the advancement of knowledge since the Renaissance, it has also become a potentially destructive force in cases where specialists have become so narrowly focused within their disciplines as to lose the ability to communicate their knowledge to others. In his book *The Moral Collapse of the University*, philosopher Bruce Wilshire argues that specialization has reached such an extreme in twentieth-century American education. In his view, academic specialization in the United States has become "professionalization," with the disciplines acting as elite, closed communities whose exclusive "purification rites" answer identity needs of their own members instead of advancing learning for the larger community.[8]

The extremes of academic specialization described by Wilshire may be considered "hard-boundaried" extremes. That is, they are based on a paradigm in which clear-cut boundaries between disciplines and concepts are automatically preferred to softer, more permeable boundaries, regardless of their validity or the educational results. The paradigm of hard boundaries has worked fairly well in scientific disciplines where strict definitions of experimental controls, variables, and results are essential to the growth of knowledge. In the humanities, though, the results have been less fortunate. Because of the influence of the hard-boundaried paradigm over all academic disciplines, many humanities disciplines and scholars have attempted to emulate the hard-boundaried clarity of the scientific method with emphasis on quantifiable issues and methods, ignoring the more ambiguous areas of humanities research. But there is one inherent ambiguity in the humanities that cannot be evaded: its dependence on the communication and interpretation of ideas among human beings. The humanities must communicate to people if they are to be meaningful fields of study. If humanities scholars become too specialized in their language and concerns they may lose the ability to communicate their ideas to the public and along with that ability, their very meaning and purpose.

Some recent statistics on American education show that the humanities have indeed lost meaning in the eyes of the public. A 1993 poll by the National Cultural Alliance on the role of the arts and humanities in our lives showed that only 31 percent of the public regarded the role as "major," whereas 57 percent said the role was "minor" and 11 percent said they played "no role at all."[9] Specialization in the sciences has not resulted in similar decay in public understanding, perhaps because the relatively coherent "vertical" structuring of scientific disciplines—from the study of the smallest particles in physics to the largest cosmic bodies in astronomy—gives a clearer picture of the importance of each discipline to an understanding of human existence. In other words, from the study of the tiniest particles in physics to the largest cosmic entities in astronomy each scientific discipline can be seen as explanatory of the way the world works. By comparison, the division of the humanities into less clearly connected fields of human activity and expression—English, foreign languages, journalism, communication, philosophy, history, art, drama, and music—makes the humanities seem less important, less coherently related to understanding life.[10] In societies with one dominant cultural heritage the humanities are at least unified and given educational importance by their relationship to that heritage, but in strongly multicultural societies such as ours, humanities education lacks that tie to meaning as well.

## HARD BOUNDARIES IN THE ARTS AND AESTHETICS

The most neglected of all humanities studies in American education are the arts and the related field of aesthetics—the study of perception in the arts and other sensory experiences. Ironically, we love and need the arts because they go beyond simple words and clear definitions in their ability to communicate deeper meanings and values. Yet, for that very reason, the arts inevitably suffer under a hard-boundaried paradigm of education, because their study does not lead to monetary gain or other clearly quantifiable values; rather, it serves a broader and deeper purpose of helping us to understand ourselves and others. Where hard boundaries have led to excessive compartmentalization and isolation of the arts—as in American education today—the arts can no longer serve that purpose. And, while recent publicity about the "Mozart effect" and similar research that links arts education to higher IQ and other test scores have raised public interest in arts education, it has done little or nothing to challenge our failure to appreciate the arts for their deeper values.[11]

Actually, coverage of the arts and aesthetics has never been good in American education, but after four decades of the Cold War–inspired math and science scare, that coverage has reached its nadir. Today, the arts at the precollege level are generally viewed as mere "enhancements" and are the first subjects affected when cutbacks of teachers and resources occur.

Exposure to the arts in kindergarten through eighth grade is thus extremely limited in many if not most urban school districts (though richer suburban schools sometimes have fully staffed arts programs). At the high-school level, students are required to take only one of the thirty-six high school credits in the arts: a mere 2.8 percent of the curriculum.[12] At the college level, core requirements in the arts exist mainly for liberal arts students and are often satisfied by one or two survey courses, that is, three to six credits from a total of about 124, or 2.4 to 4.8 percent of the liberal arts curriculum. In colleges of business, engineering, agriculture, and forestry other students may graduate with no arts courses at all; their limited core requirements in the humanities may be filled by courses outside the arts. As for the related field of aesthetics, its inclusion in the curriculum is even more haphazard, limited to elective courses at the college level taught mainly to philosophy majors by philosophers whose experience and knowledge of artistic practices may be extremely limited.

There have been many attempts to address the neglect of the arts and aesthetics in American education in recent decades. For example, Howard Gardner of Harvard's Project Zero—the foremost research center on learning—has argued in numerous books and articles that artistic and aesthetic education is as important as the logical and verbal skills learned in math, science, social studies, and language arts.[13] Music educator Charles Fowler has also repeatedly warned of the dangers for the overall educational system of neglecting instruction in the arts and aesthetics. In Fowler's view, learning about the arts helps students with a variety of essential human lessons, including finding out who they are, seeing themselves as part of a larger culture, broadening their perceptions, expanding their abilities to express themselves and communicate escaping the mundane, developing their imaginations, and evaluating and making judgments.[14] In fact, Fowler says, learning about the arts "furnishes students with a crucial aesthetic metaphor of what life at its best might be."[15] When we fail to provide adequate education in the arts and the wider related field of aesthetics, we are cheating America's children and hurting our society as a whole.

Over recent decades there have been many curriculum conferences on the arts and education in general at which the need for reform has been discussed most recently in the Goals 2000 National Standards for Arts Education.[16] There is now a growing sense that treating the arts as optional enhancements to the main curriculum of math, science, and reading has not worked, even in the limited sense of raising test scores and job skills. Moreover, the mistake we have made in neglecting the larger challenges of teaching students to understand and respect themselves and others—challenges best met through humanities subjects, especially through the arts and aesthetics—has been laid bare by the shooting tragedies at Columbine High and other schools. As we enter the twenty-first century, the time now appears ripe for a reemphasis in the schools of the arts and aesthetics and the life values they teach us.

Unfortunately the delivery system for education in the arts and aesthetics is completely inadequate to the job of improving that education, even if public understanding and support is raised. The problem is that, under the hard-boundaried extremes of specialization, the arts have come to be represented in American education as single-disciplinary practices, largely unconnected to each other, to aesthetics, or to the general curriculum. Specialists are trained in college-level departments of visual arts (called "art"), music, drama, and dance and are hired as single-disciplinary specialists to teach their art forms in the schools when positions are available.[17] But positions are rarely available for each specialty, and the specialists are not trained to teach about arts outside of their specialty. Most public schools end up with one or two arts specialists— usually in music and the visual arts—who have very limited contact with students.[18] At the elementary level, the contact is limited to several sessions of thirty minutes each week while at the secondary level arts education is mainly elective, subordinate to required courses in math, science, language arts, and social studies. Repeated calls by single-disciplinary conferences and specialists for increased coverage of their art form or the arts in general fall on generally deaf ears; such coverage would have to come out of the time currently spent on other disciplines.

The relevance of the arts to general education is lost in this hard-boundaried system. Teachers of general subjects rarely have the opportunity themselves to learn about the arts and aesthetics in an interdisciplinary, integrative manner; like everyone else, they usually fill their few arts requirements by choosing among single-disciplinary survey courses in which they learn the history of only one art form. Those college students who are training to be elementary teachers usually have required art and music education courses that supposedly help them make up for the lack of arts instructors at the elementary level, but these courses are too specialized to counter the neglect of the arts with which preservice teachers are otherwise faced; while those training for secondary-level teaching usually receive no preparation at all for teaching about the arts. As a result, teachers of general subjects for which the arts should be central concerns (especially social studies and language arts teachers) are unable to incorporate them into their teaching; they cannot teach what they themselves have not learned.

The situation in aesthetics is even worse. There, specialization has resulted in the marginalization of aesthetics as a minor subdiscipline in philosophy wherein specialists formulate and debate over hard-boundaried definitions of terms like "aesthetic object" and "aesthetic experience" in a manner far removed from normal human concerns about sensory experience and the arts. Many if not most aesthetics specialists have also adopted the hard-boundaried view of the arts as separate, single-disciplinary enterprises, even though this view inevitably diminishes the importance of the arts and aesthetic experience to education and the rest of life.[19]

## A BRIEF HISTORY OF AESTHETICS IN EDUCATION

The history of aesthetics as a discipline helps to explain the special problems hard boundaries have created for American education in the arts and aesthetics. Although aesthetic issues such as beauty, harmony, and the relationship of the senses to the intellect were central to Ancient Greek philosophy and education, as well as to many other philosophical traditions, aesthetics as a specialized discipline did not develop in the West until the eighteenth century, at the very time when academic specialization was beginning to take root. Like other philosophical disciplines of the time, eighteenth-century aesthetics emphasized logic over historical and social data in its definitions and analyses, so its practicioners tended to define and discuss the arts logically as separate practices based on how they were produced and perceived. Thus drama and opera, two of the oldest and most influential genres were generally not recognized as major art forms in aesthetic writings; they were treated as combinations of other art forms rather than as important artistic practices in their own right.

The term "aesthetics" first appeared in 1735 in Alexander Baumgarten's *Reflections on Poetry*. There, Baumgarten argued that the Cartesian worldview—the dominant philosophical view of the time—had failed to provide a place for the understanding of the human experience and judgment of beauty and art.[20] Baumgarten adopted the term "aesthetics" for this new field from the Greek word "aisthesis," meaning perception, and later used it in the title of his major two-volume study of 1750–1758, *Aesthetica*. After Baumgarten, "aesthetics" became generally accepted in other eighteenth century works of David Hume, Edward Burke, and Immanuel Kant as the discipline involving the study of beauty and the more intense experience of sublimity in encounters with nature and the arts.

The relationship between aesthetics and the arts was defined most clearly in Immanuel Kant's *Critique of Judgment* (1790), still probably the most influential work in the discipline. Aesthetics, Kant said, has to do with cognitive judgments of taste in engagements with sensory experience. ("Cognitive" refers to the mind and the process of knowing, including perception, emotional response memory, and judgment.[21]) The arts, or the "fine arts," to use Kant's comparable term, are areas of sensory experience for which aesthetic judgments are necessary and appropriate. In aesthetic judgments of sensory experience in the arts and in the larger realm of nature, the cognitive faculties of imagination and reason engage in an attempt to understand the experience in a manner quite distinct from their functioning in judgments in the areas of practical and pure reasoning, discussed by Kant in his two earlier critiques. Experiences of beauty and the sublime were said by Kant to produce a response of "disinterested pleasure," quite apart from the usefulness of the experience in promoting ordinary pleasure, profit, or other values.

Kant's view of aesthetics as one of the three main types of cognitive functioning placed it at the center of human concerns, on an equal basis with moral and scientific reasoning. This was clearly a promotion of aesthetics from its earlier position in the works of Baumgarten and Hume. Even more striking was the position of Kant's contemporary Friedrich Schiller, who held in his *Letters on the Aesthetic Education of Man* (1799) that aesthetics was essential to morality, because it helped human beings make the crucial connection between the physical and the intellectual:

It is therefore one of the most important tasks of culture to subject human beings to form even in their purely physical lives, and to make them aesthetic as far as ever the realm of Beauty can extend, since the moral condition can be developed only from the aesthetic, not from the physical condition.[22]

Aesthetics had moral implications to Arthur Schopenhauer as well. In Schopenhauer's *The World as Will and Representation* (1819), the experience of aesthetic appreciation is portrayed as a purely unselfish one, almost comparable to the highest moral experience (to Schopenhauer) of sacrificial love.[23] Implicit in Schiller's and Schopenhauer's views is the idea that aesthetic experience can transform a person for the better. That idea may appear to be easily challenged by the evidence of art-loving monsters like Adolf Hitler. But on the other hand, both Hitler's narrow tastes in art and his deadly anti-Semitism could be said to demonstrate an absence of aesthetic competence. That is, Hitler failed radically in the aesthetic challenge of learning to understand and appreciate a variety of forms of sensory experience and being in the world: to appreciate and love "the other." That kind of aesthetic failure may be at the root of much evil in the modern world, including the recent brutal mistreatment of Bosnians and Albanians in Yugoslavia, women in Afghanistan, and blacks in South Africa, and also including the extremes of careless greed practiced at times in the business world when hundreds of thousands of workers are fired to make room for more corporate profit. By contrast, the kind of aesthetic competence Schiller calls for goes far beyond appreciating particular forms or styles of art; rather, it requires a full commitment to connect sensory experience to emotional response and intellectual judgment.[24]

The high status that aesthetics enjoyed in the nineteenth century was also shared by the arts, which were viewed as idealized pursuits to be practiced and admired for their own sake, or as the French Romantic slogan had it, "l'art pour l'art." Unfortunately, the idealization of the arts and aesthetics by some Romantics has had a negative impact on education in them ever since. In our less Romantic time, education has focused more and more on scientific and technological skills connected with contemporary culture, not transcendent pursuits removed from it. As twentieth-century educator Harry S. Broudy has put it, "The mystique of art . . . has created a sharp boundary between knowledge and art, knowledge and feeling, between art and everyday experience. In schooling it has meant a division between the arts and the academic subjects that has prevented the arts from achieving a permanent place in the roster of studies required for general education."[25]

The status of aesthetics has also been undermined by the emergence in the twentieth century of psychology as the primary discipline for studying the human mind and by the dominance of experimental, empirical psychology over the earlier nineteenth-century model of "faculty psychology." Faculty psychology was based on the Kantian view that the mind consists of the faculties of reason, understanding, and imagination. As in Kantian philosophy, aesthetics was an important focus of faculty psychology, because aesthetics was a field in which the faculties of imagination and reason were both engaged in a very distinctive manner. However, empirical psychologists were not interested in trying to understand the faculties or any cognitive constructs that could not be actually observed and measured. Rather, they sought to achieve scientific status for the discipline of psychology by focusing on observable, measurable behavior prefered instead.[26] American psychology in particular was dominated by behaviorists such as B. F. Skinner, who went so far as to deny the existence of "the mind." American psychologists also focused far more on pathology than on psychologically healthy functioning. Thus, the study of aesthetics as the healthy functioning of cognitive judgments about sensory experience became a marginal concern in psychology as well.

In 1939, philosophers interested in aesthetics attempted to raise its status by establishing the American Society for Aesthetics (ASA) and, shortly thereafter, the *Journal of Aesthetics and Art Criticism* (JAAC, started in 1942 by the ASA). At first, there was recognition among the leaders of the society and the journal that it was important to join forces with teachers and practitioners of the arts in order to really have influence. Otherwise, as JAAC editor Dagobert Runes wrote in 1943, they would "remain a corner group in the Philosophical Association."[27] Then, as American philosophers fell under the dominance of the Anglo-American analytic approach—a highly arcane approach to argumentation learned, practiced, and understood only by professional philosophers—concern with collaboration and cooperation with arts educators and practicioners declined. Instead, many analytic philosophers in aesthetics hoped to raise the status of the discipline by showing that one could be just as rigorous in argumentation about the arts as about other more purely rational subdisciplines of philosophy. Under the influence of the analytic style, aesthetics became further removed from the concerns and understanding of arts educators and practitioners, and even more so from general educators, students, and the public, without any corollary rise of its status within the discipline of philosophy.

Today, the role Kant and Schiller envisioned for aesthetics has diminished to the point of nonrepresentation in American general education. Far from a universal educational concern, aesthetics has become a subdiscipline of philosophy whose study is required of almost no students, not even philosophy majors. In fact, the prestige and power of aesthetics within the discipline of philosophy has reached such a low that the American Society for Aesthetics has recently formed a Committee on the Status of Aesthetics as a Discipline to study and address the problem.[28] The connection of the arts to aesthetics has languished as well, as the arts have emphasized single-disciplinary concerns and skills of production and performance. While some arts educators, most notably music educator Bennett Reimer and the Getty Institute for Education in the Arts, have urged educators to connect artistic practices to aesthetic concepts,[29] others claim that aesthetics is irrelevant and even harmful and that the arts should be experienced and understood as practical rather than intellectual activities.

For example, in *Music Matters* (1996), David Elliott argues for teaching music as a set of human behavioral skills, performed by "musicers" for "listeners."[30] In so doing, Elliott is attempting to correct for what he sees as an overly intellectual emphasis in Reimer's approach, wherein aesthetic education has been taken to mean purely intellectual inquiry into the relationship of aesthetic concepts of form and style in music and the other arts.[31] As Elliott and others have rightly argued, that emphasis has lent itself too easily to a disregard for the inherent, experiential values of actual music making as well as the values of non-Western and popular traditions of the arts.[32] Wayne Bowman and Thomas Regelski have similarly argued that the term "aesthetic" has been wholly compromised by this formalistic tradition of aesthetic education; thus they now prefer the term "philosophy of music" to "musical aesthetics."[33] On the other hand, the assumption that the term "aesthetics" is inseparable from formalism is belied by recent highly influential research and publication in pragmatist, Marxists feminist, non-Western, environmental, and other nonformalist aesthetic theories that emphasize the relationship of artistic experience to cultural contexts.[34] Also, Elliott's position seems to give support to the current practice in K-12 schools, where students learn practical skills in band, choir, or art studio with little or no consideration of their relationship to historical, philosophical, or cultural contexts. The problem is, teaching the arts as skills without intellectual considerations encourages a merely utilitarian view of the arts, wherein they are valued and supported solely for their entertainment value at football games, parent's

nights, and similar occasions.[35] James Mursell warned with foresight in 1943
that if aesthetics was not made a primary value in music education "Worthless
materials may be used; routine procedures may be followed; emphasis may
center narrowly on technical skills; the great literature of the art may never by
opened up; nothing may be done to inspire and stimulate children to love and
appreciate the beauty and the expressive possibilities of the art."[36] Today the
question remains: how can students learn to love beauty and expression in the
arts unless they see schools valuing them in more than a utilitarian manner?[37]

The hard disciplinary boundaries of the arts and aesthetics have been more
harmful in American education than elsewhere. Traditions of training in the arts
in Europe and Asia go back to professional guilds of ancient and medieval times
and have not been as much affected by the development of the discipline of
aesthetics and other disciplinary structures in the last two centuries.[38] In America, though, schools and universities have been the primary site of education in
the arts, so the structure and the definitions of academic disciplines have been
the main influence on the training of specialists and the development of discourse in those disciplines. Too, while students of less multicultural societies in
Europe, Asia, and elsewhere commonly learn about the arts in connection with
their cultural heritage in general, the broad mix of cultures that make up American society make that connection more difficult and complex. Understanding
the complex fusions of multicultural artistic influences in American life requires
more rather than less time and attention, a requirement that has never been met
in American education.

In short, as a result of the hard disciplinary boundaries of the arts and aesthetics, the arts today exist as separate disciplines unconnected to each other
and the general curriculum in American education, mainly oriented to the training of specialists by other specialists. Arts that cross the boundaries of media
(including many of the musical arts and postmodern genres) and arts that are
strongly social in their performance practices (again, including music) are poorly
represented and poorly explained in our schools and universities. Hard-
boundaried specialization has also led to a strong, elitist distinction between
serious art and popular art, which, had it existed in ancient Greece or Elizabethan
England, would have turned proportionally as many people away from engagement in Sophocles and Shakespeare, as today turn from so-called "serious" or
"high" art.

American students and the general public usually feel excluded by the specialists' academic language and their dominant focus on European-based "high"
or "classical" art traditions to the neglect of American and other art traditions.
The growth of European art traditions out of a class-based system of patronage
has given these traditions an aristocratic association in America that has led to
ambivalence about the value and meaning of those traditions to our culture.
Twentieth-century American comedy has regularly exploited our ambivalence
about European art traditions; consider what the Marx Brothers, Victor Borge,
and Bugs Bunny have done to opera over the years. Recently ambivalence has

turned to outright ignorance, as education in the arts has worsened. Concert audiences and museum goers are growing older and older as younger generations increasing lack the preparation to understand classical art forms. As for aesthetics, Americans are usually ignorant of the term altogether.[39]

Public ignorance of the arts and aesthetics is, of course, harmful to future funding and other support for public programs and education. It is also harmful for our mental and emotional health as individuals and as a society. If we view the arts in the largest sense as an aesthetic realm of sensory imagery, this is an era when the ability to recognize and interpret such imagery has become essential to leading a rich and thoughtful life. In this highly technological age we have become consumers of sensory imagery in everything that we do, every thought that we have, every decision we make. Accepting, for argument's sake, the ancient Greek view of the arts as imitative of reality, Americans now live in an age when electronic media can imitate reality at a level of sensory intensity never before achieved. Indeed, the actual aesthetic function of the human brain in imagining and objectifying experience is now reproducible on a massive scale by machines. The ability to function intelligently and morally in the midst of this sensory immersion has become a greater challenge than ever, at least as great as the challenges of understanding modern science and mathematics. Without adequate education in the arts and aesthetics we cannot meet that challenge.

## WHAT WOULD PLATO THINK? A CLOSER LOOK AT AMERICAN EDUCATION IN THE ARTS AND AESTHETICS

Before the fragmentation of the arts and aesthetics into separate disciplines run by specialists, the importance of the arts and aesthetics to education was far better recognized. Two scenes from the history of education—one from ancient Greece and the other from late-twentieth-century America—may help to highlight the problem of increasing specialization in the arts and aesthetics. Let's listen in:

### Scene 1. Athens, 4th Century B.C.

*Athenian*: By an "uneducated man" we shall mean a man who has not been trained to take part in a chorus; and we must say that if a man *has* been sufficiently trained, he is "educated."

*Cleinias*: Naturally.

*Athenian*: And of course a performance by a chorus is a combination of dancing and singing?

*Cleinias*: Of course.

*Athenian*: And this means that the well-educated man will be able both to sing and dance *well*?

*Cleinias*: So it seems.

*Athenian*: Now let's see just what that word implies.

*Cleinias*: What word?

*Athenian*: We say "he sings *well*" or "he dances *well*." But should we expand this and say "provided he sings *good* songs and dances *good* dances?" Or not?

*Cleinias*: Yes, we should expand it.

*Athenian*: Now, then. Take a man whose opinion about what is good is correct (it really *is* good), and likewise in the case of the bad (it really *is* bad), and follows this judgment in practice. He may be able to represent, by word and gesture and with invariable success, his intellectual conception of what is good, even though he gets no pleasure from it and feels no hatred for what is bad. Another man may not be very good at keeping on the right lines when he uses his body and his voice to represent the good, or at trying to form some intellectual conception of it; but he may be very much on the right lines in his feelings of pleasure and pain because he welcomes what is good and loathes what is bad. Which of these two will be the better educated musically, and the more effective member of a chorus?[40]

## Scene 2. An American University, Late Twentieth Century

*Adviser*: Have you decided how you want to fulfill your fine arts requirement?

*Student*: No, I don't know anything about art. Why do I need to study it? I'm pre-med and I've got my hands full with the science requirements. Isn't there some way I can get out of the art requirement?

*Adviser*: If you were a business major, you wouldn't have a requirement, but as long as you're in the College of Arts and Sciences, you have to have some art. Actually as a pre-med you qualify for the Bachelor of Science degree plan, so you only have to take one fine arts course. Here's the list.

*Student*: Okay, let's take a look. Hmm, survey of art, music, dance, film, architecture, landscape architecture . . . I don't want to specialize in any of those things. Isn't there some course for art appreciation in general?

*Adviser*: There was an interdisciplinary program with team teachers from each art discipline, but that was discontinued when the professors found they wanted to treat their subjects in their own way. I'm afraid you'll have to choose one.

*Student*: Well, I like movies pretty much, so I guess I'll take the film course. How hard could that be?[41]

The first scene is a conversation between a student and Plato, the most critical of all philosophers in his attitude towards the arts. Yet even Plato takes the arts and aesthetics far more seriously than Americans do today. In fact, the dialogue suggests that Plato regards the arts and the perception of them ("aesthetics" per se was not a recognized discipline in Plato's day) as highly important subjects for education. Moreover, it is clear that in asking his students questions about artistic meaning and value, he is assuming considerable previous education in this area. Plato's focus in this passage is on whether performance virtuosity should be valued more than a moral understanding of the artistic experience. (His answer is, predictably, "no.") This question gets to the heart of how we are influenced by popular artists, a subject that American education sadly neglects, to the detriment of many young people who need someone—parent or teacher—to help them balance the powerful media that surround them with skills and experience in making intellectual and moral judgments.[42]

What a contrast we have in the second scene! Here there is no apparent recognition on the part of the system, the student, or the adviser that education in the arts and aesthetics might be important to personal development, and one doubts whether a specialized course in one or another art discipline will lead to that understanding. Rather, the student will most likely study one or, at most, two, specialized art canons—lists of terms, names, and dates as taught by specialists in the individual art disciplines. After studying the canon of one art discipline and passing the necessary tests (often in a lecture class of 200 students), one suspects the students will still think, and probably rightly, that they "don't know anything about art."

Clearly the standing of the arts and aesthetics in education has fallen precipitously since Plato's time; yet the arts themselves have not in the least diminished in their social influence and accessibility. In fact, through public museums, concerts, recordings, books, and electronic media, there is probably greater public access to the arts now than at any other time in history. In America in particular, young people's lives are made up of artistic experience from the moment they wake up to the sound of the Top 40 on their clock radio. They spend more money on musical recordings in a year than the gross national product of some developing nations. They watch on the average over seven hours of comic and serious dramas and other productions on television each day.[43] The decor of their rooms shows that visual arts are important to them as well, as does their love of music videos, and "hot" web sites. Indeed, American students may be the most avid consumers of the arts in the history of the world. How, then, can they know and care so little about them?

Some will argue that such a question should distinguish between the "high" art traditions and the popular arts, which are mass produced and distributed. In fact, the argument goes, our students' wide access to popular art forms has actually driven out time for knowledge and appreciation of "high" art: time with *Friends* leaves less time for Shakespeare (not to mention less time with real friends). Memorization of the complete works of Bob Dylan leaves no mental room for Beethoven opus numbers.

While there is some truth to the argument that popular culture has disenfranchised the traditional fine arts in America, the argument is far from adequate as an explanation for the neglect of the arts in our culture. After all, popular and folk arts have always existed next to the more aristocratic "high" arts, and their relationship has often been a mutually enriching rather than an exclusive one. In William Shakespeare's day, popular songs were the basis of highly complex and virtuosic harpsichord music played for the nobility and in homes of the educated classes. In our time, jazz and rock performers draw on the influence of Western classical or art music and also on classical, folk, and popular musics of other traditions. American composers and painters of "high" art have throughout the century enriched their works with the influence of folk, popular, and classical traditions of a variety of cultures as well. Indeed, the hard-boundaried definition of popular arts as inherently separate and inferior to high art and thus irrelevant to education is probably harmful to the overall cause of education in the arts and aesthetics. If not for the disdain of academic arts specialists, the immense amount of time and money American students spend on popular arts could act as an excellent introduction to their exploration of the arts of different times and cultures, including high art traditions and the study of aesthetics. Moreover, the enormous influence of popular arts in our culture should be directly addressed by arts educators as a factor requiring rational thought, not just passive enjoyment. Were Plato alive today, it's hard to believe that he would ignore that omnipresent influence as twentieth-century American educators have done.

A better explanation for the neglect of the arts in our culture lies in the specialized nature of American education in the arts and aesthetics: in essence, education of specialists, by specialists, for specialists. The assumption in our hard-boundaried educational system is that knowledge is best pursued and taught by specialists. Accordingly the arts have become separate disciplines at the college level, where extensive programs in history, theory, and practice of individual art forms are designed mainly for students majoring in those disciplines. At the secondary school level, arts specialists—a limited and declining number— focus their attention on identifying and teaching students with talent in their disciplines through the few available electives in band, choir, and art.

Many specialists do an outstanding job of teaching talented students to produce artworks and performances, but the results of their work are not shared by general students, who arguably need education in the arts as much or more than the talented students. There is little opportunity in the single-disciplinary instruction offered in K–12 education to introduce artistic and aesthetic concepts, let alone to allow for the repeated experience and thought that leads to genuine understanding. The situation in the colleges and universities is not much better. There, one or two courses in the fine arts usually suffices to fill the fine arts or humanities requirement. There is no general aesthetics requirement at either the college or precollege levels.

Because education in the arts and aesthetics is so specialized, teachers of general subjects that should incorporate the arts and aesthetics—including social studies, language arts, and, yes, science and math—are unable to do so because of their own inadequate knowledge. Among nonspecialists, only teachers of primary grades are required to have instruction in the arts as part of their teacher training. If future teachers of social studies or English wish to incorporate the arts into their understanding of their disciplines, they have to find the instruction that will help them do so on their own. Usually such teachers have had only the required art survey course or two in college, and they are no more likely than the other 200-some students from that class to feel comfortable incorporating the lecture and test material from the survey course into their worldview and their teaching. In addition, arts specialists themselves tend to discourage general educators from teaching about the arts. Understandably they don't want the few arts positions in the schools to lessen or disappear, so they often insist they are the only ones who can teach their subjects.

For aesthetics the hard boundaries of our educational system have been even more damaging. As previously mentioned, aesthetics is now represented in our educational institutions only as a subdiscipline of philosophy rarely required of any students. This hard-boundaried specialization has produced rigorous philosophical argumentation and historical research about individual art forms and practices as well as extraordinary skill among their practitioners. However, it has also had the effect of separating philosophical inquiry about the arts and aesthetics from education in the history and practice of the arts to the detriment of philosophy, history, and practice; and it has led to the omission of aesthetic issues and values from the teaching of math, science, business, law, engineering, and other disciplines that in my sensory view also need connection to aesthetics. Are beauty, ugliness, and other sensory pleasures and pains irrelevant to decisions in these areas? If so, the world is poorer for it.

## SEPARATING INTELLECTUAL INQUIRY FROM PRACTICE: ANOTHER HARD-BOUNDARIED MISTAKE

Separating intellectual inquiry from practical experience in the arts is another serious mistake stemming from our academic culture's preference for hard-boundaried separation over integration of knowledge and skills. Practical experience of the sensual basis of the arts is a necessary key for opening the imagination of every student, talented and untalented, to aesthetic questions about the style, form, meaning, and purpose of those arts. Teaching about choral music or painting in the absence of actually doing them is a barren approach that inevitably leades to disinterest, and not of the Kantian variety. Separating practice from intellectual inquiry also results in an overly technical approach to making art among the artists and precollege students—disconnected from questions about what the arts mean to us. At the precollege level, the separation of practice from intellectual inquiry has led to a singular emphasis on getting students "ready" for contests, concerts, and exhibits and a neglect of philosophical questions and historical information that would add intellectual meaning to the performing experiences. Then at the college level, many arts majors have trouble understanding why difficult and often dry history and theory classes are important to performers and artists at age 18 when they had no importance before.

Recognizing the weakness of the arts in precollege education, many states have recently mandated the provision of high school fine arts survey courses for students not involved in the music and art studio classes. These courses, too, are problematic because they are usually entirely intellectual in nature and because they are typically separated into nine-week units in music and art, taught by single-disciplinary specialists trained to present only their art form—thus omitting the other arts and the opportunity to educate students in aesthetic principles and judgment about sensory experience in general. Such courses seldom integrate history and philosophy with experience of the arts, although the students who are required to take these courses—those *not* enrolled in performance and studio classes—probably need the opportunity for experiential learning more than anyone else. Since the 1980s, the Getty Education Institute for the Arts has worked hard to develop "discipline-based art education," wherein education in artistic practices is integrated with study of the intellectual foundations of each discipline. Unfortunately, the Getty Institute has directed its attention mainly to the visual arts, although music educators are more firmly established in the public school system.

## FURTHER SEPARATION: HISTORY VS. PHILOSOPHY

The separation of experience from intellectual inquiry is part of the reason American education has failed to engage students and the general public in recognizing the importance of the arts to life. Moreover, intellectual inquiry has also been fragmented into separate areas of history and philosophy, especially at the college level. As I will further argue in chapters 2 and 3, hard boundaries between philosophical and historical inquiry have led to isolated, highly esoteric research and writing in both areas. At the college level, academic study in aesthetics courses or "philosophy of the arts" (the other common title for aesthetics-related courses), this philosophy is completely isolated from study of the history of the arts, which is itself fragmented among the separate art disciplines of drama, music, art (i.e., visual arts), architecture, film, and dance.

There are several problems with college-level aesthetics courses. First, as mentioned earlier, they are not a regular enough part of the curriculum to influence the public understanding of meaning and value in the arts. Second, they are generally taught by philosophers trained primarily in analytic philosophy who tend to focus on the definitions of concepts rather than on the meaning and function of the arts in life and society. The standard texts in aesthetics courses are anthologies of readings in which definitions of art, works of art, and aesthetic experience are debated in a very specialized manner. For instance, consider this excerpt from the introduction of *Philosophy Looks at the Arts: Contemporary Readings in Aesthetics*, written by highly respected philosopher Joseph Margolis:

The distinguished Polish aesthetician, Roman Ingarden, represents an entirely different approach to the aesthetic. Ingarden (even more than Maurice Merleau-Ponty) is the influential phenomenologist best known to Anglo-American philosophers of art. Ingarden's account (1964) links the aesthetic not only to appreciation—the appreciation of art—but also, in an essential way, to the very structure of artworks themselves. It is critical to Ingarden's thesis that a work of art is inherently "schematic" or at least "partially" indeterminate. This of course raises serious difficulties about the sense in which artworks are real at all, since the idea that something is both actual *and* indeterminate in structurally important respects (not concerned with issues of vague boundaries or the like) verges on the incoherent or the ontologically monstrous.[44]

Philosophers specializing in aesthetics will understand this excerpt as part of a summary of recent attempts to define the nature of artworks and aesthetic experience. But what are nonspecialists to make of it? What human experiences are illuminated here? If the instructors of aesthetics and philosophy of art courses succeed in getting students to learn who has taken what position in the various conceptual debates, what has been achieved?[45] In my view, such debates do not lead to increased understanding of the importance of the arts and aesthetics in our lives.

There are just as many problems on the history side of this fragmented picture. For example, college-level courses in the history and appreciation of the arts generally consist of canonical histories, that is, the study of successions of "great" artists and artworks in individual art disciplines, often with exclusive emphasis on the Western tradition. Relying on canons to teach history in general is problematic, for it encourages students to memorize a traditionally accepted list of names and dates rather than to attempt to understand historical relationships themselves. The emphasis on rote memorization is undoubtedly why so many students consider history boring and are unable to place the Civil War and other central historical events in the right half-century despite repeated years of lessons on the subject. However, canonical teaching of the arts is even worse because it leads to an inescapable paradox. On the one hand, there is no point in teaching the history of the arts before students are mature enough to appreciate "greatness" (the usual basis for the canonical status of a work), so precollege arts education has remained fixated on practice to the exclusion of historical and philosophical inquiry. On the other hand, however, if history and philosophy of the arts are only dealt with later on, the message is that the study and understanding of the arts is not very important, and students lose the opportunity, available in other mainstays of the curriculum to reinforce and deepen lessons learned in earlier years.

As for the singular dominance of the Western tradition in most art-historical canons, it is understandable given the inherent conservatism of the canon-forming process (see chapter 2); nonetheless it is extremely unfortunate, perhaps even tantamount to encouraging racist assumptions of European superiority in our culture and among our students. If it was ever appropriate to ignore other cultural and artistic traditions in favor of emphasizing the affiliation of the United States with Europe, it no longer is today. As we turn to a new century, American students need a global perspective in history, culture, and the arts in order to understand our traditions in context with those of the wider world. In fact, the arts may be the most important part of the global perspective we owe our students, because it is the arts that give us the most profound insights into the alternate values and workings of other cultures, inviting us literally to see, hear, and otherwise experience the world as other cultures do. Such a perspective should include a strong background in the art traditions of one's home culture, but not to the exclusion of experience and appreciation of others.

As a teacher of music history I know from painful experience how much the current music-historical canon has lost touch with the reality of students who are being required to learn it.[46] Even today this canon remains exclusively Western, despite the strong influences from Africa, Asia, and Latin America on musical developments throughout the century. The canon includes many names of composers whose music my students will likely never hear outside of a music history class, but it excludes such prominent names as Madonna, Michael Jackson, Elvis Presley, and John Coltrane, about whom students have many questions. I can add those names and other information to make the history more relevant to student's concerns in my own classes, but that is only a piecemeal correction. Again, the root of the problem is the isolation of history from philosophical inquiry: if it were not so isolated, some hard philosophical questions would be asked about the meaning and purpose of the information provided in textbooks and conveyed in these classes. Actually, students already ask these questions privately; we just don't hear them and we don't provide the answers they need. (This problem will be explored further in chapter 2.)

## AN ALTERNATIVE APPROACH: SOFT BOUNDARIES

The hard times we have reached in the arts and aesthetics operate as a classic vicious cycle in which inadequate education for one generation leads to more inadequate education for the next. What we need is a more interdisciplinary, integrative approach to education in the arts and aesthetics: an approach that will create teachers and practitioners who can communicate and interact with the general public about meaning and power of artistic imagery in the contemporary world and the past, as well as specialists to maintain old traditions and create new ones.

In this book, I recommend "soft boundaries" as a new paradigm for re-visioning the position and power of the arts and aesthetics in American education. Soft-boundaried education in the arts and aesthetics means integration of historical and philosophical inquiry with practice and experience of artistic production, within and beyond the traditional boundaries of arts disciplines. Soft boundaries may be used to construct concepts and communicate about them across disciplinary boundaries; but they are also permeable—continually open to redefinition and change as additional experience is received and examined; they are the kind of boundaries that allow for thinking and making distinctions pragmatically, without making those acts into ends in themselves. Soft-boundaried thinking leads to definitions that are working hypotheses, functioning for the exercise, or *play*, of the mind rather than for the fixing of definitions and hierarchies of value. With soft boundaries, the emphasis in aesthetic judgments moves from rating levels of excellence in the internal features of artworks—a hard-boundaried enterprise of reification and hierarchization—to questioning and appreciating the meaning of artworks and artistic practices for artists, communities, cultures, and ourselves.

Following a paradigm of soft boundaries does not mean the destruction of disciplinary boundaries and specialization in the arts and aesthetics, but it does mean that education should no longer be designed primarily for specialization. Instead, interdisciplinary education in the arts and aesthetics should be a part of general education at all levels as well as an important part of the education of future teachers of general subjects. Disciplinary specialization should remain available at the college and secondary levels, as the means for specialists to explore and understand the connections of their art form to the wider realm of the arts and aesthetics and to education and life in general.

Soft boundaries means more interdisciplinary contact among teachers and students in the separate disciplines of the arts and aesthetics and more contact and communication with the wider public. With softer boundaries and broader coverage, historians of the arts will learn enough about other art disciplines to allow for a fuller perspective on multidisciplinary art forms and on new art forms that cross the boundaries of disciplines. Teachers and students in aesthetics will learn enough about the history and practice of the arts to make their concepts and debates more relevant to current problems and public understanding. General students, including future schoolteachers, will learn enough about the arts and aesthetics as a whole to incorporate them into their understanding of the world. At the same time, more specialized education will remain available for those students who wish to become artists, performers, historians, and philosophers of the arts.

Our failure to provide integrative, interdisciplinary education in the arts and aesthetics has been a matter of hard-boundaried tradition and convenience, resulting in disciplinary and subdisciplinary specialists that interact mainly with one another. Ultimately this approach leads to isolation and irrelevance. The way out lies in softening the disciplinary boundaries of the arts and aesthetics and reconnecting with the world.

# 2

# History, Philosophy, and the Canons of the Arts

The need to raise public understanding about the arts in America is taking on special urgency as we approach the twenty-first century. The initial exclusion of the arts from the precollege curriculum proposed in the 1990 Education 2000 plan for national education reform spurred recognition around the country that the importance of the arts in our educational system and in American culture as a whole is very poorly understood. In the wake of that omission a consortium of educators in music, visual arts, dance, and drama formulated a set of national standards for precollege arts education that contains new emphasis on teaching about the history, theory, and interpretation of the arts, along with the more traditional emphasis on teaching practical skills of artistic production, such as, singing or painting. The passage in 1994 of the revised Education 2000—since renamed the Goals 2000: Educate America Act—means that the new standards for arts education have now become part of our national educational policy and are now being established at state and local levels.[47]

In my view, the approval of national standards has played a positive role in focusing attention on the need for arts education in this country. However, more than standards are needed to make a lasting improvement in that education. If the new standards are to be more than rhetoric, it will be necessary to train arts educators very differently, so that they can integrate practical experience with intellectual understanding in their various classes in painting, theater, dance, choir, and band and so that they can make interdisciplinary connections with other arts and nonarts disciplines. It will also be necessary to prepare nonarts specialists teaching social studies, English, and even math and science, to incorporate knowledge about the arts into their courses. (How this can be done

This chapter appeared in an earlier version in the *Journal of Aesthetic Education* (1998, University of Illinois Press).

will be further addressed in chapter 7: "Towards Integrative, Interdisciplinary Education in the Arts and Aesthetics.")

This chapter addresses one aspect of the changes I believe are necessary in order to truly integrate education in the arts into our general curriculum. My concern here is the problem with our reliance both at the precollege and college levels on historical canons of the arts as our main intellectual approach to arts education—a reliance resulting in separate chronologies of historical style periods, artists, and works for each individual art form. The trouble is, these separate historical canons are confusing, often inconsistent with each other and with social and political history, and altogether unhelpful in explaining the central relationship of all the arts to human culture. What I recommend instead of separate historical canons of the arts is an interdisciplinary, philosophical history of the arts in general. In philosophical history of the arts, philosophical, aesthetic questions about form, style, meaning, and value in the arts are used to guide historical inquiry.

I believe that philosophical history can be the key to bringing intellectual knowledge about the arts into the standard curriculum and to making that knowledge memorable through strong connections to other fields. Specialists and specialized courses in individual art forms would remain important for study in depth, especially at the college level, but philosophical history would be the means by which students are introduced to the study of the arts. Indeed, if the move to philosophical history is not made, arts educators may run the risk of having to refight the battle for inclusion of the arts in our curriculum on a regular basis. That battle may be particularly daunting now, when consensus for limiting public expenditures in order to balance the budget is high and when many of our public institutions for arts funding have been under attack.[48] By contrast, philosophical history could achieve a more permanent integration of the arts into our standard curriculum, without inviting future political battles.

## THE RELATIONSHIP OF HISTORY, PHILOSOPHY, AND THE ARTS

How are history and philosophy best related in inquiries about the arts? In my view, history and philosophy are complementary modes of inquiry about human existence that function best in balance and connection with each other. In fact, history and philosophy both spring from the same quintessential human need to "Know thyself," as the Delphic oracle put it. With philosophy, we seek knowledge through the process of questioning and defining ourselves and the world.[49] With history, we seek knowledge through preserving and studying the past, including that of art.

When separated or heavily imbalanced, both history and philosophy suffer. Because of the absence of philosophical questions about the meaning of the historical data gathered, history tends toward positivism—an uncritical amassing of facts—while in the absence of contact with the actualities of historical and cultural practices, philosophy tends toward arcane debates over definitions. Despite their similar Delphic roots, history and philosophy seem also to have opposing tendencies that need each other's balancing influence. The tendency for history specialists, for instance, is to study how times change, whereas the tendency in philosophy is to transcend change and seek stability in definitions and understandings that will stand "the test of time." On the other hand, the techniques of recording history emphasize stability in the preservation of past records and artifacts while philosophers are more oriented to change than stability because philosophy must continue questioning and defining the world, regardless of the work of past philosophers. In respect to both their tendencies and techniques, history and philosophy seem thus to be inversely positioned to each other, like opposite sides of a coin. It may be, then, that each needs the other for balance. Without that balance, history and philosophy each may lose touch with the human realities they attempt to understand and collapse instead into mere speculation (in the case of philosophy), or into mere positivistic fact gathering (in the case of history). Examples of this kind of collapse exist in the histories of both philosophy and history, and they do seem to correspond to periods in which history and philosophy lose their balance, as in the speculative nominalist-realist debates in fourteenth-century Europe, when scholars famously argued over the number of angels that could stand on the head of a pin, and—sadly—in American education today.

Throughout most of the twentieth century, history and philosophy have been in separate and distant academic camps. Under the influence of science and scientific thinking—the dominant intellectual paradigm through most of the twentieth century—historians and philosophers have disdained the grand metaphysical tradition of the nineteenth century—in which the pursuits merged into Hegelian philosophy of history—and instead sought separate, scientifically oriented methodologies and areas of inquiry. In recent decades, history and philosophy have been drawing closer with the interdisciplinary spread of historicism and the increasing awareness of the limits of scientific theory.[50] Indeed, as Arthur Danto suggested in *Narration and Knowledge* (the 1985 update of his 1964 *Analytical Philosophy of History*), history may have taken the place of science in providing the unifying intellectual outlook of our time.[51]

As history has gained prominence as an intellectual force, there are signs that history and philosophy of the arts have grown closer as well. One sees evidence of the history boom in the frequent citations in arts and aesthetics journals of Michel Foucault and other relativist historians and philosophers, and in the frequent appearance of the formulations "historicism" and "historicity." The discipline of aesthetics, in which value and meaning of the arts (and sensory experiences in general) is debated, has clearly been affected and challenged by the history boom—so much so that even ahistorical Platonists in aesthetics may make extensive reference to historical details in their writings.[52] The increased emphasis on history in these philosophies reflects the growing consensus that, as philosopher Anita Silvers puts it, "valuation's logical structure itself assigns historical and social forces or events a central role"; that is, you can't make sense about issues of aesthetic value without considering their historical and social context.[53]

Still, the distance between history and philosophy has remained very great in the study of the arts, mainly because of the way these disciplines have been represented in our academic institutions. Since the rise of the discipline of aesthetics in the eighteenth century, there has been a gaping institutional separation between philosophical inquiry about the arts, conducted in aesthetics, and historical inquiry, conducted within many separately defined arts disciplines, including the visual arts (studied in departments of "art"), architecture, literature, dance, theater, music, and film. The result of these separations has been positivism at its worst for many historians of artistic practice: a seemingly endless proliferation and fragmentation of separate canons of facts in music history, dance history, history of theater, history of German theater, history of German puppet theater, and so forth and so on—canons that only specialists can hope to learn and love. This proliferation is the inevitable result of positivism applied to history; the "narrow beam" of scientific inquiry, unmediated by philosophical questions about meaning, encourages the uncovering of more and more specialized information and the development of new, more specialized fields as the proliferation of information becomes too great for members of the original field to comprehend.[54]

The effect of positivism is most fragmenting for historians of the arts, who often lack even the modest philosophical orientation that general historians receive in their required historiography classes. As musicologist Philip Gossett has noted, "what differentiates music, art, or literary history from other historical enterprises is the historian's relationship to the primary 'facts' of these disciplines, the works of art themselves."[55] In other words, historians of the arts are trained and professionally oriented to identify the artworks of their field as their focus. Accordingly they have tended to view artworks in an autonomous manner, separate from their social contexts, and they have traditionally taken their theoretical issues to be those connected to the creation and interpretation of the works, rather than those connected to the art form or the culture in general. Unfortunately, for those outside the disciplines, the theory and specialized language developed for individual art forms often become more of a barrier than an aid to understanding.[56]

The separation between history and philosophy has been equally unfortunate for philosophers of the arts. While wisely leaving historians of North German puppet theater to their own devices, philosophers have sometimes failed to educate themselves adequately in historical details of artistic production and transmission that clearly do bear on the questions of artistic value and meaning they debate. Too, many philosophers of the arts have neglected to question the content and legitimacy of the historical canons, and some have developed theories and definitions of artistic practices that reinforce the canons or that rely heavily on canonical examples for proof. While historians of the arts have increasingly questioned the content of the canons in the recent years, the reliance on canons as the main basis for critical understanding in the arts remains strongly entrenched in the absence of a strong philosophical challenge. The problems stemming from this canonical entrenchment go far beyond the frequently stated feminist and multiculturalist concerns of Western male dominance in education—as strong as those concerns may be; indeed they are probably at the heart of why the importance of the arts is so poorly understood in our society today.

## THE TROUBLE WITH HISTORICAL CANONS

In order to explore more fully the weakness of historical canons of the arts as a critical basis for understanding the arts, one must consider what canons are in general and why they develop. The word "canon" itself derives from the Greek word *kanon*, meaning "rod" or "bar," and the Latin word *canon* meaning "measuring line" or "rule." In Ecclesiastical Middle Latin, "canon" acquired the meaning of "sacred writings admitted to the catalog according to the rule."[57] By extrapolation, historical canons of the arts consist of successions of artists and works in a particular art form for which a claim of universal merit or relevance has been established. What is omitted from the canon, sacred or artistic, is presumed to have failed to meet the "rule." Accordingly, those who wish to revise the canon are frequently charged with wanting to dilute the quality that canons are believed to represent. However, examination of the roots of canonicity—where canons come from and how they develop—reveals that canons emerge, not from a priori standards of merit, but from identity needs of the groups by whom and for whom the canons are formed.

For example, the very earliest canons were books of sacred scriptures determined by religious specialists to have met the rule of sacred authority, and they served to define and maintain the group identity of sects of believers. The gradual formulation and canonization of the books of the Hebrew Bible served the purpose of maintaining Hebrew identity through the diffusions in and out of Palestine and against the challenges of other cultures and religions. Similarly, histories and historical canons have evolved from stories told and codified in the purpose of defining and maintaining a sense of identity among people of the same tribe, nation, or other binding community. As historian Erich Kahler has stated, "history presupposes a concept of communal identity, of nationality, or humanity."[58] Historical canons are "canonized" histories; that is, they are successions of the most significant events and figures that have been communally authorized by long use and by the sanction of history specialists.

One can best understand the relationship of identity needs to historical canons by considering history's relationship to myth. In prehistorical, preliterate cultures, needs for communal identity are filled by engagement in tribal myths, which are regularly enacted in tribal rituals.[59] Like histories, the myths of a tribe are usually narratives of actual events experienced by past tribal members, except that in myth the events are heavily interpreted through the medium of the tribe's spiritual beliefs. With the development of writing and the emergence of centralized, semiliterate agrarian societies out of local tribal cultures, history and religion begin to separate from local, tribal myth and to define and preserve communal identity for larger groups of people over longer spans of time and space.[60] It is at this point that the identity interests of the canonizers, be they priests or historians, begin to diverge from those of their audiences; for as their professional standards and practices develop, the canonizers begin to base their own identities on concepts of professional behavior rather than on tribal, national, or religious membership. Thus modern "scientific" historians who disavow the pull of national or religious ties in order to render history "exactly as it happens" can be seen to be acting out communal allegiances that are primarily professional, rather than as having disdained all communal allegiances.

As the dissemination of canonical writings widens, the communal identity of their audiences becomes more diffuse and hypothetical, based on common reading interests or favorite web sites rather than on actual human contact and shared activity. If and when the gap between the specialists and their audiences becomes too great, the canon may cease entirely to speak to the identity of a general audience, instead becoming something that the specialists attempt to enforce against rather than with the identity interests of the general reading public.

This is the point we seem to have reached at the turn of the twentieth century with the historical canons of the arts, especially in the United States. Since the institutionalization at the beginning of the century of arts historians within academic departments—each with their own accreditation programs, scholarly societies and journals—histories of the arts have seldom reflected public concerns, as they frequently did in earlier times (for example, the nationalistic histories of the nineteenth century). Rather, historians of the arts have become very professionalistic, viewing themselves as members of global, scholarly communities. Yet, their global view has remained, even amid feminist and multiculturalist challenges, strongly centered on Europe and on an aristocratically based tradition of fine arts that excludes the great majority of artistic activity, past and present.

The use and maintenance of these elite, European-based canons of the arts has been particularly problematic in American education. American scholars whose identification with European canons helped form their group identity have ignored issues of American identity and have underemphasized the history of American art forms and artists. They have also neglected research and teaching of non-Western arts and aesthetics to a degree that at the end of the twentieth century now borders on racism. When courses in the arts and aesthetics cover only the Western tradition, students are encouraged to believe that other traditions are inferior and unimportant, and they lose the opportunity to use the arts as a key to appreciation and understanding of different cultures. In a multicultural society such as ours, that opportunity could be the key to increasing civic understanding and to lessening intergroup hatred and violence.

Given the odd, largely unexamined relationship of Eurocentric historical canons of the arts to Americans, those canons are problematic at best in their ability to engage American students' interest. Nonetheless, historical canons remain the primary basis by which American students are introduced to the academic study of arts (if indeed, they are introduced at all) and by which public discussion about the arts proceeds as well. In the case of the students, one or two courses in the fine arts are generally all that is required to fill college distribution requirements; and a single survey of the fine arts is all that is required before college, and only from those students who are not taking practical instruction in choir, band, or the visual arts. The college courses are typically large lecture courses on a single art form taught by a specialist in the art field. Often a student's entire academic coverage of the arts is limited to a canonical Survey of Landscape Architecture or Survey of Dance.

What are the negative effects of relying on historical canons as a basis for understanding the arts? First and most important, the reliance on historical canons results in the neglect of questions about the meaning and connection of the arts to life. The claim of canons to represent successions of the most significant works and figures diminishes all issues except that of value or greatness, the criteria of which are then circularly formulated to correspond with artists and artworks that have already been canonized. Canonical histories also underplay the meaning and function of artworks and artistic practices for the artists and their cultures, instead emphasizing mainly technical issues of form, style, and technique. These technical emphases speak to the identity interests of the historians since they reflect the issues that historians of the arts have learned to regard as important during their training, the continued attention to which tends to bring them professional approval. The technical emphases also lend themselves to the development of complex concepts and technical vocabulary that may flatter the sense of professional exclusivity of specialists. Among the historians of the arts, as with all specialists, complexity has an inherent tendency to appear as a value rather than as a drawback. The constant increase of information and the regular discrediting of earlier, less sophisticated historical data and interpretations seem to offer continuing proof of the validity of specialized research and the increasingly fragmented and detailed canons that result from it. Meanwhile, the structural founding of canons on identity needs makes the identity needs of the canonizers themselves invisible, and so their claim to represent pure value goes largely unchallenged. Thus, in the current debate over revising the canon, only the multiculturalists are said to be motivated by identity interests; the defenders of the canon claim concern only for universal standards and values or, as Reagan–era National Endowment for the Humanities Director Lynne Cheney has put it, for "the truth."[61]

Another problem with relying on historical canons of the arts is that the institutional separation of the arts from each other and the relatively closed nature of each art-historical canon have resulted in art-historical narratives that are inconsistent and that involve complexities far beyond the knowledge or interest of nonspecialists. Because of the closed nature of the disciplines and the further subspecialization of historians of the arts within more specific historical, geographical, and biographical limits, there are few scholars with broad enough knowledge and interests to notice and correct the inconsistencies produced by separate historical canons. Those inconsistencies are, nonetheless, extensive and very confusing to nonspecialists: even terms for the most basic historical style periods—Medieval, Renaissance, Baroque, Classical, Romantic, and Modern—are described and dated differently depending on the art form and, in any case, are based on Eurocentric views of history. For instance, the Renaissance begins in the fourteenth century in historical canons of Italian painting, in the fifteenth century in music, and in the sixteenth century in English literature (just as the "modern period" in philosophy begins), while it has no meaning for the arts outside the West. Chronologically, the Classical period in European music (c. 1750–1800) corresponds to Neoclassicism in European architecture and to the beginnings of Romanticism in European literature.[62] Similarly, European Baroque architecture, painting, sculpture, and music are contemporaneous with Classicism in French literature. Thus, the same comédie-ballets on which Jean-Baptiste Molière and Jean-Baptiste Lully collaborated may be considered Classical comedies by Molière in literary histories, while in music histories they may be classified as Baroque comédie-ballets by Lully.

The incoherence that results from separate canonical histories of the arts can best be seen in the case of drama, perhaps the most important art form in world history and one involving a combination of literary, visual, and musical aspects of artistic experience. The study of drama is fragmented among many art disciplines, each of which approach it with different emphases as to period, place, and style, each in a Eurocentric manner. In this fragmented approach, a few heavily canonized playwrights such as Shakespeare and Sophocles fare well in literary studies (though their plays are distorted by treatment as solely literary products), but the rest of the history of drama is incoherently fragmented into separate, inconsistent historical canons in the performing arts. There is a separate historical canon of (European) dance, for instance, in which issues of style and succession bear little relationship to the history of the dramatic genres and social practices in which context dances were usually developed and performed. As a result, scholars and students of dance history may remain largely ignorant of the connection of narrative dance to opera and their emergence from the same social institutions and stylistic circumstances.[63] And again, the canons neglect drama and dance outside of the Western tradition.

Opera, itself a dramatic genre of immense importance in European and Chinese cultures, receives a completely incoherent treatment under canonical history. Institutionally the study of opera is generally confined to students majoring in music, and is presented in context with the history of Western music, and with emphasis on elements of Western musical form and style. With a few exceptions, histories of opera tend to be specialized, historical canons of European musical composers and works, despite the interdisciplinary and multicultural breadth of the genre, its social import, and the fact—well known to opera historians but obscured by institutional structure and pedagogy—that an opera composer was not considered the *auteur* of the opera until the nineteenth century.[64] The fact that opera is not solely a musical genre invented by the Florentine Camerata at the end of the sixteenth century, but rather part of a worldwide human tradition of combining music, words, and scenery for purposes of dramatic representation, is lost on music students under these circumstances while other students receive little or no education about opera at all. Perhaps worst of all, the canonical approach to operatic history omits or discourages consideration of modern-day musical dramas such as American musical theater, performance art, MTV videos, films and television shows, and even commercials, all of which operate similarly on multiple lines of artistic practice and are similarly powerful in their influence and/or reflection of society.

Historical canons of art forms that are less fragmented by our institutional distinctions are also problematic. For example, let's take the case of painting, identified as a separate art form in eighteenth-century Europe in the aesthetic writings of Sir Joshua Reynolds, among others.[65] Although the historical canon of painting does not actually fragment and distort the history of painting as a social practice, it still distorts our view of paintings themselves because it encourages us to view them totally out of context from their intended purpose and the other social circumstances of their production, according to their place in an artificial chronology defined primarily by reference to formal elements of style and technique. The modern institution of the museum promotes this decontextualized formalist view, since museum visitors typically view paintings out of their original context, in stylistic and formal comparison with each other. In fact, the museum and its musical counterpart of the concert hall are primary agents in the formation and dissemination of historical canons of the arts in America today. Historians move easily back and forth between museums and educational institutions, and museums (and often concert programmers) more often than not organize their exhibits according to historical canons.[66]

There is, however, an immense difference between seeing, say, Titian's *Assumption of the Virgin* in a canonical context next to other paintings of the Italian Renaissance (as it appears in an art history book or, hypothetically, in a museum), and experiencing it in its actual original context, as the altarpiece at the church of Santa Maria Gloriosa dei Frari in Venice.[67] When one enters Saint Mary's church and sees, amid the candles, incense, stained-glass images, and liturgical chanting, the painting of Mary's own rapturous entry into heaven, one doesn't think primarily about Titian's style or canonical status, even if the visit is a tourist stop rather than a religious pilgrimage. On the contrary, one senses above all the expressive effect of the altarpiece in its depiction of Mary's ascent to heaven: in essence a ritual reenactment frozen in time and space. Titian's style, that is, his use of colors and forms, is not irrelevant to his painting's effect as ritual reenactment. Inside of the church, though, the style of the painting cannot be viewed out of context with its figural meaning and with other shapes and colors in the church, as it is likely to be viewed in the historical canon of painting. The point is not that canons are wrong; in fact, they may lead to interesting discoveries and speculations about the development of artistic styles. Nonetheless, canons are very limiting and distorting if they are the main or only way by which the arts are studied.

## CAN PHILOSOPHY HELP?

Challenging the weakness of historical canons as a basis for understanding the arts would seem to be a natural task for philosophers specializing in aesthetics (also referred to as philosophers of art). More than most other academics, philosophers seem to be fully alert to the inadequacy of history alone as a route to understanding. They also have the advantage of not being as institutionally fragmented in their consideration of artistic practice. The main journals and organizations of the subdiscipline of philosophical aesthetics concern all the arts rather than individual art forms and are open to interdisciplinary participation of historians of the arts, as well as psychologists, sociologists, anthropologists, and others. However, the institutional distance of philosophy from history has apparently served to stall philosophical critiques of the historical canons of the arts. What critiques have emerged have usually come from the historical specialists themselves, whose lack of philosophical training leaves them less well situated to make an effective challenge.[68] While history has become a greater concern for many philosophers of art in the late twentieth century the result has been even more reinforcement of the historical canons of the arts, rather than in the challenge of them.

For example, recent aesthetic writings that deal with the history of the arts can be seen to fall into three different categories: (1) strict constructionism (a term I have borrowed from legal studies), (2) foundationalism (also known as realist historicism, also to be discussed further in chapter 3), and (3) pluralism (also known as relativist historicism, also to be discussed further in chapter 3). Strict constructionism involves the use of historical texts and/or data to argue against the historical relativity, or at least radical relativity, of values and judgments, and for the fixation of a particular historical view, either as a universal standard of judgment or as the basis of more contextualized arguments about meaning, value, or intention. Among strict constructionists of the legal profession (from which the term is extrapolated), the main historical point of reference is the U.S. Constitution, the strict construction of which is thought to guarantee continuity of national values.[69] In aesthetics, strict constructionists also use the eighteenth century as a preferred point of historical reference, perhaps because the discipline of aesthetics, like the Constitution, originated at that time. The influence of strict constructionism on aesthetics has led to a fixation on eighteenth-century definitions and commentary about the arts, usually without consideration of the relevance of eighteenth-century thought to current or general aesthetic problems.

Unfortunately, strict aesthetic constructionism tends to reify rather than challenge the historical canons of the arts. The preoccupation with debating the timelessness of certain artistic works, values, and judgments leads strict constructionists to choose heavily canonical examples as the basis or support for their arguments. For example, Peter Kivy supports his argument for "enhanced formalism" as a universal standard for the appreciation of music, with illustrations of music by canonical European composers, including J. S. Bach, Wolfgang Amadeus Mozart, and Josquin Des Prez.[70] Since Kivy's theory is rooted in the same eighteenth-century ideas of art that helped give shape to the historical canonization of composers and works that was just beginning at the time, his canonical illustrations are at best circular support for his theory (as his theory is a circular support of the works' rights to canonical status). Moreover, his formalist analyses of such works as Josquin's sacred motet *Ave Maria* are as ahistorical and acontextual as is the formal assessment of Titian's *Assumption of the Virgin* in an art history textbook.[71]

Kivy's negative attitude towards the movement for historical performance practice is a good example of how strict constructionism, and canonical history as well, can find itself in opposition to actual historical data about artistic practices. Since the 1960s, scholarship on historical performance practice has been deconstructive of the music-historical canon, challenging long-held assumptions about the meaning of notational symbols in musical scores and about the relative authority of musical scores and composers' intentions compared to issues of social, historical practice—including the ways that early musical instruments were constructed and played. Kivy has opposed the deconstruction by making philosophical arguments about the meaning of "authenticity" and other words used by performance practice advocates, while ignoring the issue of the different sound worlds created by use of early instruments and techniques, probably because he views issues of sound quality as being irrelevant to music "qua art."[72] Yet, according to a less canonical view of music, musical sound and the ways in which it has been socially produced and perceived is not a side issue; it is central to the understanding of music, historical and philosophical. Thus, Kivy's legalistic analysis of the multiple senses of "authenticity" is a weak counterargument to the appeal and ease of the sound of Baroque music played with Baroque instruments and techniques.[73]

Unlike the strict constructionist view, the foundationalist, or realist-historical, view of the history of the arts recognizes that styles and values change over time. Like strict constructionists, however, foundationalists still believe in one correct interpretation of history. Because of this, foundationalists also tend to reinforce the canons of the arts because their belief in a single historical truth fits with the canonical tendency to marginalize all perspectives except that of the official account. Almost inevitably the account foundationalists accept is the canonical one, taken wholesale from the consensus of historical specialists.

For example, foundationalist philosopher Jerrold Levinson bases his definition of a work of art on whether the artistic creator intended the created object for "regard-as-a-work-of-art, in any of the ways in which artworks existing prior to [it] are or were correctly (or standardly) regarded."[74] Although Levinson intends his definition to allow for historical relativity, it is actually a very ahistorical definition, because it implies universality for the historically relative concepts of the work of art and its creator. (This problem will be more fully discussed in chapter 3.) Most important for our purposes, Levinson's definition depends on the existence of a canon or, in his terms, a continuing tradition of "correct or standard regard" for the "artness" of objects. He leaves the gathering and organization of data in support of an object's canonicity entirely to historians of the arts under the assumptions that (1) a single historical truth exists as to the "correct regard" for an object, and (2) historians can supply the necessary information about the creator's intention in an objective manner. The task Levinson's definition outlines is entirely a canonical one; if historians attended to it, they would be occupying themselves wholly with creating correct, canonical narratives of artists and works.[75]

Pluralism, or relativist historicism, allows for the more radical contingencies of history, including the existence of multiple, historically relative frames of reference among historians and peoples, and of radical change and difference in the concepts and values surrounding human artistic practices. Aesthetic pluralists have been highly critical of the failure of analytic philosophers and methods to connect with actualities of art-historical practices, but they have so far done little themselves to challenge the weakness of historical canons as a basis for artistic understanding and discourse. David Carrier comes close to the issue of historical canons in his analysis of the practices of art historians.[76] Lydia Goehr is also close to the issue in her analysis of the historical relativity of canonical concepts, such as the "musical work."[77] Anita Silvers touches most directly on the subject with her recommendation for canonical revisionism to be a regular task for philosophers and historians, so that wrongfully omitted figures can be rescued with "authorizing stories."[78] Silvers views canons as entities created by political authority, rather than out of a priori, universal standards of value; her answer to canonical disenfranchisements is the establishment of political authority for previously marginalized voices. This is a workable approach, similar to the actual practice of many feminist and multiculturalist historians. We should be clear, however, that the main effect of applying Silvers's approach would be to produce more canons and longer canons. In the absence of a direct challenge to the legitimacy of canons, and in the face of limited public memory and understanding, Silvers's newly authorized voices are likely to continue to be marginalized, viewed as representative of particular identities rather than of the universal merit on which canons are believed to be founded.

So far, then, a thorough challenge to the critical legitimacy of historical canons as the basis of academic education in the arts has been missing from philosophy. The apparent lack of interest of philosophers of art in challenging the canons of the arts may stem from the association of canons with education—ironically, a matter of low intellectual status in philosophy, as in many disciplines. It may also stem from the identity interests of philosophers, whose training has led them to find debate over definitions more engaging and more professionally rewarding than research on issues of historical practice.

## TOWARD A PHILOSOPHICAL HISTORY OF THE ARTS

However, while academic philosophers have done little to challenge the legitimacy of historical canons of the arts, that doesn't mean that philosophy in the broadest sense can't be of help in the effort to broaden the basis of academic education in the arts. What is needed more than philosophical debate over definitions is the use of philosophical questions by philosophers, historians, students, and others to challenge traditional canons and conventions of what is and is not worth knowing. Philosophical questioning should not be reserved for philosophical specialists alone; we all need it, just as we all need the arts.

In my view, the best way to correct for the narrowness of historical canons of the arts is to combine philosophy with history to form a philosophical history of the arts.[79] In this approach philosophical questions about the nature and meaning of artistic practices help to determine what data should be remembered and how. Moreover, the emphasis in philosophical history is on identifying and analyzing large-scale functions in history, rather than on tracing canons of succession within smaller-scale disciplines or fields of activity. Thus, philosophical history can have the salutary effect of challenging the conceptual reifications of the separate art disciplines, which otherwise are too readily accepted by the academic specialists trained in accordance with them.

The arts are more in need of philosophical history than are other fields, for artistic concepts appear to have changed more radically than have concepts in, say, political history—where chronicles of battles and ruling dynasties have been a consistent focus for three millennia. By contrast, many of our modern concepts for the arts, such as the artwork, the creator, and the creator's intention, do not apply well over centuries, let alone the millennia over which they are often applied.

Philosophical history encourages consideration of interdisciplinary questions about the relatedness of the arts to other social practices, which are otherwise only sporadically discussed by historians trained primarily in a single art form. It is also more compatible with multiculturalism, because it dispenses with Eurocentrically based periods and concepts in favor of a broader, structural view of the role of the arts in human history, for which consideration of all cultures is clearly relevant. Most important of all, philosophical history focuses consideration on the larger human meanings of artistic styles and forms and their evolution, something that has been missing from canonical education in separate art disciplines. Such meanings are not to be found in detailed lists and data about influential Great Artists and Works, but rather by means of reconnecting our knowledge of artistic practices to the whole of human history.

There are a number of examples of a philosophicohistorical approach in recent writings about the arts. Most notable, in my view, is Ellen Dissanayake's *Homo Aestheticus: Where Art Comes from and Why*, which views human artistic activity in a philosophical way, as a species-central behavior of "making special" that developed because it encouraged the communal cooperation necessary for survival and advancement of the species. Unlike canonical histories, Dissanayake's approach encourages us to consider what the species-centric functions are of canonized artworks and of popular and contemporary artistic activity, including everything from clothing design in Africa to avant-garde academic composition in American universities.[80]

For another example, Arthur Danto has frequently written in a philosophicohistorical manner about the evolution of artistic styles.[81] Danto's interest is primarily on the internal, technical forces affecting stylistic development, an issue that has also been treated philosophically by art historian George Kübler in *The Shape of Time: Remarks on the History of Things* and by philosopher Richard Wollheim in *Painting as an Art*.[82] Danto's view that photography disenfranchised naturalism in painting, and that philosophy has now disenfranchised visual art (in the sense of an evolving tradition), can be seen as a philosophical history of modern painting, at least in industrialized cultures.[83] It has the kind of broad interest, beyond a specialist audience, of which philosophical history is especially capable—thus his success as an art critic. Unfortunately although these works and insights are available to general readers and often to students of aesthetics, they do not fit within the canonical curriculum of the arts departments themselves, so they are rarely read or considered in core arts survey and history courses taken by most college students.

Philosophical history may proceed best from a standpoint outside the specialized disciplines of the arts, where the categories of the arts are no longer assumed and the activities normally assigned to those categories can therefore be seen in a broader philosophical perspective. In my view, historian Ernest Gellner provides a very useful model for a philosophical history of the arts in a work entitled *Plough, Sword and Book: The Structure of Human History*.[84] Although he does not discuss artistic activity per se, Gellner's analysis helps to explain the development and differences in artistic practices among hunter-gatherer, agrarian, and industrial societies. For instance, according to Gellner's threefold model of human activity (including cognition, coercion, and production), it is clear that what we call the arts falls under the cognitive function of developing, instilling, and affirming social concepts (along with activities in areas of what we call science, religion, and philosophy). In hunter-gatherer societies, the cognitive function takes place in the form of rituals for the instillation of social concepts that we think of as myth. In agrarian cultures, the development of specialized classes for owning and maintaining land leads to the emergence of sophisticated artistic entertainments, with specialists trained to create and perform art works for the entertainment (and sometimes edification) of the landed aristocracy. Industrial cultures are then characterized by increasing specialization, as the arts become separate arenas for increasingly complex production and technology. The fact that in industrial cultures the preference for a particular artistic style may be a matter of cold conscious choice is one of the most troubling aspects of life in our times. That is, amid the industrial-age crush of data and choices—in which an authoritative sense of widely shared concepts has long since been lost—we seem, nonetheless, to continue the struggle for shared concepts of authenticity, identity, and community, or at least a fleeting sense of them. What we call the arts would appear to be the main expression of that cognitive struggle.

A general philosophical history of the arts can serve to refocus our attention from memorizing sequences of artists and works to considering questions of how and why the arts function in societies. Unlike historical canons of the arts, which require extensive knowledge of dates and names, philosophical history can be made coherent and consistent with other studies of history and culture in increments of any size, depending on the class or reading time available. Indeed, the emphasis on the connectedness of the arts to life makes philosophical history of the arts relevant to all kinds of disciplines and to people at every age and educational level. Used as a general introduction available to everyone, philosophical history of the arts makes art-historical knowledge accessible and memorable to historians, philosophers, and educators of all types and to students and the general public at all levels.

How would philosophical history affect the presentation of the art of, say, drama? As we saw earlier, drama receives an incoherent historical presentation within our current single-disciplinary curriculum; dramatic genres such as dance, opera, and film, are treated one-dimensionally by the departments that teach them, instead of as genres combining literary, visual, and musical aspects. In a philosophical history, though, drama would lose its separate canons and single-dimensional treatments and would be viewed in context with its large-scale social function: as representational ritual consisting of literary, musical, and visual aspects, used by its patrons and creators for the instilling of concepts. The philosophicohistorical narrative of drama would include all kinds of representations, from religious pageants to opera to film to music videos to home videos and even to television commercials, and it would focus on the nature and meaning of these dramatic genres and their connection with the societies and social practices from which they evolved. Through philosophical history, drama could become the means for students to study the most crucial questions of existence, as interpreted by people of many different times and places.

Education in the philosophical history of drama could begin in the earliest grades, in context with the appearance and discussion of any dramatic representation. For example, grade school students could not only see, perform, and compose children's plays (as they currently do); they could also discuss the concepts in them, how they were enacted, and what they teach us about life in general.[85] Later, when these same students began to read and view canonized dramas, they would be ready to consider critical issues of meaning and value in reference to them, rather than viewing them, in the canonical manner, as the means of acquiring cultural literacy at best and as old, elite, and irrelevant at worst. Aesthetic theories about the meaning and purpose of drama could be discussed in context with the performance and/or study of canonical works and of popular dramas on film and television today. Stylistic changes in dramatic genres, such as the development of dialogue in Greek tragedy or the use of musical leitmotifs in opera and film, would not be viewed primarily as individual achievements by canonized artists, but in the fuller context of stylistic evolution within artistic traditions, as well as of external social forces. For further information on individual styles, artists, and works, veterans of philosophical history could proceed to consult the specialists and the historical canons.

In short, the reform of arts education in the direction of philosophical history could result in a rise of understanding of the role of the arts in all our lives, among the general public as well as among specialists in the arts and aesthetics. One more soft-boundaried reform will be necessary to insure greater appreciation of the arts in American education: that of integrating experience and practice of the arts more fully into academic study, and vice versa. This reform will be discussed in Part III, "Soft Boundaries and the Future," following further consideration of the problems with hard-boundaried education in the arts and aesthetics.

# 3

# Uses of History in Some Recent Aesthetic Writings

Aesthetics, the study of cognitive judgments of sensory experience, is a subject that touches on every aspect of human life, from seeing, hearing, eating, touching, and smelling to thinking, learning, and loving. Why then, do Americans seem to dislike or resist learning about aesthetics? One reason is that almost no one knows what aesthetics is, or even how to spell it correctly ("esthetics" is preferred in some circles). The Greek roots of the term give it an arcane flavor that deters many, and the often convoluted debate of aesthetic specialists tends to deter the rest. Also, the meaning of the term and the breadth of the discipline have shifted many times since their formal origins in the mid-eighteenth century. The initial focus of aesthetics was on understanding the experiences of beauty in nature and, to a lesser degree, in the arts. This focus was supplanted in the nineteenth century by an emphasis on beauty and other aesthetic values specifically in reference to the arts. In the twentieth century analytic philosophers have made aesthetics into a complex field of debate about the meaning of relevant concepts, such as "aesthetic object," "aesthetic experience," and "work of art."

So, when students seek a straightforward definition of the already intimidating term of "aesthetics," what they are likely to receive from teachers or authors of writings on aesthetics may intimidate them all the more. A simple and memorable definition would help immeasurably to make this important discipline seem more accessible to students and the public. I like the definition "the practice of making sense of sensory experience": it's short, simple, and—with its asso-

An earlier version of this chapter appeared in the *Journal of Aesthetics and Art Criticism* in the special issue *Philosophy and the Histories of the Arts* 51 (1993): 363–75, under the title "History and the Philosophies of the Arts." It was first presented to the American Society for Aesthetics at the 1993 Philadelphia meeting as my response to the 1991 Institute on Philosophy and the Histories of the Arts.

nance, meter, and internal repetition—somewhat poetic, as I think a definition of aesthetics should be.

Aesthetics—the practice of making sense of sensory experience—is a broad interdisciplinary field of study. According to the major academic organization in the field, the American Society for Aesthetics, aesthetics includes "all studies of the arts and related types of experience from a philosophic, scientific, or other theoretical standpoint, including those of psychology, sociology, anthropology, cultural history, art criticism, and education." In practice, though, psychology, sociology, anthropology, and especially history have been marginal concerns in aesthetics, probably because aesthetics originated and became institutionalized as a subdiscipline of philosophy, dominated by philosophers specializing in the arts.[86] The tendency of philosophers in aesthetics to prefer debate over definitions to the study of actual artistic practices has led to an almost anti-historical perspective in some cases, with many aesthetic specialists arguing without much knowledge of the historical contexts in which their concepts originated.

The rising influence of historicism in many disciplines has had some effect on aesthetics, as philosophers in that discipline have come to recognize that understanding value depends on historical context.[87] However, even recent, historically influenced aesthetic writings reflect the imbalance of history and philosophy. In various ways, these writings depend on the bracketing of so many of the pesky realities of historical practice in the arts that they often fail to connect with issues on which historians, artists, and the public need the most philosophical direction, that is, issues of the meaning of the arts in our lives. In some cases, the bracketing is so extreme that the resulting definitions lose all credibility as explanations of artistic practice. Although sometimes fascinating in terms of their complexity, such definitions have had little influence on artists, historians, and educators within the separate disciplines of the arts because they are so obviously by and for professional philosophers.

To illustrate, let's take a brief survey of some current historically oriented aesthetic writings: those of Arthur Danto, Jerrold Levinson, Nöel Carroll, Anita Silvers, and Joseph Margolis. Roughly speaking, these fall into the categories of the foundationalist, or realist-historical position (Danto, Levinson, and Carroll) and the pluralist or relativist position (Silvers and, more radically, Margolis). (These positions were also discussed in chapter 2 in context with their relevance to art-historical canons; here the focus is the credibility of their theories for explaining the arts and their history in general.) According to the foundationalist position, the historical relativity of aesthetic styles and values over time is admitted and accounted for in the formulation of aesthetic definitions and judgments, but the presence of a single historical truth is nonetheless asserted. According to the pluralist position, the foundationalist notion of a single historical truth is rejected since, among other things, historical and cultural relativity applies to the minds of historians who do the preserving and narrating of historical data, as well as those whose statements and actions they record.[88]

## THE FOUNDATIONALIST-HISTORICAL POSITION: DANTO, LEVINSON, AND CARROLL

The most conservative of the foundationalists would appear to be Arthur Danto, who has theorized in rather hard-line Hegelian fashion of the "end of art" and whose historicist theory of interpretation was the first of the institutional theories of art, for which George Dickie is best known.[89] Danto's position is complex, to say the least, perhaps because despite his foundationalist stance, he is more aware than most philosophers of the complexities of practice in both art and history. His roping off of these complexities is done with considerable irony, as he deals, for example, with the gaps between what he thinks the "Ideal Chronicler" must know and what the mere human historian can detect of the fabric of history.[90]

Style is one of Danto's central aesthetic concerns: how to understand its evolution in a single artist, in artistic movements, and in the whole movement of art in history. These are large-scale issues in the face of which relativism must appear inadequate. In approaching them at all, Danto asks for a distinction between "narrativism de dictu"—presumably the belief that the historian can capture the narrative structure of history—and "narrativism de re"—the belief that the history of art itself is narratively structured.[91] He wants the historian to seek out, if not necessarily to find, "some credible internal relationship between beginning and end," something which is not structured by the historian, as relativist David Carrier would argue, but is in the structure of history itself. Metaphorically speaking, Danto wants a peek at God's plan, or at least the tools to facilitate a peek. The fact that his position is so compelling is an indication that God, and the metaphysical quest thereof, may not be so dead after all, in late-twentieth-century analytic philosophy or elsewhere.

But, although Danto's philosophy of art may succeed in the Delphic respect, in raising powerful questions about ourselves and our art, it runs the risk of isolating and alienating philosophy from history and art because of its apparent arrogance in identifying "the end of art" and because of the much lower role it assigns to artists and historians in the art-historical narrative. That is, philosophy in Danto's theory not only plays the central role in creating art (through interpretation), but it also inevitably leads to the disenfranchisement of art and history, when artists come to the end of stylistic development, recognize the meaning of their actions, and do historically insignificant, philosophical art from that point on.[92] According to Danto, this philosophical disenfranchisement of art took place in the mid-1960s, about the time of his critical encounter with Andy Warhol's Brillo cartons. However insightful Danto's claim turns out to be, it cannot help but be a jarring one to historians, who are trained to be cautious in interpreting the meaning of events close to their own time, particularly when it comes to the identification of a world-historical (to use the Hegelian term) ending. It also suffers from circular argumentation (that is, theory leading to interpretation and back again), for it is Danto's foundationalist historicism that causes him to seek a single narrative line of explanation for postmodern art and, failing to find it, to declare the end. Were he a historical relativist, the multiplicity of artistic expressions would not be problematic and might even suggest by extension the presence of more multiplicity in the past than earlier historians and philosophers have recognized in their narratives and definitions.

There is also the problem of extensive developments since the 1960s in the art of marginalized groups such as women and African Americans, developments that are clearly of some historical import. To say or imply that they are not significant is to raise questions about the hidden criteria upon which one's view of art-historical import is based. In general, the belief that there is one correct narrative of art through time may necessarily lead to insensitivity, however unintended, to the patterns of marginalization in history and historical narrative. This is one of the main reasons that history is needed by philosophy (and other disciplines): to remind philosophers of the human potential for marginalization and other failings, so that they can be on guard against them in their own process of questioning and defining.

Less metaphysical (despite the title of his book) is Jerrold Levinson's philosophy of art as contained in *Music, Art, and Metaphysics* (1990).[93] As the most explicitly historical of current philosophies of art, Levinson's approach deserves full discussion here, although otherwise one hesitates to add much to the already extensive commentary upon it. In its historical context, Levinson's philosophy is one among the many analytic attempts to surmount the main definitional dilemma of aesthetics in the wake of Morris Weitz's influential article "The Role of Theory in Aesthetics" (1956), where he argued that Ludwig Wittgenstein's theory of games made analytic definitions of the arts unnecessary and illegitimate. Contrary to its purpose, Weitz's article led to renewed vigor among analytic philosophers competing to best define the necessary and sufficient conditions for recognizing works of art.[94] In Levinson's solution to the dilemma, the defining of artworks occurs according to the historically fixed intentions of artistic producers: "a work of art is a thing intended for regard-as-a-work-of-art, regard in any of the ways works of art existing prior to it have been correctly regarded."[95]

What problems and variables of history are roped off and overlooked in Levinson's approach? First he overlooks or at least seriously underestimates the problem of the historical relativity of the concept "artwork" and its resulting weakness as a basis for a general philosophy of art. He also implicitly overlooks the historical relativity of the concept of the autonomous artistic producer, or as he puts it, the "independent individual (or individuals)" whose intention fixes the correct regard of the artwork; and he relies on the equally contingent concept of property rights as a universal basis for deciding whose intentions and interpretations will apply.[96] Actually, though, the concepts of the autonomous artist and artwork, not to mention property rights, are far from universal. In fact they only apply consistently in the Western tradition to literary and visual artworks from after the Middle Ages, and to musical works from the latter eighteenth century and on; and they are even more problematic in application to non-Western traditions. Levinson's reliance on these nonuniversal concepts makes his definition highly questionable for any but the most limited use.

Even where creative autonomy can be reasonably established, Levinson's definition raises another serious historical problem: that is, how can something as complex and psychological as intentions be clearly enough fixed by an art producer to be understood by themselves, let alone future scholars who must reconstruct them in order to make the determination of artness, according to Levinson. (This is a problem for Richard Wollheim and Anthony Savile as well, both of whom rely on intentionality as a central factor in defining and understanding works of art.[97])

Levinson's concepts of the autonomous artwork, the autonomous producer, and the artist's intentions are most problematic in the art of music, on which he has written and theorized the most. Music is a performance art for which the most easily identifiable object—the notated score—is a highly relative factor in musical production. For instance, many substantive musical repertories (for example, song, dance, and improvised instrumental genres) exist in Western and other cultures for which scores are rarely made or contemplated and for which the notion of an autonomous, intention-laden producer is thus highly problematic. Even where the preparation of scores is a standard part of musical performance, the practices of which musical features are notated precisely, which features are implied, and which features are left entirely to the performers are different for different cultures, periods, composers, genres, and so forth. Levinson is aware of the pitfalls of identifying music by the notated score; he instead proposes that a musical work is an indicated performed-sound structure.[98] But he still insists on the objectified concepts of autonomous work and composer, saying that the notion of artist as creator is "a deep-rooted idea that merits preservation if at all possible. . . . If it is possible to align musical works with indisputably creatable art works such as painting and sculptures, then it seems we should do so."[99]

But is the notion of artist as creator "a deep-rooted idea"? Not within the balance of human experience. Rather it is a notion with very shallow roots, going back little further than the European Renaissance among painters and sculptors and less far for musicians. If the artist-as-creator cannot be fairly called a deep-rooted idea, there is no reason for Levinson or anyone else to align the definition of music with that of the "indisputably creatable artworks such as painting and sculptures." For that matter, Levinson's fixation on "creatability" places unwarranted emphasis on the physicality of art, considering that the physical material of sculpture, painting, and even architecture decay over time, just as do musical sounds. What is left, according to a less objectified view of art, are cultural artifacts that can help us understand the artistic practices of the past, but which are not themselves art.

Since we are dealing with a historically oriented theory, it may be useful to consider which historical art forms might be included and excluded under Levinson's definition. Here again the problem of historical context intrudes, because "art" itself is a historically relative concept (a factor which Levinson mentions but minimizes).[100] We cannot correctly assume that the art objects canonized in museums and history books were produced under the same understanding of what art is and does under which we operate. But even if we rope off that problem, we still face others. Consider, for instance, that Levinson's definition requires a starting point somewhere, some object whose art status is certain. From the standpoint of the relativity of the concept "art," the best place to start would appear to be in the recent past, where we can be most certain that the concept is close to our own. But the definition also implies a causal chain spreading forward from the most distant past, with each artifact's art status dependent on the producer's intention for it to have "regard in any of the ways works of art existing prior to it have been correctly regarded." The paradox is that we cannot be certain of correct regard for any part of the chain unless we start at the beginning, but, at the same time, the beginning is precisely where we are least sure that "art" exists as a comparable concept to ours. So where do we start the chain, at the beginning or at the end?[101]

Actually, these are merely academic quibbles, because Levinson does not appear to expect that anyone, philosopher or historian, will actually construct the chain. His theory is not meant to bring philosophy and history together, but to compete in the post-Weitz sweepstakes for the best, most defensible definition of art. Whether the definition is institutionally applied and with what actual consequences is an issue that Levinson leaves to others, presumably the art historians. The fact that they might get it wrong (because it's doubtful that it could be applied successfully) is not a central concern, since the foundationalist-historical position allows for the possibility of many, perhaps all, incorrect narratives in actual practice.

Nonetheless, in the interest of thoroughness, let's consider how Levinson's theory would apply to an actual case. Does a piece of Gregorian chant fit his definition of music, for example? With Levinson's theory we approach this question by asking if a particular piece of Gregorian chant was intended for regard-as-a-work-of-art, in any of the ways works of arts existing prior to it had been correctly regarded. To answer this question requires historical evidence of authorship and intention that is seldom available or understandable to the musicologist, let alone the philosopher. In the case of our example, the "composer" of the great majority of Gregorian chants is anonymous, and even when authorship is known there is little likelihood of finding evidence of intentionality about "regard." What evidence there is suggests that Gregorian chant should be excluded, since it was more a part of liturgical practice than something regarded as a work of art (whatever that might be inferred to mean circa 800 A.D.). According to the myth recorded by Franconian scribes in their manuscript illustrations, for instance, the "composer" of Gregorian chant is God, who dictated the sacred liturgical language through a dove into the ear of Pope Gregory the Great.

Still, Levinson admits Gregorian chant as music,[102] perhaps influenced by the fact that it is canonical; that is, it has long been accepted and taught as music by music historians. The question of how Gregorian chant got to be canonical and whether the canonization is logical is evaded here (although such philosophical questions are exactly what is needed by music historians). And indeed, if the foundationalist-historical position is correct, Levinson doesn't have to address it, because according to that view there is only one correct narrative, that of real historical truth. If mistake of identification occur, it is due to a mistake in the facts, not the theory.

Let's assume for the moment that a mistake has been made in the identification process that is subsequently corrected, resulting in the exclusion of Gregorian chants as musical works. We are still left in this case with another historical problem: that of when and how the vast numbers of polyphonic compositions based on Gregorian chant come to attain the status of musical works, if indeed they can make the transition under Levinson's prescription from regard-as-liturgy to regard-as-art at all. This vast repertory includes all the polyphonic music that used Gregorian chant for an underlying cantus firmus from the tenth century forward to J. S. Bach and even beyond. It thus extends into the Romantic concert-hall repertory, since many Romantic composers quote from the "Dies Irae" chant. One can argue, even with Hector Berlioz's "Dream of a Witches' Sabbath" in his *Symphonie Fantastique*, that regard-as-liturgy still applies; otherwise the use of the "Dies Irae" to illustrate the damned would not have the emotive and descriptive power it does.

The case of Gregorian chant and its decendants is far from an unusual one, for human practices in and out of music do not appear to evolve in a single, causal chain, guided by a godlike or Hegelian narrative plan. Rather, artistic practices and the cultural artifacts that they leave frequently evolve along very different lines than those of original intent, as can be seen in many cases where historical evidence of intent is plentiful. Certainly J. S. Bach, to use what should be among the safest of canonical examples for Levinson's definition of art, never intended his then-unpublished sacred works such as the *B Minor Mass*, the sacred cantatas, the Passions, and the organ chorales, toccatas, and fugues to be attended to in the cognitive manner some philosophers of art prescribe or assume, instead of in religious manner during church services. If even Bach and canonical Romantic music doesn't work unambiguously in support of Levinson's definition, what music does? Also, even if some music can be found and defended as unambiguously doing so, shouldn't the far greater body of excluded and questionable music throw this philosophical enterprise into question? In short, Levinson's definition may be a strong contender in the post-Weitz sweepstakes of philosophical aesthetics, but its detachment from actual practice in art and history renders it of questionable value for artists, historians, and others who might wish to engage in aesthetic inquiry.

The practical problems of art and history are more credibly dealt with in Nöel Carroll's approach to history. Carroll calls for a reorientation from looking at art in the objectified form of artworks towards looking at art as a historical, cultural practice, wherein "the question of whether or not an object (or a performance) is to be regarded as a work of art depends on whether or not it can be placed in the evolving tradition of art in the right way."[103] With Carroll's approach, the task of historical narration is not just a theoretical construct to be carried out or not by someone else as they choose but is more central to the art philosopher's task, since it is the history that produces the knowledge of the details of art practice on which the philosophic questions and definitions are to be based. Carroll also avoids the trap of requiring necessary and sufficient conditions to separate art from other cultural practices; in fact, he admits the likely conjunction of art to other cultural practices, as, according to his narrative procedure, art's processes of repetition, amplification, and repudiation are traced back through time. He further admits the messy, ill-defined character of many cultural practices in their origins and evolutions.[104] Of art, then, it can safely be said that Carroll excludes nothing. His approach is necessarily narrower in its philosophic aims than is Danto's or Levinson's, but at the same time it is broader in its ability to account for complexity in art practices.

What Carroll does not account for, however, is the complexity and relativity in art-historical practice, as each historian approaches the necessity of preserving, organizing, and telling a coherent story of art's past. In this respect, Carroll is perhaps the furthest of the foundationalists from the consensus among historians and philosophers of history, most of whom recognize the necessary entrance of imagination and perspective into the historian's processes. Carroll's narrative approach to defining art also brings to mind a caveat from recent narrative theory: that the structure of narrative inherently functions to impose unities over experience, unities that may correspond more to the controlling myths of the time than to the experience narrated. It is no accident, according to some narrative theorists, that certain practices and groups, especially women, have been omitted or marginalized from historical narratives and that those whose stories have been told have been distorted.[105] Indeed, the historical evidence for marginalization, omission, and distortion in the practice of art-historical narration is overwhelming and has been the focus of much feminist revisionary work since 1970 and the rise of academic feminism.[106] The foundationalist-historical position leads to the rejection of all this evidence as merely proof that art historians can and do write incorrect narratives. The historical problem that a single "correct" narrative may be impossible is thus not seriously considered in Carroll's philosophy of art.

## THE PLURALIST APPROACH: SILVERS, MARGOLIS, AND GOEHR

Pluralism is much less problematic in its conception of history than is foundationalism. It doesn't have to try, as foundationalism does, to rope off the contingencies of which history is so full in order to make plausible the notion of a single historical truth. Rather, pluralism allows for historical and cultural variability in every concept that has evolved in the philosophic search for knowledge about art; in fact, pluralism of the radical relativist variety revels in its variability. For some, this is precisely the problem with radical relativism in application to history and elsewhere: it seems to require deconstruction of the individual ego strength necessary to human life, particularly the philosophical task of trying to define oneself and the world. If truth is only relative and contextual, then the point of life and philosophy is thrown into more radical question than many wish to handle.

Prominent among the pluralists is Anita Silvers, who has argued that the foundationalist-historical position (represented under the term "traditionalism" in her article) inevitably fails to come to terms with an oft-overlooked but central concern in the philosophy of art: the issue of the canon, or the determination of artistic value over time.[107] Contrary to the concerns of some foundationalists and essentialists, Silvers maintains that pluralist revision of canons need not "minimalize the importance of aesthetic value by making it instrumental."[108] Indeed, she criticizes art philosophers for failing to heed the central issue that Weitz actually posed in his influential essay of 1956, that of moving beyond the issue of definition (which he thought he had resolved) and addressing the issue of value.

In seeking to address the issue of value herself, Silvers focuses on the authorizing power of narrative, saying that "art which endures does so in virtue of being the subject of powerfully authorizing stories."[109] While she is aware of the postmodern criticisms of narrative and artistic authority, she rejects that position in favor of a revisionism, whereby marginalized or omitted artists and art practices can be rescued and authorized by later historians.[110] She thus admits the relativity of historical perspective and truth, without sacrificing the human claim to subjective authority.

Silvers's position is very promising in its allowance for a full conception of art, history, and philosophy, in theory and practice. In particular, her emphasis on the canon shows concern in the practical results of art-philosophical inquiry that many other art philosophers appear to lack. Postmodern feminists may question her trust in heroic narrative, to many a masculine-identified means, as a way by which "her(oine's)" story can be told, and they may disagree with her emphasis on the need for subjective authority in the feminist project. On the other hand, however, Silvers is suspicious that the postmodern demotion of the author should come at the very moment when the authority of women has become a possibility in the art world.

Remaining on the radical-relativist left of Silvers is Joseph Margolis. As far back as 1974, Margolis theorized that both artistic producers and objects are "physically embodied and culturally emergent entities," after the influence of Foucault and against the analytic fashions of the time.[111] Since then he has continued to raise questions about the evasion of the complexities of art practice by analytic philosophers. Thus according to a recent article by Margolis, analytic aesthetics "is an extremely narrow gauge of thought," with

almost no emphasis to be found in it on the complexities of history, the historicizing of cognition and inquiry, the praxical context of judgment, taste, description, explanation, interpretation, the discontinuities of cultural movements, horizonal blindness, and, most particularly, the social forces that form and preform the conceptual orientation of human selves apt for any of the pertinent roles belonging to the world of art.[112]

Similar to poststructural hermeneutic theory, Margolis's radical relativism makes room for the historical past to change the future and for the future to change the past, in the sense of reinterpreting works and intentions according to contemporary standards. He is therefore critical of the philosophical attempt to fix artworks by historically based intentions, since in his view the future will inevitably reinterpret those intentions.

While Margolis's radical relativism may appear destabilizing in some respects, it actually provides a more stable stance in others, particularly in the problem of making sense out of the proliferating tangle of currently produced versus museum-preserved artworks and practices. According to Margolis's reasoned view, every artwork, be it old, new, folk, classical or pop, is a culturally emergent entity whose historicity and relevance to the culture in which it is currently emergent must be considered. Hamlet's recent emergence in the physical embodiment of Mel Gibson on film is an event of our time, as is the release of *Teenage Mutant Ninja Turtles III.* To be a philosopher of art would seem to commit one to deal with the meaning of such events, as Margolis does. If more philosophers were to accept the challenge of radical relativism, they could be of great assistance to historians and teachers of the arts, who have been facing a near crisis of identity as to what artistic knowledge is necessary to cultural literacy and who are not helped by arcane disputes over whether this or that practice fits a particular aesthetic definition. In fact, the frequent mix of uncontextualized concepts from different historical epochs in philosophical debates has the effect of turning the field of aesthetics into a Tower of Babel, with unanalyzed historical frames of reference, rather than separate languages, confusing and scattering the participants. By comparison, Margolis's radical relativism poses less of a threat to the ability to constitute oneself as a coherent subject than does the acontextual use of historical positions as they appear convenient to one's arguments or views.

Margolis's treatment of artists as "physically embodied, culturally emergent entities" may also be a better approach than the heroic idealization of Silvers particularly in light of twentieth-century psychological findings on the artistic process. Without necessarily agreeing with Freud, Jung, Klein, Kristeva and others as to the problematic psychology of artists, there is nonetheless something highly suspicious about our Romantic myth of the heroic artist when it leads in practice to so much alienation between the individual artist and society. Death of the author, at least as alienated hero, could be a very positive development if it allowed for the reemergence of art as an important cultural practice in the lives of people throughout society, rather than just in the specialized professions of art. By comparison, the task of continuing canonization that Silvers lays out would seem to emphasize the isolation of art in society if, as seems likely, the authorizing stories continue to focus on heroic artistic proficiencies beyond the abilities of ordinary people.

Another recent and influential pluralist approach is that of Lydia Goehr, who has explored the normative functions and functional lives of such aesthetic concepts as "the musical work" in their historical contexts.[113] The idea of time-bound concepts and with it the assumption of different concepts for different cultures and epochs is an attractive and useful one in countering the certainties of strict constructionists and foundationalists. Yet the time-bound approach can lead to arguments that are almost as distant from the actualities of historical and cultural practice as the strict constructionist debates over eighteenth-century definitions if those involved are more interested in philosophical argumentation than in public understanding of the arts.

## CONCLUSION

The failure of philosophers in aesthetics to come to terms with the realities of history and practice in the arts is a prime example of how the hard-boundaried paradigm has hurt understanding and communication in the arts and aesthetics. At the same time, the paradigm covers up its own negative effects, for as long as specialists in aesthetics debate only one another in professional conferences and journals, their failure to communicate general understanding about the arts and aesthetics will not be noticed.

Only when philosophical specialists in aesthetics attempt to spread their debate to students and the general public do difficulties appear, as nonspecialists turn away in dismay from the debate. The lack of interest by nonspecialists then has the effect of making the specialists even more insular, seeking "mimetic engulfment" (in Bruce Wilshire's term) in ever more elite professional circles where understanding and approval of their scholarship is available.[114] Outside of those circles insular language and concerns of the specialists convey the impression that understanding the arts and aesthetics is not a matter for the general public; it is merely a matter for a small group of specialists who are not particularly well paid or well respected.

Meanwhile, Americans need the help of philosophers to understand how and why the arts are functioning in society today, just as we need their help with ethics, logic, epistemology, and other philosophical problems. If philosophers in aesthetics debate terminology with one another instead of engaging with issues in the arts that affect us all, they do not help us.

I cannot end this chapter better than asking again, what would Plato think?

# Part II

# *Boundaries in Music*

We have seen in Part I that American education is hurt by the hard-boundaried fragmentation of the arts and aesthetics into separate disciplines and subdisciplines. In Part II, the analysis of hard boundaries is extended to the discipline of music, probably the most fragmented of all the arts in our educational system. Chapter 4, "Fragmentation in the Musical Field," provides a brief sketch of the development and the perspective of each of the many groups of music academics: from musicologists to music theorists and composers to music educators, to performers and conductors. Chapter 5, "Soft Boundaries and Relatedness: A New Paradigm for Understanding Music," discusses the need for a new paradigm of soft boundaries to alleviate the fragmentation in the musical field and reconnect musical concerns with the wider public. Chapter 6, "Soft Boundaries, Autonomist/Formalist Aesthetics, and Music Theory" extends discussion of the need for soft boundaries in music to research and teaching in music theory, recommending a more culturally connected approach to the analysis of music. Further ideas on how to integrate the study of music theory with other aspects of music appear in Chapter 7 of Part III, "Soft Boundaries and the Future," entitled "Integrating History, Theory, and Practice in the College Music Curriculum."

# 4

# Fragmentation in the Musical Field

As discussed in Part I, hard-boundaried specialization has had a very negative effect on education in the arts and aesthetics: it has marginalized them as single-disciplinary concerns of specialists, unconnected to each other and to the general curriculum. Within the individual disciplines of the arts, hard-boundaried specialization has further led to the development of separate subdisciplines of history, theory, and practice in various art forms. Some of the arts are more divided and subdivided than others. In drama, issues of theory, history, and practice are often integrated in the study and preparation of historical works for performances. In the visual arts, issues of history and theory are merged in undergraduate art history classes. In music, however, there are sharp divisions between history, theory, practice, and there are many other divisions as well.

Specialization is so advanced in the discipline of music that is more properly called fragmentation: a fragmentation of the musical field into separate subdisciplines of musicology, ethnomusicology, music theory, composition, music education, musical aesthetics, music therapy, music psychology, music sociology, popular music, music in general education, music performance, and conducting. Actually it is difficult to list all the separate subdisciplines that currently fragment the musical field because there are separate academic societies, journals, and programs for virtually every instrument and musical activity under the sun. Most of the specialties in music are contained within the discipline of music and its departments, but not all of them: music therapy and music psychology are typically under psychology; music sociology is under sociology; popular music is under cultural studies, communication, or even English; and musical aesthetics is under aesthetics in philosophy. Each specialty has a different perspective on what is important in research, education, and practice, with the result that music departments feature more factional relationships than typically exist elsewhere in academia. There is one organization, the College Music Society, which brings the factions together; otherwise music academics are a highly frag-mented, fractious bunch.[115]

Fragmentation also characterizes the curriculum of college-level music de-partments. Except where the small size of a music department disallows spe-cialization, music departments are generally divided among musicologists, theorists, educators, conductors, composers, and performers, all of whom offer separate courses and programs in their specialties. Precollege education in music rests on specialization as well: music, like all of the arts, is considered to be under the purview of music and art specialists, who unfortunately may not be available on the teaching staffs of many schools. Because of the overall domi-nance of specialists in American education, there is no contrary force that can act to limit or control the entrenchment of specialization in music, regardless of the harmful extremes of fragmentation that have resulted from it. Instead, spe-cialists typically work to maintain or increase the power and position of their specialty, even when that specialty is rendered less important by social or tech-nological change. During the last century, changes in technology and society have altered the nature of musical knowledge, production, and distribution. Yet because of the entrenchment of multiple groups of specialists on music faculties, music curricula have changed very little.

## FROM WHENCE FRAGMENTATION? A BRIEF HISTORY OF AMERICAN MUSICAL EDUCATION

In order to gain a better understanding of the problem of fragmentation in the musical field, we need to examine the history of American musical education and how and why the separate musical subdisciplines and perspectives have developed as they have. (I use the term "musical education" here to indicate musical education in general, as distinguished from the subdiscipline of "music education," which refers to education of precollege students in music and, at the college level, future music teachers.)

Ironically, the problem of fragmentation in our musical field is partly due to the comparative strength of general musical education in our past, in contrast with education in the other art forms. Surprisingly, given the current margin-alization of the discipline, music and musical education have played a prominent role in American history. Institutionalized musical education began in the church singing schools of the eighteenth century, which functioned to teach church-goers how to sing the hymns of their liturgy without the help of the organs and professional choirs (the mainstay of European church music, at least until sixteenth-century Reformation leaders discouraged their use). In the New World, the predominance of Reform worshippers over Catholics among the colonists led to a more democratic, less professional form of music in worship, organized around the unaccompanied singing of hymns. The simpler style of Protestant sacred music was more easily achieved than the Catholic style, given the comparatively rustic circumstances of the colonial settlers—that is, the scarcity of musical instruments and skilled professionals.

Because of the hymn-singing tradition, the American colonies had a fairly literate musical culture, in which music was spread through published collections of psalms, and other settings of sacred texts that were learned in singing schools and performed in church. By the late eighteenth century, the unique traditions of musical education in America had resulted in distinctive American musical practices, including the development of shape-note singing, the proliferation of the unaccompanied polyphonic genres of a so-called rougher style of counterpoint in which conventional European rules for avoidance of parallel 5ths and octaves between voices were habitually broken (mainly because of the practice of men and women singing the same parts in octaves). Of course, the education offered in the eighteenth-century singing schools was predominately practical and performance oriented; that is, it was designed to produce adequate musical performances rather than any more general understanding of music.

In the nineteenth century, the movement for universal public education in the United States was accompanied by strong advocacy for regular music education as well, and the concept of what that education should consist of was influenced primarily by the practical and performance-oriented traditions of the singing schools. To the extent that an academic focus existed in American musical education, it took the form not of academic learning in music history and theory, but rather in the emphasis on European musical styles. In particular, Lowell Mason and his followers believed that a proper musical education meant rehearsal and performance of European music as opposed to more generalized study of music in culture or of more indigenous American styles. Thus, while outside the United States public (and private) music education included academic focuses on history and theory, American musical education focused entirely on performance.

Along with public education in music came the need for education of music teachers. Teacher education in music began in Boston in 1834 with a series of conventions led by Mason and George Webb on methods of teaching music, mainly by means of rehearsal and performance of musical works. The 1830s also saw the adoption of music as a regular publicly supported subject in the curriculum first in Boston and the states of New York, Maryland, the District of Columbia, Connecticut, Rhode Island, Pennsylvania, New Jersey, Kentucky, and Ohio; and by the 1850s in the cities of San Francisco, San Antonio, Chicago, Memphis, St. Louis, Terre Haute, Cleveland, and Columbus.[116] As America became industrialized in the years following the Civil War, musical education became widespread in the public school system, but the reconsensus was still far from universal for its need. General music instruction became standard in the lower grades partly because the movements for child-centered and progressive education viewed music as essential to early education; but its inclusion in early education has never been very extensive.

In order to promote music as a general curricular subject in the schools, music educators formed national and state organizations. The largest and most influential of the organizations was the Music Educators National Conference (MENC), originally founded in 1909 as the Music Supervisors' National Conference, with the name change following in 1934. The Music Teachers' National Association, founded in 1875, was less influential, focusing mainly on promoting individual student achievement as opposed to curricular policy. The MENC's greatest success in promoting inclusion of music education at the secondary level was in the area of large music ensembles: chorus, orchestra, and band. These ensembles were popular with administrators in that they were economical—large groups of students could easily be placed with a single instructor—and they were useful in promoting schools through their performances in concerts and contests put on by the ensembles. Large-ensemble-based music education made it difficult for instructors to go beyond rehearsal and performance of simple music in a few limited genres, but this problem became largely invisible at the secondary level, because those students and teachers who might have preferred a broader form of music education were likely to have already left the system. Thus, the system worked to reproduce itself by encouraging and rewarding students and teachers that liked the large-ensemble-based approach, to the neglect of other musical skills and knowledge.

With the growth of music programs at the secondary level, there was increasing demand for programs in higher education, as well. By the end of the nineteenth century, departments and schools of music were widespread. Yet even as college-level musical education spread through the country, the scholarly study of music—musicology—had yet to gain a foothold in American education. A mere nine individuals established the American Musicological Society in 1934, long after musicology had become a force in European musical education. Further, although musicology grew after World War II, its influence was still limited by the tendency toward hard-boundaried specialization at that time, leading to the fragmentation of musicology into separate camps of history and theory and the establishment in the 1960s of a separate discipline of music theory (to be discussed in chapter 6). Also, the limited focus of most musicologists on Western music alone weakened the influence of the discipline and led to the development of another separate subdiscipline of ethnomusicology, the study of musical cultures outside the Western art music tradition.[117]

With musicology acting as a late-arriving, divided influence in American musical education, the curricula of college-level music departments and secondary schools were controlled primarily by music educators and performers, both of whom were trained to view the practice of music as the primary educational concern at all levels of study. In the nineteenth century, musical performance in high schools had been confined mainly to choruses singing music from the European art music tradition, while in colleges performance was mainly extracurricular, with student groups like the Whiffenpoofs of Yale teaching and directing themselves. Some schools, especially in communities with high German populations, developed orchestras, but the performance difficulty was often beyond students. Gradually experience with orchestral music depended more and more on Young People's Concerts, an approach begun by Frank Damrosch in 1898 wherein professional orchestras and conductors acted as music appreciation teachers for young audiences.

In the early twentieth century a new and very powerful influence entered the American music curriculum: band. In comparison with European-style orchestras, bands were a more popular, more indigenous part of American culture, and the tradition of band performance, as developed by John Philip Sousa among others, emphasized entertainment, which reached a wide audience. Marching bands first appeared in the schools in the early twentieth century, transplanted from the battlefields of the Civil War to the playing fields of athletics. Marching band quickly became a powerful influence in American music education. Band director Mark Hindsley's 1932 rationale for marching band explains why:

The value of the marching band to music education in general lies in its advertising power. It provides a strong incentive to all youth to study music so as to participate in band activities. Parents are quick to realize the worth of such an organization in a disciplinary way and as an outlet for some of the child's leisure time and surplus energy, and accept it also as providing an entrance to further musical culture, in which they are at the time probably more interested than the child himself.[118]

Unfortunately, the "advertising power" for which Hindsley and others most value marching bands is only indirectly connected to the goal of actually learning about music. Far from providing "an entrance to further musical culture," the dominance of marching bands draws energy away from the broader array of musical and artistic traditions towards a singular focus on marching band repertoire, which then becomes a primary focus on college-level music study as well. Out of football season, concert band performance provides students with a wider array of musical challenges, but the repertoire is still quite limited compared to the repertoire available for other ensembles and instruments.

The popularity of band and the availability of athletic-based funds for recruitment of college-level music majors to fill their ranks has, nonetheless, led to enormous power and dominance for band programs in musical education at both the college and precollege levels. Indeed, the dirty secret of many large state music departments is that many if not most music majors are high school band members recruited by means of scholarship money funded by well-funded college athletic programs, with the expectation that the recipients will serve the programs' interests. The opportunity to get a sizable college scholarship in exchange for doing something found enjoyable in high school is attractive to students and their parents, but in terms of the time required to participate in the ensemble the student would probably be better off working for McDonald's and choosing their own major.[119]

The dominance of large bands in American music education since the 1930s is the most peculiar, fragmenting factor in the musical field today. Although band music was initially popular and indigenous to American culture when it entered the schools in the early twentieth century, its dominance in schools today is singular and unrelated to the popularity and significance of large bands outside of the schools; thus it constitutes a "school-music culture."[120] Yet the power and influence of athletic programs keeps schools and colleges in the business of producing bands and band directors, far above any other musical activities and skills.

The dominance of large bands is not the only fragmenting factor in American musical education today. In fact, all the fragmented perspectives of the various types of music educators have created a system in which communication is difficult and curricular reform next to impossible. Besides the limiting perspectives of band directors there are other limiting perspectives that are harmful to the cause of representing music in education as the rich human pursuit that it is. The system in music is overwhelmingly replicative, not transformative, the students and teachers it attracts are those who are content with the status quo. The following is a brief sketch of the backgrounds and perspectives of other specialties regularly represented in music departments and how they interact with each other. (Specialties that are structural subdisciplines outside of music such as music psychology and music therapy are not included here. Their perspectives are drawn from that of their controlling disciplines, and influence and interaction between them and the music department–based specialists is extremely limited.)

## MUSICOLOGY AND ETHNOMUSICOLOGY

Musicologists (also known as music historians) are the definers and teachers of historical knowledge in Western music; ethnomusicologists deal with musical cultures all over the world. Musicology developed in Europe in the late eighteenth and early nineteenth centuries and thus it reflects the beliefs of European historical specialists in that era in individualism, nationalism, male dominance in the workplace, and European primacy in the world. In fact, because German musicologists were most influential in the nineteenth century, music history ever since has remained under the spell of the "three B's": the German composers. J. S. Bach, Ludwig van Beethoven, and (to a lesser extent) Johannes Brahms.

Despite the rejection by modern musicologists of much nineteenth-century research, modern music history has retained much of its nineteenth-century character as a canon of European composers, or as some put it, of dead, white European males. That canon has excluded study of music of non-Western cultures to such a degree that the separate discipline of ethnomusicology became necessary to address those concerns. (Actually, the terms "ethnomusicology" and "musicology" should more logically be reversed, with ethnomusicology as the ethnocentric study of Western music and musicology as the comprehensive term.) Ironically, now that ethnomusicology have their own discipline, many of them oppose efforts of musicologists to incorporate non-Western music into their teaching on the grounds that the subject should only be taught by specialists.

In the twentieth century, musicology and ethnomusicology have, like many other humanities disciplines, been heavily influenced by the ideal of an objective, scientific methodology, which Joseph Kerman has called "positivism." The obscure topics of articles in major research journals in musicology have demonstrated this positivism. For example, the table of contents of the Spring 1987 *Journal of the American Musicological Society* shows a list of articles unlikely to be of interest to musicologists in general, let alone musicians or the general public:

1. Charlemagne's Archetype of Gregorian Chant—Kenneth Levy
2. Landini's Musical Patrimony: A Reassessment of Some Compositional Conventions in Trecento Polyphony—Michael Long
3. Musical Evidence of Compositional Planning in the Renaissance: Josquin's "Plus Nulz Regretz"—Christopher Reynolds
4. Historical Interdependency of Music: A Case Study of the Chinese Seven-String Zither—Bell Yung.[121]

Obviously, these are articles based on research by specialists in particular areas of musicology, and they are read primarily by other specialists in that area. The status and success of musicologists depends on their ability and willingness to engage in such research. How this research reaches and affects other music specialists and the general public is a question that is rarely, if ever, raised.[122]

Since the 1980s, musicology has become less purely positivistic under the influence of the "new musicology," style of musicological scholarship in which more notice is taken of the cultural influences and meanings of historical styles. The influence of "new musicology" on the discipline has resulted in, among other things, research in popular music styles, the development of feminist and gay musicology, and the rise of musical semiotics—the interpretation of musical signs and symbols. A listing of articles from the Spring 1997 issue of the *Journal of the American Musicological Society* shows the greater cultural connectedness of recent musicological research:

1. Frames and Images: Locating Music in Cultural Histories of the Middle Ages—Phillip Weller
2. Schumann and Romantic Distance—Berthold Hoeckner
3. For Those We Love: Hindemith, Whitman, and "An American Requiem"—Kim H. Kowalke[123]

These articles still clearly involve specialized research probably beyond the understanding of most musical specialists and enthusiasts, but at least the titles reflect more interest in connecting musical research with other scholarly discipline. Unfortunately, given the drop of enrollments in music and the decrease in numbers of faculty positions in musicology in recent decades, relatively few of the younger, more culturally connected musicologists have been able to get jobs teaching music history. Instead, music history courses remain in the hands of traditionally trained musicologists or, at smaller colleges, in the hands of nonmusicologists whose reliance on a narrowly defined canon may be even more entrenched.

Indeed, the canon of music history is a particularly narrow and conservative one. It presents a series of European male composers improbably "begetting" each other with little help from women, non-Europeans, or traditions of popular and folk music. Recent textbooks have redressed the imbalances a bit. Even Donald Grout's staunchly conservative *History of Western Music* (6th edition, co-authored by Claude Palisca)[124] now actually includes a few musical examples by women composers. But these improvements are relatively slight and do nothing to address the structural deemphasis of popular and world musics in the curriculum. The music history canon is also problematic in its inconsistency with other arts canons and with the political and social history of the world. The long-standing lack of interest of most musicologists in pedagogy and curriculum as, presumably, unscholarly concerns makes these problems very difficult to address in a systematic manner.[125]

## MUSIC THEORY AND COMPOSITION

One hopes for a more coherent view of musical practice from the discipline of music theory, the study of how music "works." Unfortunately music theorists are often even more isolated in their approach to understanding music than are musicologists; they tend to approach and teach music as a set of formally analyzable chords and other pitch structures. The history of music theory as a discipline helps explain the pitch-oriented nature of its focus. Unlike music theorists of previous times, who were academic or liturgical scholars concerned with many aspects of musical structure, modern music theorists are mainly composers, absorbed into American universities in the post–World War II period when universities needed music faculty and prestige, and the composers needed a dependable income to make up for their loss of the market to electronic reproductions of old and of popular musics.

It was typical for the new composer-theorists, whose intellectual backgrounds varied widely, to be assigned basic theory classes on terminology and taxonomy in common practice period music, that is, the identification of pitches, scales, chords, and chord progressions. The post–World War II focus of American composers on developing new atonal pitch structures to replace functional tonality may also have influenced them to emphasize pitch in their research and teaching over other aspects of musical style and structure.

Had music theory been in the hands of genuine theorists or philosophers of music, there probably would have been more questions raised about music theory's dominant emphasis on issues of pitch and on Western common-practice-period and early-twentieth-century examples. Instead, very little questioning or change has taken place in music theory teaching despite the enormous changes in the American musical scene since the 1950s. Rather, the composer-theorists have increased both their isolation and their control over the music theory curriculum, establishing music theory as a discipline separate from musicology, with its own journals, academic programs, and its own academic society, the Society for Music Theory (SMT, founded in 1977). In the process, the pitch-based analytical methods of music theory have become more formalistic and complex, beyond the understanding and interest of almost everyone aside from the composer-theorists themselves. In the 1990s, music theory has taken a turn towards cultural connectedness, similar to that of musicology.[126] Still the table of contents of a recent issue of *Music Theory Spectrum*, the SMT journal, shows their concerns to be rather narrow as well:

1. Steven Block, " 'Bemsha Swing': The Transformation of a Bebop Classic to Free Jazz";

2. Matthew Brown, Douglas Dempster and Dave Headlam, "The #IV(bV) Hypothesis: Testing the Limits of Schenker's Theory of Tonality"(3) (3) (3);

3. James Hepokoski and Warren Darcy, "The Medical Caesura and Its Role in the Eighteenth-Century Sonata Exposition";

4. Ramon Satyrenda, "Liszt's Open Structure and the Romantic Fragment";

5. Peter A. Hoyt, "Haydn's New Incoherence."[127]

The most disturbing effect of the narrow focus of music theory is on musical education at the college level. There, music theory's formalistic approach is imposed on college students in the form of two to three years of music theory course requirements, both for students majoring in music and for nonmajors interested in other music courses. In effect, composer-theorists are gatekeepers for the college-level study of music, whose imposition of formalism over music serves to discourage the entry of nonmusicians and the continuation of some talented music majors as well. The result of their gate keeping is the academic ghettoization of music as a mere professional specialty, instead of a critical inquiry into an essential, universal human practice. Moreover, because of the isolation of music theory from musicology, there is now no widely read criticism of music in the sense of an intellectual debate about musical style, form, and meaning comparable to the critical debates in other art forms. What is called music criticism is more like sportswriting: comparative discussions of the technical skill of musical performers, rather than discussion of musical style, form, and meaning. By comparison, the visual and literary arts continue to integrate theory with history at the college level, and they enjoy a critical discourse that is more widely read in and outside of the academic community.[128]

While composer-theorists have generally demonstrated more concern with educational issues than musicologists, their limited interest and knowledge in the history and philosophy of music have resulted in a rather narrow emphasis on producing "competencies" in common practice period music, rather than pursuing broader inquiries into the nature and purpose of music and its various styles.[129] And so, while music is a multibillion-dollar industry with immense significance to American culture as a whole, Americans—scholars and public alike—mainly lack the theoretical resources and knowledge to understand how the music of our world works.[130]

## MUSIC EDUCATION

Music education is the category of academic music with the deepest roots and greatest influence on American education. In their role as teachers of precollege students and future precollege music teachers, music educators focus on developing the best methodologies for learning and teaching music. Today music education research tends to be in the nature of scientific experimentation on the perception of various kinds of musical sounds; humanistic research is discouraged. Researchers often rely heavily on experimental findings in music psychology to determine how to teach and evaluate musical skills, not always with ample consideration of the historical context of the concepts on which the experiments are based. Under this approach, easily objectifiable and measurable concepts, such as "perfect pitch," may receive the most attention as criteria for musical aptitude, even though, in this case, perfect pitch is a historically relative aptitude, irrelevant and possibly even harmful to the understanding and performance of music before pitch was fixed at A = 440 in the mid-nineteenth century.

The long list of articles in, for example, the Fall 1997 issue of the *Journal of Research in Music Education* reflects the narrow, scientific and pedagogical focus of the discipline:

1. Structured and Unstructured Musical Contexts and Children's Ability to Demonstrate Tempo and Dynamic Contrasts—Patricia Flowers

2. Factors Relating to Pitch-Making Skills of Elementary Education Majors—Claire Wehr McCoy

3. Perception of Tempo Modulation by Listeners of Different Levels of Educational Experience—Deborah A. Sheldon and Diane Gregory

4. Effect of Selected Recruiting Strategies on Beginning Instrumentalists' Participation Decisions—Glenn E. Nierman and Michael H. Veak

5. Psychological Sex Type and Preferences for Musical Instruments in Fourth and Fifth Graders—Tiffany J. Sinsel, Wallace E. Dixon, Jr., and Elizabeth Blades-Zeller

6. Effects of Audio- and Videotape Models on the Performance Achievement of Beginning Clarinetists—Fraser Linklater

7. Effects of Multicultural Music Experience on Preservice Elementary Teachers' Attitudes—Judith M. Teicher

8. Sequental Patterns and the Music Teaching Effectiveness of Elementary Education Majors—Judy Bowers

9. Self-Reported Versus Observed Classroom Activities in Elementary General Music—Cecilia Chu Wang and David W. Sogin

10. Teaching Behaviors of Middle School and High School Band Directors in the Rehearsal Setting—Larry Blocker, Richard Greenwood, and Bentley Shellahamer

11. Effects of Physical Attractiveness on Evaluation of Vocal Performance—Joel Wapnick, Alice Ann Darrow, Jolan Kovacs, and Lucinda Dalrymple

12. Effects of Audience on Music Performance Anxiety—Albert LeBlanc, Young Chang Jin, Mary Obert, and Carolyn Siivola

As with the articles in musicology and theory, these articles are strictly for specialists. They all involve readily obtainable measurements of current behavior in music or music education, as opposed to more challenging inquiries about what we teach and why. Studying the effects of such parameters as recruiting strategies, multicultural experience, physical attractiveness, and audience presence on the performance and evaluation of musical skills is not likely to lead to a broad understanding of how best to teach music to students and the public. Since music educators are not required to become expert in musicology, theory, or performance, they may design their research on the basis of a very limited perspective on human practices in music (which is of course not helped by the failure of general music history and theory courses to adequately cover music outside of Europe).

The emphasis of music educators on methodology has resulted in some cases in the invention of new simplified instruments, notation, and theoretical concepts for teaching purposes, as in the Orff, Kodaly, and Dalcroze methods.[131] These methods have their advocates, but unless they are kept in a limited context, they can result in teaching students about an artificial "school music culture" instead of teaching them about the instruments, notation, theory, and history of actual human cultures. When emphasis on methodology rises to the point of creating a school music culture, that culture sustains and reproduces itself by creating the appearance of the need to produce more specialists in the dominant areas of that culture, as when the dominance of large ensembles in K–12 education creates the apparent need for more training in large ensemble performance and direction at the college level, rather than for other types of musical knowledge and skills. Meanwhile, outside of our educational system, large bands and choirs are far from the dominant modes of musical expression in our society. The fact that they are prominent at all is probably largely due to the school music culture created and sustained by music educators. The problem is not that large ensembles are not valid means of musical expression and musical education, but rather that their emphasis, spurred on by music educators' focus on methodology, has left little room for other forms of musical expression and education.

Because music educators are more concerned with the education of others than in the pursuit of more specialized skills and knowledge, they suffer from an image of intellectual inferiority among specialists in musicology and theory, an image that is in fact related to the hard-boundaried view of what constitutes academic excellence and prestige. Indeed, the lack of rewards and prestige in academics for scholars committed primarily to education in all the disciplines is one of the worst legacies of the hard-boundaried paradigm; the system functions to reward specialized research far more than it does successful teaching. In the case of music educators, they may be less knowledgeable about music history and theory than specialists in those areas, but they are often far more knowledgeable about the interdisciplinary areas of aesthetics, cognitive science, learning theory, and psychology—areas that offer much insight into the needs of musical education. Because of the inferior image from which music educators suffer, however, their interdisciplinary insights into curricular needs at the college level are rarely given sufficient attention by other music academics. Even the best research by music educators into methodology cannot result in broad curricular change unless the discussion reaches other quarters.

Actually, music educators themselves are currently too divided about their goals and methods to speak with a coherent voice about curricular needs. Many music educators advocate Bennett Reimer's tradition of—as critic David Elliott plus it—"music education as aesthetic education."[132] That is, they accept Reimer's view that musical skills should be taught in context with aesthetic concepts about their meaning and value. Others, including David Elliott, Thomas Regelski, and Wayne Bowman prefer a praxis-based approach to music education: teaching music as doing music, but doing in a contemplative manner that goes beyond contemporary school music culture, mainly devoted to rehearsals and performances of large ensembles.[133] Both the Reimer and Elliott camps are sincere and thoughtful about the problems and needs of American musical education, but neither has had sufficient influence on educational policy in general to make a strong impact, either on other college-level music specialists or on K–12 music education.

## PERFORMANCE

The fragmentation of musical knowledge by music theorists, historians, and educators can only be confusing to the specialists who concentrate on performing music. Like music educators, performers have enormous influence in musical education: they act as the frontline teachers of music to their individual private students and to the audiences at their concerts. Unfortunately, musical performers are sometimes ill-suited for their role at the front lines, because their orientation tends to be more physical than academic. Indeed, the representation of performers at college-level music departments, as opposed to conservatories, was only recently a controversial matter.[134] Given their more practical orientation, musical performers often know and teach little about music history or about historical performance practices that are not represented in musical scores, such as improvised ornamentation. Yet, for good or ill, historical works and styles are a constant focus of music performers, to a far greater degree than in other arts departments. Like museum curators and guides, performers have the most influence in communicating historical information about the works they feature, both through their performances and through their teaching of other performers. When applied teachers are historically uninformed there is little time in music history classes to make up for the misunderstandings conveyed in the private studio, such as whether J. S. Bach wrote his Inventions for grand piano or even marimba, rather than for the very different-sounding keyboard instruments of his time.

The traditional focus of academic musical performers on historical works creates another, even more serious, problem for the field of music: it isolates them from the reality of practice on their instruments in contemporary culture, a reality much more likely to involve knowledge and performance of popular idioms than it was when they were trained. Once isolated from that reality, music department faculty and students are often unable to perform contemporary skills and compete for jobs outside the academic market. That inability translates to loss of credibility for music departments as training grounds for future musicians, especially in the case of more traditional instruments such as piano and violin. It is no wonder that, for example, piano enrollments have fallen precipitously around the country, when college-level teachers of piano ignore all practices outside of the Western art tradition, including jazz, rock, country, and synthesizer techniques, not to mention non-Western practices. By contrast, guitar enrollments have grown, because instruction on that instrument rarely omits reference to contemporary popular practices.

Performers tend to be better represented in large music departments than any other group, in part because they are the means for recruiting majors. That is, the majority of entering college music majors identify themselves as performers, mainly because performing skills are the only ones visible in precollege music programs; i.e., in the bands and choirs from which college music majors are recruited. Even if there are only a few students in bassoon, clarinet, flute, cello, viola, and violin, there will still be a perceived need to staff these specialties in order to recruit students. The strong representation of performers on music department faculties means that their perspective is better represented in voting changes to curriculum, personnel, and other department matters. Given their conservative background, they are unlikely to recognize the need for curricular coverage of musical styles and technologies for which they received no training; more likely they will want to maintain or raise credit hours in traditional areas in order to fight against their students' declining interest and skills in those areas.

Although performers study pedagogy more regularly than do other music specialists, performers tend to be very unadventurous, basing their teaching almost entirely on the master-apprentice model. Unfortunately, the master-apprentice model is very old and inefficient in terms of department credit-hour accounting, and that in turn leads to the overloading of introductory music clas-

ses in order to improve statistics. The master-apprentice approach is also ineffective for many, if not most, students, who do not have the experience and
discipline to apply the instruction of the private lesson in the long, lonely hours
of solo practice. When private applied students come to their lessons without
sufficient outside practice, they lower the morale of their teachers. Low morale
may lead to further conservatism and certainty that curricular change is dangerous, that traditional requirements must be maintained or increased in order
that the students be adequately educated.[135]

Finally private applied study tends to be indoctrinative: it often does little to
promote students' independent responsibility for critical inquiry about the
traditions and social functions of musical performance. This kind of inquiry is
more needed now than ever, since the Eurocentric performing traditions of academic musicians are not the only ones of importance to tomorrow's musicians.
Students who lack training in non-European traditions are at an enormous dis-
advantage for competing in the popular music market, and the (Western) classical market is not large enough to contain those who are being trained in that
tradition. Moreover, our popular music culture suffers from the lack of influence
by the best-trained musicians in our society. What passes for avant-garde "alternative" music, to take one example, is sadly lacking in the kind of originality
that comes from knowledge of a variety of historical and cultural musical practices. The greatest musicians of every tradition, from J. S. Bach to Igor Stravinsky, the Beatles, Ravi Shankar, and the Kronos Quartet, seem to be those who
interest themselves in a wide range of musical expressions. Our system of musical education does little to encourage that spirit of inquiry; rather, it serves
actively to discourage it.

## CONDUCTORS

Conductors are a category of performers who may actually play no instruments themselves (a fact that greatly amused cartoonists in the nineteenth century, when the profession of conducting was new). Conductors hold considerable
power in music departments because of their control over recruitment for the
large ensembles that they direct. In many music departments students are being
paid to be music majors, for no better reason than that conductors wish to fill
their ensembles. The power of conductors in American musical education is
partly due to the fact that music was established in American education at a
time when the status of conducting was at its height: the era of Gustav Mahler,
Arturo Toscanini, Leopold Stokowski, and John Philip Sousa. It is also a result
of the fact that until recent years music educators in the United States have
virtually all been conductors as well, so the curricular frameworks they have
developed for American music emphasize conducting and performing ensembles
as a mainstay of the curriculum, particularly at the precollege level. Accordingly
conductors are perceived as leaders and mainstays of college music departments

by students, faculty, and administrators, although their outlook on music may be no broader than the boundaries of their specialty.

At their best, though, conductors are positioned to help their ensembles and their conducting students integrate their knowledge of music history, theory, and practical techniques into thoughtful and exciting interpretations of musical works and to deeper understandings of musical styles. In fact, at the precollege level, conductors are often the only teachers of music, so they alone have the opportunity of teaching a comprehensive approach to music. Unfortunately many conductors view their job solely as training students to perform in concerts and contests. This limited view then affects musical education at the college level by giving future teachers a very narrow idea of what they need to learn and, when they become high school or junior high conductors, teach others.

## IMPLICATIONS OF FRAGMENTATION

Fragmentation in the musical field makes broad critical discussion of musical issues difficult because of the lack of knowledge and interest of specialists in one another's subdisciplines. It also makes curricular reform very difficult because of the tendency of each subdiscipline to protect its turf. As a result, American music departments have not kept up with the enormous musical changes in the world in the last half-century, especially the growth in music technology and musical multiculturalism. Our departments are still mainly organized around studying and performing canonical works of Western art music from the common practice period (c. 1700–1900, the period of J. S. Bach, Mozart, Beethoven, Frédéric Chopin, and Brahms). The separate subdisciplines of music may not agree about much, but they are united in their conservative, formalistic approach to understanding music primarily as a set of structural relationships. With the rise of nonformalistic postmodern and feminist theoretical approaches in the 1970s, scholars in the literary and visual arts moved away from formalism to explore other, more culturally connected forms of interpreting and understanding the arts. Those developments in turn have led to a softening of the literary and artistic canons in the direction of including study of non-Western and popular arts. In the music curriculum, though, the stunning growth and fusion of popular musics, world folk and art traditions, and "World beat" have yet to receive appropriate coverage in the curriculum.

The worst thing about the fragmentation of our musical field is that as long as music departments are fragmented, they will fail to have a real impact on present and future education. In order to reform our curriculum, we must join forces and dedicate ourselves, as educator Benjamin Willis put it back in 1954, "to the stake of *music in education* and not to the individual *music specialist's stake in education*."[136] In my view, what is needed to address the fragmentation of the musical field is soft-boundaried thinking and structural reforms; these will be discussed in chapter 5.

# 5

# Soft Boundaries and Relatedness:
# A New Paradigm for Understanding Music

In view of the recent rising influence of postmodern thought and feminist theory in music, the time appears to be ripe for the emergence of a new music-theoretical paradigm to challenge the highly formalistic conception of music found in Western music history, theory, composition, and practice. The paradigm I am proposing is that of soft boundaries and relatedness, wherein the covert valuation of "hard" (i.e., clearly distinct) boundaries in traditional concepts and judgments about music is replaced by recognition of the relatedness of music and musical entities across "soft" (i.e., permeable) boundaries, including relatedness to social context and function. The soft boundary of the paradigm is not a hard-and-fast line or rule for defining and judging music as in traditional aesthetics but is similar to Heidegger's sense of boundary: "that from which something *begins its essential unfolding.*"[137] Thus, the focus of the paradigm is on how the unfolding proceeds within and across permeable boundaries, rather than on the definition and reification of the boundaries themselves. Or, in other words, the focus is necessarily the whole musical experience rather than any particularized musical entities such as motives, phrases, sections, movements, and so forth.

In its attention to relationship rather than singular fact or thing, the paradigm of soft boundaries and relatedness has strong ties to contemporary postmodern and feminist theory. The ties to postmodernism are most obvious, for as Jerome Klinkowitz has stated, the key to the postmodern habit of thought is "that the authentic phenomenon in any event is not *fact* but *relationship.*"[138] The re-

This chapter first appeared in the *boundary 2* special issue on "Postmodern Feminisms" (1992) under the title "Soft Boundaries and Relatedness: Paradigm for a Postmodern, Feminist Musical Aesthetics." It is slightly revised here, in keeping with the orientation towards education rather than feminist theory. I might add that since 1992, softer-boundaried, culturally connected research has entered musicology and music theory to a surprising extent, but music curricula have been little affected by this development.

orientation from fact to relationship has roots in existential and pragmatist philosophy,[139] and it has received particular emphasis in the French poststructural
theory of, for example, Michael Foucault, Jean-François Lyotard, and Jacques
Derrida, wherein the traditional "logocentric" claims to epistemological universality and objectivity have been deconstructed and replaced by a recognition of
the validity of multiple perspectives of reality, each related to its own context.[140]
Thus, postmodernism has become the philosophy of pluralism and relativity or
as Lyotard puts it, that which "denies itself the solace of good forms."[141] In the
case of music, that denial extends to all supposed norms of musical structure,
as we shall see.

The connections of the paradigm of soft boundaries and relatedness to feminist theory are more difficult to define but just as important. Note, for example,
that the definition of relatedness as a feminine-identified function started in
Freudian psychoanalytic theory and was counterfeminist in some respects. Many
feminist theorists, however, have found validity in the connection between relatedness and the feminine, usually more in terms of enculturation than of nature.[142] Another tie to feminist theory is in the implicit emphasis on experience
and the body, an emphasis that leads away from reification and hierarchization
toward a more communal, shared conception of the arts.[143]

Although a relevant response to the hard boundaries of traditional Western
thought and culture in general, the paradigm of soft boundaries and relatedness
is especially well suited to the task of changing the subject in aesthetics because
it directly reveals and counters the otherwise covert valuation of hard boundaries
that has prevailed in aesthetic definitions and judgments going back to classical
Greek culture and the categories of Aristotle. In the seventeenth century, these
hard boundaries took the form of Cartesian dualism, which has since been very
influential in the development of scientific method and research in the Western
world. Only in the latter twentieth century has Cartesian dualism been strongly
questioned, first by poststructuralist theorists in the 1960s and later by feminist
theorists in the 1970s and 1980s. Most notably, feminist theorist Susan Bordo
has found evidence in René Descartes's diaries of what she calls "masculinist"
projections of fear and rage onto the feminine-identified, sensual realm of nature.
Bordo argues that Descartes's view of the feminine reflects other misogynistic
elements in early modern European culture, including the hundreds of thousands
of witch trials and burnings of unattached older women who were perceived as
powerful and dangerous to social stability. To Bordo, Cartesian dualism is the
scholarly side of the contemporary attempt to control the dangerous feminine
realm with the masculine-identified realm of reason and judgment.[144]

In the eighteenth century, the hard boundaries of Cartesian thought took further form in Immanuel Kant's insistence of a pure, intellectual disinterestedness
in the aesthetic perceiver and on a purely autonomous artist and artwork. Kant's
concept of aesthetic disinterestedness lay the groundwork for the Romantic aesthetic revolution, or what Marxist literary critic Terry Eagleton has called the
"ideology of the aesthetic." According to Eagleton, the Romantic aesthetic ide-

ology was a kind of politically charged denial that served to prevent consideration of the relatedness of art to culture, as well as to the possible psychological or political agendas of the critics making that denial.[145] Once culture was cleared from the field, the way was clear for the critic to fill the vacuum with projections of supposedly universal definitions and criteria for judgments and then to build canons and hierarchies of "greatness" on their basis. Because of their construction in the cultural vacuum, the resulting definitions, judgments, and hierarchies have since tended to suffer from circularity; that is, the judgments of merit serve as argument for the criteria, and the criteria serve as argument for the judgments.

The above critique of aesthetics in Western culture applies most powerfully to music, the realm of "risk-free identification" as Catherine Clément puts it. There, the greater ambiguity of musical meanings has tended to give freer rein to critical denials and projections, especially since the rise of the Romantic "aesthetic ideology" in the early century.[146] In 1854 Eduard Hanslick's *On the Musically Beautiful* translated the Romantic aesthetic into the autonomist, or formalist, theory of music, a theory that denies the aesthetic importance of music's emotional effects and cultural functions and instead regards music as a purely autonomous configuration of "tonally moving forms."[147] Most influential music philosophers since Hanslick have continued his formalist views at least to some extent. Moreover, since the 1950s and the rise of analytic aesthetics, the discipline of music theory (in which musicostructural concepts are developed and applied) has separated from musicology and formed a distinct profession with its own societies, journals, and credentials. Both music theorists and analytic music philosophers tend to view music in particularly hard-boundaried manner, excluding practical, historical information about the cultural context of music and relying instead on formalist concepts and circular argumentation.

Even a brief examination of the academic products of music theory and analytic music philosophy serves to underscore the importance of a new softer boundaried paradigm for musical aesthetics. For instance, theorist Leonard Meyer unwittingly provided an excellent example of the pitfalls of formalism and circular argumentation in his much read and reprinted essay "Some Remarks on Value and Greatness in Music" when he referred to the question "What makes music great?" as the "$64,000 question." In the essay, Meyer gives the formalist answer that music's greatness depends wholly on "syntactical organization," and he argues for his position in a covert circular manner. "If we ask," he says, "Why is Debussy's music superior to that of Delius? the answer lies in the syntactical organization of his music, not in its superior sensuousness."[148] This is a circular argument because it starts from the assumption, based on Claude Debussy's higher canonical status over Frederick Delius, that Debussy's music is superior and that the reason for its superiority will provide the universal criterion for understanding musical greatness. In other words, the answer, the syntactical organization of Debussy's music, leads in circular fashion to the question, what makes it superior, which leads to the formalist theory, which in turn leads to the proof of the superiority of Debussy's music (which, however, was never in real doubt in the first place). Here and elsewhere circular argumentation functions so smoothly that issues of substance, such as an explanation of how Delius's or Debussy's musics are more or less sensuous or syntactical, fall by the wayside.

Those who recall the 1950s TV game show *The $64,000 Question* also may remember the scandal that broke out when it was revealed that winning contestants in a competing but very similar game show had been told the right answers in advance of receiving the questions. (This scandal was the subject of Robert Redford's 1994 film, *Quiz Show*.) Unfortunately, the circular equation of the right answers preceding and following the questions is so common in musical aesthetics and criticism that no such scandal breaks out in the academy when the musico-aesthetic value fix is in. Again, it is the greater confusion about what constitutes musical content and meaning—a confusion fostered by the denial of cultural connection—that allow weak arguments like Meyer's to pass as authoritative.

A more complicated example of the pitfalls of formalism and circular argumentation is found in Peter Kivy's *Osmin's Rage: Philosophical Reflections on Opera, Drama and Text* (1988). Following a highly questionable assertion that "all art requires theory—not just for its creation but for its appreciation," Kivy compares the judgment of Mozart's *Cosi fan tutte* under Joseph Kerman's theory of "opera as drama" with the judgment under his own theory of opera as "drama-made-music,"[149] and reaches almost comic heights of dialectic:

On Kerman's interpretation, *Cosi* emerges as a deeply flawed though (I am sure Kerman would agree) estimable work. On my view it emerges as Mozart's most perfect opera—which may be to say the *most perfect opera*.

What does this tell us about *Cosi* as a work of art? What I want to emphasize is this: it by no means follows that *Cosi* emerges as a greater work of art under my description than under Kerman's. Or, to put it another way: under my description of opera as drama-made-music, *Cosi fan tutte* is a more perfect example of that kind than *The Marriage of Figaro*; but this in no way implies that, under my description, *Cosi* is a greater work of art. Indeed, I think the opposite: that although *Cosi* is the more perfect opera, which is to say, the greater drama-made-music, *Figaro* is the greater work.[150]

Unfortunately amid these tortured efforts to clarify the appropriate theory on which to judge *Cosi fan tutte*, the actual experience of the music is lost to consideration. Kivy's argument here, rather typical of his musico-aesthetic work in general, demonstrates how formalist thinking tends to evade and/or control human aesthetic experience within the sharp boundaries of the theory which supposedly gives it birth "*qua* music, *qua* art, *qua* aesthetical object," as he puts it.[151] In the narrow sector of contemporary academic music, where composers' written and published theories about their music are often better known than are the compositions themselves, Kivy's view may appear reasonable. It may even make sense in the somewhat wider context of the classical concert or, to cite

Primat Conehead's analytic-style definition, "a gathering of humans to absorb sound patterns."[152] In a more vital, life-connected musical culture, however, the notion that music needs theory for its existence, especially theory of the formalistic, culturally disconnected kind, is ridiculous. What music more probably needs, at least from scholars, is a greater understanding of its relatedness to life, something it may receive when the covert valuing of hard boundaries is replaced by a more soft-boundaried approach.

## MUSIC'S RELATEDNESS TO THE BODY

There are at least three aspects of musical experience to which the paradigm of soft boundaries and relatedness can usefully apply: (1) relatedness of musical experience to the body; (2) relatedness among the constituencies of musical experience, including the composer, performer, audience, critics, and community; and (3) relatedness of musical style to culture. Recognition of music's relatedness to the body appeared prominently in late eighteenth-century expression theory, but such recognition receded in the nineteenth century, when most aesthetic theorists tended to make a sharp Cartesian division of mind and body and to project sensuality away from the male-identified cultural norms, onto the feminine-identified realm of the Other. Indeed, late nineteenth-century male authors, painters, and composers frequently exhibited this projection in extreme, sadomasochistic images of female madness, hysteria, and nymphomania.[153]

In terms of actual musical experience, the denial of music's relatedness to the body has quite literally "held sway" in the context of the Western musical concert, resulting in the sharp boundaries—taboos, really—applied against otherwise common musicophysical responses of swaying, singing, and beating time. This is especially notable during classical concerts, where permitted physical response is frozen into required clapping zones between musical works (and, acting as a signifier of the unnatural repression, some occasional spasms of uncontrollable coughing during the works). These prohibitions against the body, beginning roughly with the concert performances of Kant's time, contrast sharply with the intentional bodily engagement found in the main genres and performance situations of many other musical cultures, including parts of our own popular music culture, many ancient and tribal cultures, and preindustrial Western culture roughly up to Kant's time, that is, before the decline of aristocratic patronage and the consequent fixing of the middle-class concert as the privileged form of musical dissemination.

Indeed, one can hardly overestimate the influence of the nineteenth-century middle-class concert and its continued hegemony as the privileged form of musical dissemination in Western art-music culture on accepted modes of musical style and experience. One notes, for instance, that the formalist theory of music arose out of the context of the concert hall. There, emotional and physical responses that had previously been welcome, accepted parts of musical experience among friends and family could now have the unwelcome effect of alerting nearby strangers to one's innermost feelings, not to mention inhibiting their ability to hear the music. Moreover, at the same time bodily response was ruled out of bounds for the concert audience, it began to be expected in the creator and performer as one of the signs of genius (a condition Kant had defined as out-of-normal bounds); and so images of the intensely sensual, physically abnormal, or even contortional performer (and composer) began to appear in published sketches and verbal accounts of Beethoven, Chopin, Berlioz, Niccolò Paganini, and Franz Liszt. Jacques Attali argues that these alienated artist-celebrities carried the denied sensual projections of their audiences and learned to feed off them in sadomasochistic demonstrations of power.[154]

It is easy to see how, in this repressed context, the notion could take hold that one's proper approach to music as composer or listener was to attend to a set of "tonally moving forms," disembodied from motion, emotion, or extra-structural meaning. Indeed, few would fault Eduard Hanslick for failing to understand the historical relativity of the concert and the aesthetic judgments he made in its context. Today's formalists, however, are on much thinner ground, continuing to view as universal an approach to musical production and reception that modern historical research has clearly revealed to be culturally relative, an approach that has the effect of discounting, or discrediting, the great majority of global musical cultures throughout history.

On the other hand, when we turn from formalist critics to actual musical artists, we find more awareness and response with regard to the connection between context of dissemination and style, probably because their survival and success are at stake. Just as composers of instrumental music responded with an increasingly formalist-oriented style as the performance context moved from church and chamber to concert hall, and later to private and academic meetings of avant-grade composers, so they will also likely respond to a move of art music back to connectedness with life. Given the threat of declining public interest and patronage, some have done so already. For example, the process and New Age idioms are a step in this direction, both in their emphasis on the "being-in-time" consciousness of the body and in their ready accessibility to the understanding and participation of a wide audience.[155]

The new, softer-boundaried performance contexts may include everyday settings, such as outdoor parks, restaurants, or other social communing places with a freer ambience and fewer physical restrictions on moving, talking, eating, drinking, or sleeping, and they may include settings not yet imagined for genres that cross the boundaries of current convention. To our Romantically acculturated minds, some of these settings may suggest an unacceptably humble, utilitarian status for music; but paradoxically it is probably the proud insistence on the autonomy of Western art music that has resulted in its declining influence in American public life. On the contrary, music appears to occupy a higher status culturally when it is integrated with other forms of life experience, as, for example in its evident integration with poetry, dance, eating, weaving, and religious ceremonies of preindustrial societies.[156]

## RELATEDNESS OF MUSICAL EXPERIENCE AMONG COMPOSERS, PERFORMERS, AUDIENCES, CRITICS, AND COMMUNITY

Ideas borrowed from poststructural theory strongly suggest the value of softer, less-hierarchical boundaries among the constituencies of artistic experience—in the case of music, the composer, performer, audience, critics, and community. For instance, the deconstructionist view of the literary work as "text," of writing as "textuality," and of reading as involving a cooperative "intertextuality" is a model that in effect softens the boundaries between writer, reader, and community and emphasizes not the fixing of absolute or hierarchical value but the play of meanings among readers and writers.[157]

In the case of experience-oriented performance arts like music, the deconstructionist view is particularly applicable, not only because of the likelihood of widely variant performances of any given work but also because of the limitations and variations in the specificity of notational practices over the history of Western art music, not to mention popular music and music of other cultures. For example, in contrast to the relatively stable historical practices of "notation" for, say, novels—which arguably preserve the author's intentions in the written words, music-notational practices have been neither universal nor stable. Those practices range from an absence of notation (a vast quantity of music in the area of song and improvisatory instrumental genres and passages) to the merely mnemonic indications of phrase direction in ninth-century chant notation to later Medieval, Renaissance, and Baroque practices (where notation of pitches and rhythms is often incomplete, misleading, or ambiguous and where little or no information is provided on timbre, dynamics, tempo, and articulation). These crucial musical elements all required the co-creation of musical performers. Even in the case of our "common practice period" (circa 1700–1900), notation of the main musical elements is still usually incomplete without the interpretation of a skilled musical performer who is knowledgeable in the terms and techniques of performance practice for the period and genre involved.[158]

Thus, not only is the score a bad gauge of a composer's intentions, its very inadequacy to that purpose suggests the need to reevaluate the Western art-musical view of the composer as isolated genius-creator at the top of a hierarchy—whose intentions alone determine the musical work—and to consider a demotion, if not a death, of the composer's authority.[159] The reigning notion too closely resembles Ronald Reagan's "trickle-down" theory of economics and has parallel results in terms of the musical disenfranchisement and impoverishment of the majority of the public (and it hasn't worked very well for the composers, either). We should note that many of the most vituperative proponents of this compositorial domination were composers themselves (e.g., Berlioz, Wagner, Schumann, Brahms, Mahler, Schoenberg, and Stravinsky). Indeed, starting in the nineteenth century, the tendency of composers less toward performance and more toward theory and criticism as a method of supporting themselves and/or disseminating their music and is itself a sign of the triumph of hard-boundaried theory over musical experience in the Western art-music tradition.

Sadly the composers are only apparently the victors in this evolution, since the disenfranchisement of music's other constituencies has had the effect of alienating most of us from an active connection with music, leaving us passive receivers, not only for the art and popular music industries, but also for the multibillion-dollar industries of civic and corporate Gebrauchsmuzak, if I may coin a term. By Gebrauchsmuzak, I mean the football fight songs, supermarket music, advertising jingles, movie and television soundtracks, and other artificially produced sound environments, not to mention the mass-produced music videos and sound recordings that feed the chain of demand in the popular music world. The problem is not the supposed gap in value between high and low culture but, rather, the largely unnoticed disenfranchisement and disengagement of people from active engagement in a musical culture of their own. Where popular music as a whole fits in this picture is difficult to say, since it comprises so many highly variant subcultures. Chances are, though, that the extent to which popular music plays on us like elevator tapes (i.e., without our awareness and involvement), it is part of the Gebrauchsmuzak problem as well. On the other hand, with the paradigm of softer boundaries and relatedness among musical constituencies, the process of hierarchization, disenfranchisement, and disengagement might be turned around, and a more equitable relationship might be sought between music and its various constituencies.

Some composers from the art-music community have blazed a trail for this kind of turnaround. (Ironically, they may be freer to do so than more commercially tied popular musicians.) For example, in writings going back to the 1930s, proto-deconstructionist John Cage has challenged every assumption of Western art-musical culture, and, in particular, he has emphasized greater engagement of the performer and the audience in the experience of music.[160] Feminist composer Pauline Oliveros has also repeatedly crossed the boundaries of genre and constituency in her music. For example, in *Sonic Meditations* (1971), dedicated to "the elevation and equalization of the feminine principle along with the masculine principle," Oliveros invited audience members to engage in the musical experience as performers themselves. In the first meditation entitled "Teach Yourself to Fly," Oliveros directs the audience members/performers to "Gradually observe your breathing become audible. . . . Color your breathing very softly at first with sound. Let the intensity increase very slowly as you observe it. Continue as long as possible until others are quiet."[161]

*Sonic Meditations* may be too radical for some, but at the very least Oliveros's instructions remind us that music is, first and foremost, experienced. Her view that valuing the feminine must mean a more egalitarian sharing of that experience, and thus a deprofessionalization and dehierarchization of it, is one that is shared by many feminists outside music as well. Do we risk "greatness" by deemphasizing professionalism? Perhaps, but if that means the reenfranchisement of more people into active participation in a musical culture of their own, it could be worth the risk.

The possibility of softer boundaries and relatedness among the constituencies of a musical culture has also been raised through the explorations by twentieth-century anthropologists and ethnomusicologists of preindustrial societies whose boundaries between musial constituencies are frequently softer and differently focused than those for Western industrial society. For example, ethnomusicologist Elizabeth Tolbert tells of the spiritual, communal function of the lament among the Finnish Karelians and analyzes the music in context with that function.[162] Anthropologist Carol Robertson finds that music, in the form of communally performed ritual, offers the individual in the African Kassen-Nankani and South American Mapuche tribes "a web of relationships within which his/ her individuality can be defined," including the web of gender relationships.[163] Communal dance, song, and religious-dramatic ritual generally figure prominently in preindustrial music cultures, casting considerable question on the Western art-musical view of these experiences as secondary to the "pure" experience of untexted, instrumental music.

The response of musicologists to this research has been slowed by their positivism and their ethnocentricity, so that assumptions of universality or at least superiority of the boundary practices and value judgments of Western culture continue to prevail in aesthetic and historical writings about music, which in turn influence curricula, textbooks, and value judgments among the general population. In the world of actual musical experience, though, hard boundaries can be their own worst enemy. Just as the triumph of hard-boundaried theory over musical experience in the Western art tradition has brought in its wake an explosion of lesser-theoried popular and folk musics, so popular and folk music have often influenced Western musical styles in their encounters, even when Western colonialism was disrupting much of the rest of the culture. The stylistic incursions of American popular music into traditional music cultures around the world could be, not an exception to this rule, but a very striking case of it. That is, American popular music today is founded largely on the music of African American culture in combination with Western European traditions. The musical cultures it has invaded and disrupted have been more hierarchic aristocratic cultures, such as those of Thai, Japanese, Indian, or Persian court music, where professional specialization had led to a level of complexity similar to that of Western art music and far removed from the abilities, understanding, or participation of the general culture.

## RELATEDNESS OF MUSICAL STYLE TO CULTURE

The mention of non-Western musical culture leads very naturally to consideration of the third area of musical relatedness under discussion in this chapter, that of the relatedness between musical style and culture. Although the influence of McClary and other culturally oriented musicologists has had a clear effect on research, music history textbooks and teaching have lagged far behind, avoiding coverage of jazz, popular, and world musics that are clearly central to the understanding of music in our society.[164]

The academic evasion of music's cultural relatedness has been coupled with a pervasive diminution of women's musical activity. Indeed, a masculinist slant continues in musicology and music history teaching to a degree that would amaze critics of other fields. Take, for example, *The Music of Man*, an expensively produced series of videos that accompanies the Brown-Benchmark textbook for music history, K. Marie Stolba's *The Development of Western Music*. *The Music of Man* clearly marginalizes women in the title and in the accounts of the music-historical periods.[165] Of the myriad of active, influential musical women of the twentieth century, this series shows only Martha Graham, Judy Collins, and Joan Baez, the last of whom is presented as a woman notable for having had a love affair with Bob Dylan and for performing his music. (In fact, Joan Baez's fame and influence as a performer and composer preceded Dylan's, and his career profited from the personal relationship with her rather than the other way around.) Clearly a new paradigm is needed in the teaching of music history in order to challenge the masculinist slant, the preoccupation with greatness, and the denial of cultural connectedness.

With respect to the teaching and analytical practices of music theory, the paradigm of soft boundaries and relatedness is intended to lead to analytical approaches that dereify the hard boundaries illustrated in the very terms with which we think about and analyze music, that is, as in pitches, chords, rhythmic motives, phrases, sections, movements, and works.[166] There is much from the Romantic tradition of musical aesthetics on relatedness as a model for musical thinking. For example, music is the beautiful play of sensations of hearing (Kant), the least representational and thus most elemental art (Schopenhauer and Nietzsche); and, as mentioned earlier, the art in which content consists entirely of "tonally moving forms" (Hanslick). Some of the analytical procedures borne out of the Romantic tradition already emphasize relatedness, as in the contrapuntal relatedness of Schenkerian theory. However, to the extent that these and other analytical modes have operated under the assumption of universality (as Schenkerian theory assuredly has), they should be reexamined; otherwise the analytical activity resulting from their use will fail to connect meaningfully to the musical experience being studied. (The effect of soft boundaries on music theory and analysis will be further discussed in chapter 6.)

Examination of the types of boundaries found in a musical repertory could lead to a stronger understanding of the relationship of the history of music to history in general. Take, for instance, the suggestion in Marxist literary and art criticism that in cultures of aristocratic patronage, where art and artists have been owned as property, the artistic styles reflect the hard boundaries of ownership, for example, in the distinct, often symmetrical phrases, sections and movements, clear meters and mainly masculine cadences (i.e., cadences that resolve on a main rhythmic beat) of eighteenth-century musical style.[167] The tendency of Romantic and modernist music criticism has been to associate the breaking of these boundaries with the Kantian concept of "genius,"[168] and to base canonical hierarchizations of greater and lesser geniuses on their tendency to break the boundaries. Wolfgang Amadeus Mozart (our archetypal musical genius), for example, is a great composer because of his constant resistance to these boundaries, which takes the form of frequent feminine cadences (which resolve off the beat), assymetrical phrases, metrical displacements, and surprises of chromaticism, tonality, and melodic contour.[169]

Putting the mythology of artistic genius aside, however, Mozart's boundary-breaking might be understood better in relationship to his resistance against playing his expected role within the patronage system and against conventions and authority, in general.[170] By comparison within Mozart's close circle of contacts, this was a resistance that did not appeal to Antonio Salieri, on whom Alexander Pushkin, Peter Schaffer, and their audiences have projected such heavy doses of Romantic ideology. Moreover, such resistance was probably psychologically impossible for Wolfgang's older sister Maria Anna Mozart, also a child prodigy but barred by family and culture from public musical activity as an adult woman.[171] These observations move the critical focus from hierarchization of greatness to cultural relatedness, but they do not in any way devalue Mozart's music. Rather, they present another, more culturally related basis for appreciating that music without requiring the devaluation and dismissal of musical repertories in which boundary breaking is a lesser factor.

In terms of current musical practice, application of the new paradigm of soft boundaries and relatedness between musical style and culture means questioning and playing with the hard boundaries of traditional and modernist styles, as in the deconstructive play of Cage, Peter Schickele (masquerading as P.D.Q. Bach)[172] and performance artist Laurie Anderson, whose characteristic electronic distortions of her own voice seem to mirror the electronic distortion and transformation of the subject in postmodern culture in general.[173] Woman composers may play a particularly prominent role in this development because they are best positioned to explore expressions of feminine identity that have been overlooked under the old paradigm, including sound imagery that is less climax oriented and more birth- and growth oriented. In *Feminine Endings* Susan McClary discusses the possibilities of new discursive strategies for women composers at length, including a fascinating description of Janika Vanderwelde's *Genesis II* as an exploration of birth imagery in sound.[174] As McClary explains, developing the new musical language of Genesis did not come easily to Vanderwelden; she first had to realize that she was in the habit of using musical imagery more related to masculine experience than to the feminine side, particularly the image of climax. This recognition came, comically enough, while Vanderwelde was fulfilling a commission to write incidental music for a children's play, *Jack and the Beanstalk*, easily the most Freudian, masculinist-oriented of fairy tales. McClary describes the climax Vanderwelde wrote as follows:

The music depicting the beanstalk's erection and penetration is a highly venerable gesture—one that marks the heroic climax of many a tonal composition. A kind of pitch ceiling consolidates, against which melodic motives begin to push as though against a palpable obstacle. As frustration mounts, the urgency of the motivic salvos increases; they move in shorter and shorter time spans, until they succeed finally in bursting through the barrier with a spasm of ejaculatory release.[175]

McClary goes on to comment that "this musical gesture appears prominently in many of our favorite repertories,"[176] and indeed it's hard to think of a late Romantic or early twentieth-century orchestral work without at least one of these "ejaculatory releases," though no one but McClary has identified them as such. At the same time, it is hard to find similar gestures in orchestral music of other cultures and times. So, though the formalist tradition of music criticism would never admit it, this practice of tonal climax appears to be a culture-specific expression, one that corresponds well with the promasculine, misogynistic imagery of much late nineteenth-century European art. Many historians and critics of the visual arts have identified this misogynistic imagery as corresponding to social fears over the contemporary rise of feminism, or, as the Victorians quaintly put it, "the Woman Question." Among musicologists and music critics, however, the idea that a particular style of musical climax, or any style, might have cultural significance has until recently been regarded as ridiculous, and McClary has been much criticized and lampooned for her views. With a new critical paradigm of soft boundaries, though, the onus would be on the formalists to defend the view that a distinctive style feature has no relationship with the culture.

In short, a new paradigm of soft boundaries could help lead to wider, interdisciplinary theoretical and critical activity that may in turn positively affect how music is taught and practiced in our society. On the other hand, the fragmentation and isolation of music professionals into composition, theory, history, education, and performance means that any new paradigm faces an uphill battle in receiving wide currency in all the relevant musical subdisciplines, organizations, and journals. Extensive institutional and curricular changes will be necessary if we are to stem and reverse the professional fragmentation and isolation of music in the academy as an arcane study of the Western canon relevant only to music majors pursuing careers in performance or in the teaching of more of the same.

In my view, the most important curricular change needed is in the area of college-level music theory. Currently music theory forms the largest part of the college music curriculum, as well as the part most strongly dominated by the study of European art music traditions. As long as Eurocentric music theory study occupies two to three years of the life of a music major—and acts as a barrier to advanced music study by other students—there is little chance of reforming academic music study. The paradigm of soft boundaries is essential in the area of music theory in order to challenge hard-boundaried concepts and assumptions about musical structure that have developed primarily in response to the study of Western art music since the eighteenth century (that is, the "common practice period" of J. S. Bach, Beethoven, and Brahms). In my view, these hard-boundaried assumptions and concepts are best understood in context with the mainstream approach in Western aesthetic theory since the eighteenth century: an approach I refer to as "autonomist/formalist" and with which I will deal at length in the following chapter.

# 6

# Soft Boundaries, Autonomist/Formalist Aesthetics, and Music Theory

The importance of new paradigms, or models of thought and action, has been a frequent theme in recent aesthetic theory. The value of a new paradigm lies in its ability to go beyond the traditional questions and answers of a discipline and challenge the underlying framework of values and practices that serve to produce those questions and answers.[177]

Since the rise of the discipline of aesthetics in the eighteenth century, its dominant values and practices have developed around the autonomist/formalist position: that is, the view that art should be created and appreciated in a "disinterested," structurally oriented manner, apart from any considerations of cultural context or function.[178] The autonomist/formalist position may be seen as an extension into the aesthetic realm of the general logocentric tendency in Western thought to contain, categorize, and hierarchize experience, so that the physical, emotional, and cultural aspects are viewed apart from the intellectual/verbal aspects and devalorized as irrational or primitive. Although this tendency was recognized before the development of feminist theory, it has since been identified by feminist scholars as a masculinist tendency because the aspects of experience that it devalorizes have regularly been associated with women.[179] It is also a quintessentially hard-boundaried position, in that it leads to theoretical concepts and analyses that are strictly contained within the boundaries of an artwork, unconnected to its cultural context.

There are three main elements to autonomist/formalist aesthetics: (1) the definition of art as a distinct activity, apart from other cultural practices; (2) the isolation and reification of "artworks" (i.e., the physical objects of art), away

This chapter appeared in the *Journal of Aesthetics and Art Criticism* in the special issue *Music 52* (1994): 113–26, under the title "Autonomist-Formalist Aesthetics, Music Theory, and the Feminist Paradigm of Soft Boundaries." This version has been revised to change emphasis from feminist theory to aesthetics and arts education, in keeping with the focus of this book.

from their origins and symbolic meanings in human experience; and (3) the use of formalist or structurally oriented concepts as universals for judging and hierarchizing the value of artworks. Only the first two of these elements were present in the aesthetic writings of early Romantic philosophers and critics of art, for they explicitly rejected the formalist concepts and judgments of eighteenth-century aesthetics in favor of a more poetic approach to art criticism. Since the early nineteenth century, however, the elements have typically appeared together as, for example, when Clive Bell assigned the highest aesthetic value to primitive sacred icons because of their "significant form," or when Eduard Hanslick defined and judged music entirely on the basis of its "tonally moving forms."[180] In part because of the abstract, largely nonrepresentational character of musical sounds, the autonomist/formalist position has reached its height in application to the art of music, producing a profusion of structural concepts and analytic procedures commonly known as music theory.

Notwithstanding its denial of cultural connections, the autonomist/formalist position itself arose in a cultural context, that of the "museum culture" of the arts.[181] Although the practice of preserving and exhibiting artifacts in museums had its roots as early as the Middle Ages, it wasn't until the latter eighteenth century that museums became the major mode for the exhibition of art, as artistic patronage passed from the upper to the middle class and from aristocratic chambers to public museums, concert halls, and other large-scale institutions of art. Despite presumptions of neutrality, the institution of the museum served to impose a radical new context on art and its public, in which the latter had to perceive separate artworks in conjunction with each other, according to themes and layouts determined by the museum personnel (or in music's case, the concert performers or organizers), and to do so in silence and physical and emotional restraint. The denial of the artworks' relatedness to culture and to physical and emotional engagement created a vacuum that could then be filled by formalist analyses and judgments. Not surprisingly, the museum culture has given rise to the institutional theories of art, according to which art is defined and artworks identified by art institutions, critics, and teachers. However, museums are at least as likely to destroy or inhibit artistic meaning, as for example, when an art museum exhibits a musical instrument with the sign "Don't touch the object of art."[182]

The rise of autonomist/formalist aesthetics with the museum culture of art served to promote an approach to artistic experience that privileged formalist intellectual judgments of isolated artworks while devaluing and deemphasizing the physical, emotional, and cultural experience of art. In so doing, it not only discouraged individuals from those vital aspects of artistic experience; it also disenfranchised communities, whose roles in forming and experiencing the cultural meanings embodied in artistic practices and artworks were ignored. Instead of envisioning a broad community of artistic participants, autonomist/formalist aesthetics promoted fragmentation into isolated "high" and "low" art subcultures, proliferation of separate professional art specialties, and a hierarchization of art participants that assigned all proprietary rights to a singular artist/creator.[183]

The ascendancy of the museum and its associated institutions of training (i.e., conservatories and departments of the arts) corresponded to a period of greater social exclusion and subordination for women—a move from patriarchal to masculinist culture as Barbara Ehrenreich and Deirdre English describe it—that affected the institutions themselves, in their practices of educating men and women artists and exhibiting their works on an unequal basis. Such exclusionary practices in turn led to an increased concentration of women's artistic activity in domestic, utilitarian arts such as pottery, weaving, genre painting and song, arts that require little institutional support but have been discounted under autonomist/formalist aesthetics. As a result, the canons of the arts, compiled mainly since the onset of the museum culture, have evolved to show a dearth of women artists, or "great" women artists, that has compared unfavorably to the genealogies of Great Men.[184]

Given the failure of autonomist/formalist aesthetics to account for so much of the world's musical experience, the time now appears to be more than ripe for the introduction of a new paradigm for the understanding of music: a paradigm of soft boundaries to challenge the framework of autonomist/formalist concepts and judgments that have developed around that art. The paradigm of soft boundaries challenges a key element in the autonomist/formalist position: the covert valuation of "hard" or distinct boundaries in the concepts that music theorists have used to define and judge music—concepts including the (supposedly autonomous) musical work, movement, section, period, phrase, chord progression, motive, and interval. With the paradigm of soft boundaries, the valuation of hard boundaries in music-theoretical concepts, analyses, and judgments is balanced by consideration of the relatedness of music and musical entities across soft or permeable boundaries, including relatedness to the physical, emotional, and cultural experience of music.

## A CLOSER LOOK AT MUSIC THEORY

Music theory is the discipline in which structural concepts and analytical judgments for music are formulated and taught, so it is music theory that one must address in order to effect any real change in academic musical discourse. Curiously music theory occupies a very different status and role in music than does theory in the other arts (where theory generally is incorporated into historical and practical study). Theory in music is a separate discipline, with little direct connection to the seemingly related disciplines of music philosophy (which functions institutionally as a branch of philosophical aesthetics) and musicology (including music history and sociology). It is the absence of close connection with practitioners and issues of music philosophy and history that has made music theory so vulnerable to long-term domination by the single aesthetic position of autonomist/formalism.[185] Moreover, because two to three years of music theory study are required of all students who wish to study music academically on an advanced level, music theorists are able to assert their autonomist/formalist views, at least to some extent, over everyone in the academic music world. A brief review of the institutional history of music theory may help to explain the control that music theory exercises on the dissemination of information about music in our society and how much a soft-boundaried paradigm is needed.

Music theory's separate status and power goes back to ancient Greece, where it was music theory, not history or practice, which was the focus of academic musical study and discourse. Greek music theorists such as Pythagoras proposed universal concepts for music, rather than concepts relating to contemporary or historical musical practices.[186] Medieval church theorists continued the universalist focus of the Greeks to aid in their agenda of discouraging popular cultural practices of the Germanic and Nordic tribes while preserving music as a realm of pure speculation, suitable for otherworldly expressions of Christian worship.[187]

The rise of humanism and historicism beginning in the Renaissance gradually led to a more balanced inclusion of historical and practical knowledge in the academic study of music while music theory came out of the clouds and into the hands of musicians, usually composer-performers, who were equally as interested in explaining contemporary practice as in speculating on universal forms.[188] Jean-Philippe Rameau, for example, was a noted music theorist and also a keyboardist and opera composer; accordingly his theoretical treatises introduce and discuss speculative universal concepts, such as the fundamental bass, alongside practical issues of composition and accompaniment.[189]

Unfortunately the balance and connection of music theory with the history and practice of music in the eighteenth century was then strained in the following century by the fragmentation of the musical field into separate subdisciplines of musicology, composition, conducting, and performance, each with specialized skills and language beyond the knowledge and abilities of the general public. As composition became separate from performance, composers were increasingly isolated from the public within a Romantic "aesthetic of originality" (as Carl Dahlhaus puts it), which encouraged them to forego pleasing audiences with familiar styles in order to maintain the autonomist/formalist dedication to the Romantic aesthetic slogan of *l'art pour l'art*.[190]

By the early to mid-twentieth century, composers of high art music were mostly so estranged from the public that they had to seek economic sustenance in the universities. There they were generally assigned to teach composition and music theory, which then consisted mainly of basic music notation and chordal identification. To the extent that music theory was a research discipline, it functioned under the umbrella of musicology. Meanwhile, the universities themselves were affected by rising professionalization and positivism, as individual disciplines within the arts and humanities each aspired to the systematic technical language and tools associated with the most prestigious fields of the natural sciences. In music, many academic composer-theorists (as well as composers outside of the universities) turned to mathematical explorations of set theory for the organization of musical tones and electronic and computer systems for the generation and analysis of musical works.[191] This was also a turn away from identification with musicologists and the history of musical styles; study of style, after all, involved the relativization of the composers' own creative activity, and it also required music-historical expertise that was often beyond the knowledge or interest of creative artists.

By the late 1950s, the composer-theorists began to break away from general musicology circles to found their own journals, organizations, and graduate programs. David Kraehenbühl's foreword to the first *Journal of Music Theory* well expresses the isolationist, ahistorical spirit of the new theory specialists, as it makes an academically respectable connection of purpose between their speculative enterprise and that of the early Greek and medieval music theorists:

In centuries past the formulation of laws regarding the practice of music was regarded as the highest aim for a musician. . . . But in our own time it is the rare musician who knows how his art offers a key to universal understanding. Music theory has become a discipline in stylistic definition or, still less, a system of nomenclature and classification that offers no valid laws even regarding music. It is [to] the restoration of music theory as more than a didactic convenience, more than a necessary discipline, as in fact, a mode of creative thought that this journal is dedicated.[192]

The two most prominent figures in the rise of modern music theory were Allen Forte and Milton Babbitt. Beginning in 1959, Forte taught at Yale, where he edited the *Journal of Music Theory* through much of the 1960s and guided several generations of theory doctoral students who later proceeded to prominent teaching positions at other universities. Forte's intellectual focus throughout his career has been on the advocacy, development, and application of universalist systems for the analysis and formulation of pitch structures: first as an advocate of Schenkerian layer analysis, then as a formalizer of pitch class and interval class sets for analysis of twentieth-century serial music, and most recently as the advocate of a linear analytic method combining elements of Schenkerian and set theories.[193] From 1977 to 1982, he also presided over the first years of the Society for Music Theory, the founding of which signalled the final institutional split of music theory from musicology.[194]

Milton Babbitt, on the other hand, inspired a generation of students at Princeton University (including Benjamin Boretz and John Rahn), where the journal *Perspectives of New Music* was founded in 1962. Although less universalist in his stance than Forte, Babbitt has been more extreme in his isolationism and in his alliance to scientific system. Indeed, Babbitt calls for music theory to drop its ties to music and the arts and ally itself with scientific theory and to produce only statements and musical compositions whose terms are verifiable.[195] His analysis of Schoenberg's deeply religious, humanistic opera *Moses und Aron* demonstrates this approach; it deals only with the location of the 12-tone pitch structures of the opera, apart from their significance in the plot, let alone the overall meaning of the epic, and without mention of any musical features besides pitch.[196] Babbitt's followers, although less extreme in their renunciation of cultural connections, have nonetheless pursued his program of developing a more scientific music-theoretical language, based on observable primitives of time and pitch. Unfortunately such language can lead to a particularly fragmented version of autonomist/formalism as, for example, when John Rahn recommends thirty-one isolated hearings of the first eleven bars of Webern's *Symphonie Op. 21/ mvt. 2* in order that the structural relationships be appreciated properly.[197] The narrowness of focus promoted by such "close reading" (as Rahn describes the Princeton approach) makes balanced consideration of the experience of the full symphony all but impossible, not to mention consideration of its cultural context and meaning. Moreover, it leads to the exclusion of nontheorists from the critical discourse (and of the music from their discourse), as well as the exclusion of all music from critical consideration but the most systematically constructed kind—just what Babbitt had hoped.[198]

Unfortunately the increased professionalization and isolation of music theory in the last thirty years has had more effect on music than just increasing research in hard-boundaried theory and analysis. Rather, because of the separation of theory specialists in graduate-level curricula and postgraduate research and professional interaction, they no longer share a strong intellectual or institutional connection with musicologists. If they did, the interaction might otherwise serve to promote communication and correction of imbalances for both disciplines. Theorists also lack contact and shared knowledge with philosophers of music; indeed the occupation by music theorists of the philosophical, or pseudophilosophical, role in academic departments of music serves to separate musicologists from music philosophers as well, to the detriment of each discipline.

The most disturbing effect of this isolation is not on music theory scholars, who may have the breadth of intellect and experience to surmount it, but on musical education at the lower levels, as promulgated by the rank-and-file teachers of music theory. At the undergraduate level, for example, the isolation of music theory from music history results in the naive presentation of Western theoretical concepts about how music works, separate from the context of the history and performance of the music and from historically oriented issues of musical style.[199] The focus is mainly on formalist analysis of harmony, to the neglect of melody, rhythm, tone color, and large-scale structure—all of which are more clearly related to culture and more accessible to listeners. Extended over the two to three years that music theory occupies in the curriculum, such a restricted presentation is bound to leave the impression on that Western harmonic concepts have universal or at least normative validity. This impression is strengthened by the monolithic program and course title "music theory" (as if there is only one) and by textbook declarations that the concepts are basic, fundamental, and comprehensive, or that, as Forte puts it in his *Tonal Harmony in Concept and Practice*, "they stand at the very foundation of the art and reach forth to include its most elaborate expressions."[200]

Actually, if anything, the reverse is true. Most undergraduate theory textbooks present a decontextualized miscellany of common practice period harmonic concepts, many of which are inapplicable to a great amount of music within Western culture, not to mention outside of it. In order to make the concepts appear relevant and comprehensive, textbooks (and teachers) focus on short phrases, carefully chosen or newly composed. This is a claustrophobic approach that can lead to a narrow, distorted view of the music under consideration and an extraordinary misuse of academic time and energies.[201] A similar approach to the college-level study of the art of literature would have students spending most of their academic time and energy applying textbook norms of one narrow aspect of writing style—say, rhyme—to isolated lines of Shakespeare, John Milton or Emily Dickinson, instead of reading and interpreting the full plays and poems. Unfortunately, when this happens in a music theory class, it is a more serious problem than it would be in literature, because students receive so little academic exposure to music that they are necessarily less aware than literature students might be of what a narrow and distorted view they are getting of the world of musical art.

In addition to the false universalism of the concepts of music theory, there is the problem of the underlying autonomist/formalist assumptions in the procedures of music analysis, assumptions that (1) music consists of separate musical works that can and should be isolated from their cultural contexts and analyzed; (2) analysis should deal with the structural organization of pitches inside the "musical work" as determined by the musical score; and (3) there are universal, or at least normative, standards of value with which musical works can be judged and compared.

The above assumptions are so standard that they may appear reasonable, but they do not stand up to the test of transhistorical and transcultural evidence. Lydia Goehr has argued against the first assumption, showing that the concept of the musical work is part of the Romantic model of the arts, which tends to distort the non-Romantic music to which it is frequently applied, whether to Antonio Vivaldi or Duke Ellington.[202] The second assumption about the primacy of pitch structure is similarly dubious. Understanding music (assuming that is still the goal) depends at least as much on rhythm as pitch, precisely because rhythm is so tangibly physical, emotional, and cultural. Even if rhythm were not generally excluded from the picture, the practice of analyzing from the notated score is highly questionable because, as Nicholas Cook has shown, the notation is not itself music, but merely an analogy that developed and continues to evolve around the teaching of music-theoretical concepts.[203] Moreover, the practice of analyzing from the score ignores strong historical evidence that composers are not solely responsible for their musical works. Rather, performers are usually to some extent the co-creators of musical structures, not to mention musical experiences, in ways that depart from the notational indications in every musical parameter, including the fundamentals of duration and pitch.

The third assumption of universal standards of value is easily disproven by the history of music theory itself, that is, the proposal of different universalist theories, by Jean Philippe Rameau, Heinnich Schenker, Leonard Meyer, Forte, and others, that are not in retrospect universal at all, but clearly reflective of their formulaters' frames of reference. (This assumption does not apply to theorists of the Babbitt school, who tend to regard each separate musical work as a theory unto itself.) Different as these and other universalist theories of musical value are, they have one thing in common: they lead to analytical procedures and data that center around the viability of the theories themselves rather than the gathering of information about, or appreciation of, the music being analyzed. Frequently the theories function in circular fashion, with carefully chosen cononical works or passages serving both to formulate and to prove the theory, as in Leonard Meyer's preference of Debussy to Delius for "syntactical" reasons.[204]

Universalist theories and judgments, and autonomism/formalism in general, can be dangerously seductive in their simplicity, especially in an era of declining cultural literacy in art music. So, although some music theorists have recently begun to explore other critical approaches from interdisciplinary sources,[205] their explorations are institutionally disadvantaged in their competition with the autonomist/formalist approach at all but the highest level of research, unless and until the hard-boundaried paradigm is displaced. Unfortunately, it is very difficult for musicians trained under the current curriculum to free themselves from the autonomist/formalist assumptions and challenge the exclusionary practices in their own disciplinary corners of music. It is also almost impossible for non-music majors, who might be more likely to challenge those assumptions, to take upper-division courses in music as they might in art history or literature, without undergoing prerequisite years of training in music theory—a requirement that further isolates music from other academic departments and the wider community. As a consequence of the isolation, music receives little or no discussion in general humanities and social science courses and curricula that otherwise benefit from interdisciplinary integration. The same omission occurs in cultural criticism; that is, music is omitted from discussion in cases where it is obviously relevant, such as film reviews, or is mentioned only superficially. In the case of many films, omitting critical consideration of the music is not unlike analyzing *Tristan and Isolde* without discussion of Richard Wagner and his musical style. Nonetheless, it happens all the time.[206]

## SOFTENING THE BOUNDARIES OF MUSIC THEORY

That is the general scope of the isolation maintained by the autonomist/formalist practices of mainstream music theory. The question is, what can the paradigm of soft boundaries do to alleviate the isolation? Simply stated, the paradigm calls for music theory to seek knowledge and formulate concepts and judgments about the relatedness of music to all aspects of experience, avoiding hard-boundaried distinctions and preferences for intellectual experience alone. Actually, there are signs that a paradigm shift may already be underway. Under the influence of ethnomusicology, Marxist aesthetics, hermeneutics and post-structural theory, many musicologists and some theorists concerned with musical style have increasingly turned to culturally related concepts in the 1980s, in the belief that, as Judith Becker states, "evaluation is only viable within a culture, particularly within a genre."[207]

Applied to practice the paradigm of soft boundaries would reorient music theorists towards the development and use of a far wider range of concepts in their own analyses and in their teaching of theory and analysis to others with emphasis on concepts that clearly relate to the experience of the music under analysis. Music theory of this kind would be accessible and interesting to many more people because it would help to explain their own experience with the music, rather than superimposing a complex formalist analysis of no apparent connection to their experience. The current isolation of music theory and music majors would thus be softened by the wider involvement of students from other disciplines and by the softer boundaries that would develop within music departments between currently separate fields of music philosophy, history and sociology, and performance. Music theory could continue to play a central role in the formation and application of concepts for music analysis, understanding and discourse, but its role would be less isolated from that of music history, sociology, and philosophy, and more like that of theory in the visual and literary arts—where specialists in theory alone are rare. Music theorists would need to gain more competence in areas other than theory and composition in order to practice and teach their discipline. As a result, the status of music theory as a separate discipline with separate graduate programs, journals, and societies would likely wane along with the power of music theory over the shape of musical education in our society.

From where would the experience-related concepts for a softer-boundaried music theory come? They could come from the ways in which the music under consideration was composed, performed, heard, taught, danced, moved, worked, or prayed to. They could include terms, preferably in the language of the period, for sequences of bodily gestures that were associated with dancing or playing the music in question or for the organization of accompanying texts, dramatic representations, sacred rites, or work functions. Something very much like phrases would probably remain valid for lots of music because of the analogous structure of accompanying poetic lines and dance motions in each case. But many other supposedly normative concepts that occupy the great majority of music theory classtime—the altered 6th-chords, functional progressions, mediant modulations, and so forth—would move from the normative column into narrower application in context with music composed under their influence. Harmonic analysis of Bach chorales according to Ramellian or Schenkerian concepts alone would be out; consideration of the source, text, and religious function of the chorale and consideration of the meaning of Bach's particular harmonizations and melodic colorations in comparison with other settings would be called for in their place.

In cases of musical repertories for which evidence of theoretical concepts and procedures are thin or lacking, the history of music writing, including notational practices, could act as a guide: deconstructing supposedly universal concepts of pitch, rhythm, harmony, tone color, and dynamics by revealing music-historical periods and repertories in which they were differently conceived or absent and reconstructing ways in which the music was actually experienced and thought about. In the case of ninth-century plainchant, for example, the fact that the notation indicates the direction of liturgical phrases, not individual melodic notes, should discourage formalist melodic analysis of the chant repertory.[208] In the case of Baroque trio sonata Adagios, the fact that the notation records an incomplete melodic and harmonic framework for the performers to elaborate, not a finished composition, should discourage formalist analysis there as well.

The emphasis on experience-relatedness of notation in music theory classes would likely serve to enliven the course material and allow students to contemplate by extension what our current notational practices suggest about our musical culture and ourselves—a form of critical thinking too often missing from music theory classrooms. Chances are that contact with the historical contingencies of music writing and notation would similarly stimulate the thinking of the music theorists themselves, as they are forced to deal with how and why they should analyze a musical work, such as a Baroque Adagio, whose pitches and rhythms (let alone dynamics, tone colors, and other features) cannot be quantified or verified. In such cases, the theorist that would choose nonetheless to fix the pitches and rhythms in a reified version that could be analyzed would be open under the new paradigm to the question of whether their analysis was being done for the sake of understanding the music, or for theory's sake alone.

Experience-related concepts could also come from general aspects of a culture such as dress or speaking style, wherein a culture's semiotic codes for symbolic representation of emotions or beliefs in color, shape, or sound might be read in a nonmusical context and applied analogously to the culture's music. Susan McClary demonstrates this approach in *Feminine Endings: Music, Gender, and Sexuality* (1991) by finding musical gestures used in opera to illustrate eroticism, for example, in untexted or "absolute" music.[209] McClary's finding of meaning in absolute music goes against almost two centuries of the claim, asserted during the contemporaneous rise of German symphonic music with German transcendental idealism, that music is not representational in the sense of the other arts but rather transcendent, or as Schopenhauer saw it, a direct copy of the will. However, the tendency to deny the representational aspect of music, while naïvely accepting its presence in the visual and verbal arts, simply reflects the privileging of verbal and visual symbolism in our culture, a bias considered by some feminists to be inherently masculinist. Is Debussy's *Afternoon of a Faun* unrepresentational of that sensual, sexual subject, compared to a picture of a faun or Stéphane Mallarmé's poem? Indeed, it would seem that music is more capable of representing some types of experience than are words or images.

The key to unlocking the meanings of supposedly autonomous structures of sound is probably rhythm because rhythm has the strongest ties to music's physical and emotional impact and the weakest ties to formalist analysis. It is obvious that musical rhythm is related to dance and other socially constructed patterns of movement and that such patterns themselves have cultural roots and functions. Use of the rhythms of a dance outside of its cultural context—as when Joseph Haydn uses minuets and Gustav Mahler uses ländlers—involves the carryover of the cultural associations of the dance that in turn contribute to artistic meaning. Even where dance steps and other socially constructed patterns of movement are not literally present, it should be possible for historically informed music analysts to consider the meaning of different rhythmic motifs and styles such as those of ragtime, blues, minimalist music and even the formalist-organized rhythms of the concert hall—just as critics of the literary and visual arts consider the cultural meanings of nonrepresentative features in those arts. By comparison, the universalist, formalist theories and analyses of rhythm which Grosvenor Cooper and Leonard Meyer (among others) have proposed appear to be rather empty exercises in isolation, judgment, and hierarchization, not at all oriented towards the understanding of the music.[210]

Under the new paradigm of soft boundaries, psychoanalytic models for interpreting artistic meaning may also be applied, much more successfully once the false universals of mainstream music theory have been cleared away and the conscious meanings of musical gestures have been more openly explored. The particular value of the psychoanalytic approach is that it gets beyond the hierarchical focus on greatness and into the analysis of the underlying meanings of artistic symbolism for the creative artist and the wider community. Of course, a soft-boundaried psychoanalytic approach would not make the universal assumptions that Freud did. Walter Abell has suggested a mixture of Freud's emphasis on the personal unconscious of the creative artist along with Jung's emphasis on the collective unconscious of the larger community as a means for interpreting meaning in art.[211] Applied to music, Abell's suggestion would involve comparison of musical gestures as used by a particular composer or performer, with the gestures common to the culture, in order to better understand the art, the artist, and the community. Given the symbolic nature of art, the ability to interpret artistic gestures and experiences could lead to a better understanding of our cultural ills and needs, just as psychoanalytic interpretation of dreams leads to personal diagnoses and recommendations.

Equally important to what the paradigm of soft boundaries will do in terms of music theory and analysis is what it will not do. For example, it will not produce theories and analyses that determine the comparative merit of different musics and musical works. This will no doubt disappoint many, for hierarchization is an honored practice in our culture, particularly in academic circles. Its honored status often leads us to imagine that hierarchization is essential to or the same as understanding, when in fact the understanding it provides is usually slight to nil—like the understanding experienced when *American Bandstand* critics give a song an "88" for a good beat. Soft-boundaries will also not produce a clear rule as to which of the possible experience-related concepts is best to use for understanding a particular example of music or a clear standard for ascertaining when an analysis has been successful. A sense of increased understanding and appreciation of the music will be the only guide as to the validity of the analysis, just as it is in criticism of literary and visual arts.

I foresee one serious objection to the paradigm and its particular application to music theory and analysis, having to do with the feasibility of increasing the complexity of music theory, as the paradigm will to some extent do. That is, how will students, who often have difficulty in understanding the simplistic universalist concepts of traditional music theory, be able to cope with multiple, experience-related concepts?

This is a difficult question, to which there are several relevant answers. First, the current pedagogy, even if one considers it successful (and I do not), comes close to academic fraud. One does not learn in college-level physics that Newton's laws are universal and unchallenged, though that would be simpler for ill-prepared students to understand. Why, then, is it acceptable to teach false universals in music? (If the comparison seems inappropriate, it may be because our society's respect for meaning and purpose in the arts is so much lower than that for the sciences.) Second, the difficulty students have in understanding the simplistic false universals results in part from the poverty of precollege musical education, which neglects virtually all aspects of music except for service-oriented ensembles of band and choir. This too is a kind of educational fraud that should be addressed, rather than adapted to with increasingly simplistic approaches to music at the college level.

Third, the false universals of music theory may be relatively simple in the context of music theory coursework, but because they oversimplify musical practice, they make other music courses, especially those in music history, more difficult. It may be, too, that the reason students currently have trouble with music theory is that they sense the falseness of the concepts and procedures while they are in school, and they find little application of them to the music they experience outside of the classroom. Although multiple, experience-related concepts and procedures would introduce more complexity, it is possible that their greater connection to the cultural, physical, and emotional experience of music by the students would make the concepts, and academic musical study in general, actually easier to absorb and retain.

In the broadest sense, the paradigm of soft boundaries will challenge the isolation of music theory and of music in general from culture, and perhaps by extension alleviate the isolation and devaluation of the arts in general. The result could be a major improvement in our society's appreciation of the need for artistic experience and education, of the necessary connection of the intellect to the sensory experience of the body, and of the values necessary for understanding others and experiencing life to its fullest.

# Part III

# Soft Boundaries and the Future

As we enter the twenty-first century, it is evident that we will need all our cognitive skills in learning to understand and engage productively with the new interactive, sensually immersive technologies that have been and will be developed. In this section, I propose specific curricular reforms in music and the arts in general that I believe will allow educators to provide students and the public with those skills. Chapter 7, "Integrating History, Theory, and Practice in the College Music Curriculum," proposes a structural realignment of the curriculum to allow for more integration of music history and theory with practical skills of composing, arranging, performing, and conducting. Chapter 8, "Towards Integrative, Interdisciplinary Education in the Arts and Aesthetics," explores ideas for curricular reforms in the arts and aesthetics in general. As discussed in Part I, hard boundaries in the arts and aesthetics have led to separation of historical philosophical and experiential approaches in the arts and aesthetics, and those approaches in turn have lost balance and meaning. Chapter 8 proposes reforms to soften those boundaries. Part III ends with chapter 9, "Virtual Reality and Aesthetic Competence in the Twenty-First Century," which examines the necessity of a more soft-boundaried approach to education in the context of the rise of virtual reality and other sensually immersive forms of art.

# 7

# Integrating History, Theory, and Practice in the College Music Curriculum

The fragmentation of the discipline of music into separate subdisciplines of musicology, theory and composition, education, instrumental and vocal performance, and conducting (discussed in chapter 4) has made curricular reform in music very difficult at a time when the need for that reform is paramount. While the American musical scene has changed immensely in this century, our curriculum is still largely founded on history, theory, and performance of European and, to some extent, American art music. Recent recognition of the academic neglect of non-Western, American and popular musics has led to strong demands to cover skills and knowledge associated with those areas, without any additional credit-hour space in the curriculum with which to do so. At the same time, the development of complex new computer-based technologies for producing music has led to the need to teach students new skills, again in the absence of additional time and resources with which to do so.

In fact, the American music curriculum has long been stretched to the limit with course requirements for theory, history, and performance of Western art music. Academic requirements for music majors now commonly involve so many credits and so little choice that music students find themselves isolated from other students, who in turn are prevented from academic study of music by the design of the curriculum for majors only. Because of the lengthy emphasis on knowledge and skills associated with the Western art music tradition, there is little or no time for the teaching of contemporary musical skills such as composing, arranging, and producing advertising jingles, popular songs, and film scores; nor is there a consensus among music academics that contemporary skills should be taught. Instead, training in contemporary musical skills takes place largely outside the academic system, with the result that music students lack training to enter recognized professional areas in music, while those hired to perform contemporary music often lack traditional musical knowledge and training. This disconnection between academic and real-world practice in music helps

to explain why the tremendous economic strength of the American music industry has not translated into a strong position for music in higher education,
as it has in the case of, say, engineering, computer science, and business. That
is, music students are learning skills for which there is little market and are not
learning the skills for which a strong market exists. The market alone is not
sufficient justification for curricular decisions, but the existence of this inverse
relationship between musical skills that are most marketable and those that are
most often taught in colleges is surely an unhealthy sign for the future of music
in American education.

Curricular reform is obviously necessary to address these problems, and so
the subject of curricular reform has become a frequent focus of academic musical organizations and conferences.[212] Yet, because of the fragmented structure
of the discipline of music, most academic conferences in music involve only
one subdiscipline and thus do not lend themselves to the development of broad
consenses on ideas for reform. Even the College Music Society, an organization
that welcomes the involvement of all college-level musical scholars and performers, is organized according to the subdisciplines, with separate board members, forums, paper sessions, and reviewing panels in each area. As long as we
maintain the hard boundaries of the separate musical subdisciplines, we severely
limit the possibility of curricular reform because each subdiscipline tends to
guard its own traditions and prerogatives in the belief that the skills and knowledge they preserve can only be taught in their way. The only way out of this
impasse is to soften the boundaries between the subdisciplines and re-vision the
ways that they can work together to cover necessary musical knowledge and
skills.

## THE CORE OF THE PROBLEM: THE SEPARATION OF HISTORY
## AND THEORY

The core of the problem is the separation of music history from music theory.
This separation is almost unique to music among the arts; history and theory
are regularly integrated in academic courses in the visual arts, architecture,
drama, and dance, because theory is by its nature historically based. As discussed in Part I, the separation of history from theory or philosophy in the study
of the arts prevents us from questioning the meaning and purpose of what we
are studying and its application to actual human activity. In music, the absence
of questioning is an important factor in the strength and sustenance of our large-
ensemble dominated "school-music culture," a culture that bears little resemblance to the real music world, popular or classical, past or present.

Unfortunately, in the great majority of college music departments, music history and theory are represented as distinct areas and subjects, and their relevance
to practical skills such as performing, composing, and arranging are often lost
in the process. Since the 1950s, there have been college music programs that

offer a more integrated, "comprehensive musicianship" approach to the teaching of music history and theory, but the influence of these programs declined in the wake of increasing specialization on most campuses during and following the 1960s. Indeed, since the institutional separation of music history and theory in the 1950s and 1960s, the technical language of music theory has become especially daunting, with the result that students and nonspecialists are often discouraged from trying to learn more about music. In philosopher Peter Kivy's memorable words, music-theoretical language has in our time become "as mysterious as the Kabala, and about as interesting as a treatise on sewage disposal."[213] Music history has suffered equally, often appearing to students and nonspecialists as a tedious collection of arcane details about musical works, composers, and styles rarely encountered outside the classroom.

One could argue, in favor of hard curricular boundaries, that the division of music teaching responsibilities between music history and music theory is logical and thus helpful to students' comprehension of the material. Yet the actual division of music history and theory subject matter is far from logical. Typically music theorists teach students, not theory in general, but the particular harmonic theory developed by Jean Philippe Rameau in the early eighteenth century and used in the "common practice period" of Western music (ca. 1700–1900). Theorists also teach "twentieth-century theory," that is, 12-tone serialism and other non–common practice period methods of organizing pitches in art music up to 1950. On the other hand, music historians teach pre–common practice theories along with history, style, and form, along with Western art in music, with some recent inclusion of American and popular musics as well.

Because of this odd division of responsibilities, there is no regular connection of theoretical concepts and constructions to historical styles and circumstances in theory classes, and there is little connection of harmonic theory to other aspects of musical form and style. Rather, the scales and chords of the common practice period are taught in music theory classes as if they were universal, while other scales and chords are overlooked. On the history side, the limited discussion of theory and, in a larger sense, philosophical questions leads to a tedious proliferation of historical data, disconnected from questions of how and why styles and practices of music change.

The separation of historical and philosophical inquiry has made it more difficult for performance students to apply relevant academic knowledge to their performances than it would be if history and theory were more integrated. Without that application, lessons in music history and theory are quickly forgotten. Worst of all, the disconnection of theory, history, and practice leads to the impression that theory can be meaningful without history and practice; that historical inquiry can be conducted without reference to theory and practice; and that practice can be meaningful without history or theory. Yet the idea that specialization is best has been undermined by recent discoveries in cognitive science that learning works best along multiple lines. Connecting historical data, theoretical concepts, and practical competencies gives students multiple paths of understanding and allows them to access concepts more easily between their long- and short-term memories.[214]

The separation of the academic study of music into specialized courses and programs of music theory and music history also makes it difficult for general students to study music beyond basic courses in music appreciation or fundamentals; the specialized language and focus developed in those courses and programs tend to exclude all but students majoring in music. The loss of opportunity for general students is ultimately music's loss, since those students will be less likely to support music and music education than if they had had more opportunity to learn about it in college. The separation of academic music scholars into theory and history has also negatively affected precollege music education—currently a program for training bands, choirs, and, occasionally, orchestras for contests and concerts. The decline in the breadth of the precollege music curriculum was a little-noted aspect in the plot of the 1997 film, *Mr. Holland's Opus*, where the Richard Dreyfuss character goes from teaching music appreciation and a variety of performance classes to an apparently singular focus on band performance thirty years later. That has been the pattern outside of the movie as well for thousands of school districts. The recent development in the Goals 2000 Educate America program of challenging content and achievement standards in the theory and history of music (and all the arts) has been a hopeful sign, but implementation of the Goals 2000 standards is next to impossible as long as the structure of college-level education remains so fragmented. (This issue will be more fully discussed in chapter 8.)

## THE ANSWER: SOFT-BOUNDARIED INTEGRATION OF THEORY, HISTORY, AND PRACTICE

The American music curriculum must be reformed if music is to be represented in our schools as an exciting, influential, and complex medium of communication instead of the training ground for bands and choirs to which it has in most cases devolved. Change is necessary at both college and precollege levels, but it must start at the college level, where we train educators to teach at all levels. The deep structural roots of this problem make the possibilities of curricular reform to solve it seem slim. Yet I believe we can improve the situation without a radical restructuring of the subdisciplines and curriculum in music. In my view, the key is a restructuring of the academic side—the music history and theory programs—so that students can learn the history and theory of major musical styles in context with each other and with a greater connection to practical application of this knowledge in the classroom and in more specialized applied study. This approach would be an extension of "comprehensive musicianship" approach of combining theory and history instruction to include connections to the performance and experience of Western art and popular music, and of prominent styles of non-Western music as well.

Coverage of non-Western music is particularly important as we approach the twenty-first century because our society is increasingly a globally directed one, and our ties with Asia, Africa, and South America are equally as important as our ties with Europe. While many colleges offer courses in world music, these courses cannot in themselves bring about a more integrated, multicultural view of the music world. Teaching world musics apart from Western music is a way of marking them as the "Other," something apart from the mainstream. It undervalues the importance of cross-cultural influences in the evolution of music and civilization in general, and it may even contribute to a continuation of racist notions of European and Western superiority. It also limits students' understanding of Western music, since they are unable to appreciate its stylistic and formal developments in context with developments elsewhere in the world.

Integrating world musics into our standard theory and history curriculum is difficult, but not impossible, and I believe the effort must be made. To that end, I offer the following six semester plan for integrating history, theory, and practice of music around the world. It is an intensive, five-day-a-week program combining music history, theory, and some practice. (It is assumed that applied performance and ensemble courses will remain available for more specialized practical training.) There is still a strong emphasis on the Western tradition in this plan; that emphasis is necessary for the understanding of the development of medieval, Renaissance, Baroque, Classical, Romantic, Modern, and for American popular music, as well as popular music all over the world. But in addition to the Western emphasis there is coverage of the history and theory of other traditions, particularly as they impact on the development of Western and American music. The following integrative music curriculum summarizes how this plan would work.

*Semester 1*. History and theory of folk and popular musics around the world including folk songs, spirituals, blues, rock and roll, and musics of Indonesia and Africa. Comparison of basic textures, scales, and harmonic systems of different world musics, including the major-minor scale system and simple chord progressions of Western tonal harmony.
*Practicum*: Computer- and keyboard-assisted recognition of folk and popular music styles and forms; exercises in singing and composing in these styles.

*Semester 2*. History and theory of music to 1600, including ancient and medieval styles in Europe and Asia and the emergence of European musical styles in the late Middle Ages and the Renaissance.
*Practicum*: Recognition, singing, and simple composition exercises of chant, organum, motets, and Renaissance counterpoint.

*Semester 3*. History and theory of music, 1600–1750, including Baroque European music, music of the Americas during the first centuries of European settlement, and the development of Indian music under the Mughal Empire.
*Practicum*: Recognition of Baroque European and some American styles and forms; singing, playing (on keyboard), and composition of basso continuo, monody, fugues, and chorale settings.

*Semester 4*. History, theory, and analysis of classical music, ca. 1750–1800, including intensive analysis of sonata form, rondo, song form, minuet, and theme-and-variations movements.
*Practicum*: Recognition, singing, and simple composition exercises in classical styles and forms, chord progressions, and modulations.

*Semester 5*. History and theory of nineteenth-century music, including European instrumental and vocal music, European and Chinese opera, and the rise and influence of American and other national styles.
*Practicum*: Recognition and analysis of nineteenth-century styles and forms; recognition, singing, and composition exercises of Romantic-style songs and chamber music.

*Semester 6*. History and theory of twentieth-century music, including the global fusions of music in minimalism and world beat.
*Practicum*: Recognition of twentieth-century styles; composition exercises in major styles of the century.

Semester 1 would cover introductory material such as notation and the basic harmonic and formal structures underlying folk and popular music, including the form of the 12-bar blues, verse refrain form, and other stock harmonic and formal patterns found in commonly heard music today. It would also introduce basic forms, rhythmic patterns, and pitch systems in popular and folk musics of selected non-Western cultures such as Indonesia and Africa. The practicum for Semester 1 would include computer- and keyboard-assisted recognition, notation, composition, and performance of simple harmonic patterns and accompanying melodies in any of the twenty-four keys in the Western system as well as recognition of non-Western musical styles. Use of computer software programs for notation and recognition of pitches, rhythms, harmonies, and forms would begin with Semester 1 and would be a key focus throughout the six-semester program. Emphasis on computers and on the basics of popular music would motivate students to pay more attention, since these skills are so obviously relevant to expertise in the contemporary musical scene. They would also engage the students' minds and ears on multiple levels in and out of class as they work to apply their new concepts and skills to all the music they hear around them. This kind of engagement is often missing in college music classrooms today, and the disappointment at its absence leads to a permanent drop of motivation for academic work in some students.

Semester 2 would cover the history and theory of musics from primitive and ancient cultures through the Middle Ages and the Renaissance, including the development of art music cultures in China, India, and the Middle East as well as in Europe. The practicum for Semester 2 would involve computer- and keyboard-assisted recognition, composition, and performance of these styles. Semesters 3 to 6 would continue the integration of history, theory, and practice for the Baroque, Classical, Romantic, and Modern periods, including developments and influences of non-Western musics during those periods. Semesters 2 through 6 would each be open to all students, not just music majors, assuming they had prerequisites of Semester 1 and of one or two world civilization courses. This would make upper-division music courses available to general students on a similar basis as upper-division courses in English, history, and many other subjects of general interest. Wider participation of general students in music department course offerings could have the effect of increasing interest and involvement in music of general students during their college years and afterwards.

Given the generally limited background and slow progress of students on Western music history and theory as covered in the current curriculum, the expansion of that curriculum to include contemporary non-Western and popular musics may appear unrealistically ambitious. But, as Jerome Bruner points out in *The Culture of Education*, the apparent slowness with which students learn may come from teachers assuming a "blank slate" model of education and failing to recognize and deal with the knowledge and theoretical paradigms that students have formed before they reach the classroom.[215] Following Bruner's suggestion, if we as music instructors recognize and connect with our students' interest in and knowledge of popular music, we can do much to improve their learning.

Bringing issues of contemporary practice around the world should enliven ears and minds of students and instructors alike and should also bring critical, philosophical questions about how and why musical styles work the way they do to the forefront of the classroom. The importance of rhythm and other non-pitch-oriented musical elements will be made more explicit through the study of contemporary world and popular musics. Many instructors may find themselves learning about rhythm and texture from the more sensitive ears of their students, which may lead to more enlivened, democratized classroom analysis and discussion. Democratization in the music classroom can be a positive thing rather than something to be feared. Contrary to the dominant large-ensemble model in school music culture, no one in the college music classroom has the final answers to how music works, and no one should seem to have them. What an instructor can do with authority to fulfill teaching responsibilities is to organize the lessons and evaluative processes to provide tangible skills and maximum excitement for knowledge about how music works—an excitement that should lead to continued interest long after course credits are completed.

## THE REALIGNMENT APPROACH: THEORY TAKES POST-1990, HISTORY TAKES PRE-1900

For colleges where major program changes are unrealistic, it may be possible to integrate the teaching of history and theory without actually joining the classes and areas. A pragmatic adaptation of the integrated approach could consist of realigning music history and theory area responsibilities so that music theory would cover theory, history, and basic practice of music since 1900, and music history would cover theory, history, and basic practice of Western and non-Western styles until about 1900. Assuming real integration of history and theory is impossible, the current era is better handled in music theory than in music history classes, because the current era is the basis on which contemporary theorists should philosophize about music (and philosophers theorize) and because it is too close to our time to be the best subject for history, at least in lower-division classes.

Under this arrangement, music theory would include history, theory, and basic practice of all types of contemporary and earlier twentieth-century music, including Western art music as well as world and popular musics; and history would cover history, theory, and practice of Western and non-Western musics before 1900. Additional emphasis on musical practices would be offered by private applied teachers as well as teachers of conducting, composition, and other advanced musical skills.

The realignment approach would be presented over seven semesters, as follows.

### Theory Courses, Post–1900

*Music Theory I*. Music notation, melodic structure, basic tonal harmony, standard forms, and styles in popular and folk music; and basic forms, rhythmic patterns and tonal systems in major non-Western music, including Indian music, Chinese music, Indonesian music, and African music.

*Ear Training I*. Computer- and keyboard-assisted recognition and notation of the basic harmonic patterns and accompanying melodies and rhythms; recognition and reproduction of rhythms, textures, chordal progressions, and forms of popular music genres and styles from around the world.

*Music Theory II*. Chromatic harmony, including secondary dominants, chromatic chords, and modulations in jazz and Western art music of the common practice period. Advanced melodic structures and forms, including irregular phrases, continuous melodic structures, and complex forms such as sonata form and fugue.

*Ear Training II*. Computer- and keyboard-assisted recognition of harmonic, melodic, and formal patterns introduced in Theory II.

*Music Theory III*. Theory and history of post-1900 art music, including the 12-tone serialism developed by Schoenberg and commonly used and extended by European and American composers in the 1950s and 1960s; electronic and computer music, non-Western influences in minimalism, texture music, microtonalism, world beat.

*Ear Training III*. Computer- and keyboard-assisted recognition and composition in these styles.

*Music Theory IV*. Composition and arrangement for contemporary music styles, including advertising jingles, popular songs, television and film scoring, and avant-garde art music composition.

*Theory IV Practicum* (in place of Ear Training IV). Alternation between private lessons with the instructor and master classes for hearings and critiques.

### History Courses, Pre–1900

*Music History I*. History and theory of ancient, medieval, and Renaissance musical styles, forms, genres, composers, and performers; including Ancient Sumerian, Egyptian, Chinese, Indian, Greek, and Roman music and the development of Western music and Near Eastern Islamic styles.

*Music History II.* History and theory of music of the Baroque and Classical Periods, including developments in Western music as well as developments and influences among European, Asian, African, and American musical styles.

*Music History III.* History and theory of nineteenth-century music, influences among European, Asian, African, and American cultures.

According to this plan, Theory I would cover music notation, melodic structure, basic tonal harmony, and simple forms and styles in contemporary popular music and folk musics around the world. Theory II could cover more complex melodic, harmonic, and formal structures found in jazz and in Western art music of the common practice period (which is still commonly heard in the twentieth century, and thus is an appropriate subject for theorizing). Theory III could cover twentieth-century art music, starting with atonal systems and techniques of the early century, and continuing with various types of electronically and multiculturally influenced styles common since the 1950s and the onset of the "global village."

Theory IV would focus on introductory training for occupations in the commercial music world, in popular music or art music, similar to the kind of training in broadcasting that students majoring in journalism and communication get in school. Topics for study would include composition and arrangement of advertising jingles, popular songs, film scores, and avant-garde art music. Instead of a separate ear-training class, Theory IV students could alternate between private lessons with the instructor (for individual coaching on their projects) and master classes in which students' works would be heard and critiqued by the rest of the class. Given only two prerequisites of Music Theory I and II, Theory IV could be made available to students in related fields such as broadcasting, journalism, communication, engineering, and business.

In this realigned curriculum, music history would take three semesters, starting with a semester of ancient, medieval, and Renaissance music; continuing with a semester on music of the Baroque and Classical periods, including Asian, African, and American developments; and concluding with a semester on nineteenth-century music. Western art music would continue to be a prominent point of reference in the realigned history curriculum, but there would also be more opportunity for discussion of interactions and influences between Western and non-Western cultures, as is common in western civilization and world civilization courses. This realignment will call for theory and, more generally, philosophy to have an important place in music history classes as the basis by which historical facts and concepts are understood and remembered.

## INTEGRATING HISTORY AND THEORY WITH PRACTICE

In addition to curricular changes, new integrative teaching techniques are needed to make connections between the study of music history and theory and the practice of music more explicit. The traditional practices of lecturing in music history and drilling on competencies in music theory do not lend themselves easily to creative critical thinking about the meaning of what is being learned. On the other hand, linking historically based lectures and theory-based drills to class and group discussions can give students a chance to question and apply the concepts they learn more critically and creatively. In my view, participatory exercises, group projects, and other integrative techniques should be used more in history and theory classes and should be a mainstay of a more integrated music curriculum.[216]

For example, participatory exercises in the experience of a musical style or concept can help students absorb the physical, emotional, and cultural implications of what they are learning. Such exercises may include—in addition to listening, which presumably is already a mainstay of music classrooms—experience in singing, playing, composing, and dancing with the styles and forms being studied or analyzed. Participatory experiences increase the impact of a lesson and the ability of students to remember and apply the knowledge gained, including in their own future classrooms if they become teachers themselves. For example, a lecture on thirteenth-century music can be combined with philosophical questions about the relationship between the development of medieval notation and of musical style, as well as the relationship between contemporary notation and musical style. Then, group performance of a thirteenth-century song like "Sumer is icumen in" using Franconian notation of the period can give the students an experience that will make the academic concepts they have learned far more meaningful and memorable.

Group projects and presentations are also useful as a way of getting students more involved in the process of integrating musical research and practice—which in turn prepares them to teach others about music in the future, as well as understanding it and the learning process better in the present. One way to use group presentations is to have students sign up for their choice among a selection of genres, works, or composers, to study and teach to the class in a series of group presentations. Then the students in each group divide the topic up into manageable parts, do their individual research, and organize and present their findings to the class together with practical illustrations. In this manner, every student becomes the teacher at some point during the class and must deal with the problems of forming meaningful generalizations about the history, theory, and practice of music in their chosen area, as well as the work of collecting, understanding, and organizing. That experience inevitably leads to greater understanding of why history and theory are important to their solo and ensemble study.

One of my favorite integrative teaching techniques is what I call the "historical happening." Historical happenings involve students impersonating historical figures in some musical activity or debate. Some examples of historical happenings I have used in music history classes are as follows: a Medieval Feast of Fools, a discussion of Renaissance composers and religious figures about style and form in sacred music; a debate among eighteenth-century patrons and composers about the virtues and vices of the patronage system; a Romantic salon; and a debate among twentieth-century composers about their respective musical aesthetics and styles. Typically, historical happenings help students understand the relationship of theory, history, and practice in a historical period, as well as giving them an opportunity to get fully into the spirit of the time. Extra credit points may be used to encourage students to come with period food, dress, and performances so that the historical happenings become festive and creative occasions. Many students who are reluctant to take part in regular class discussions may have their minds and mouths set free by role-playing in a historical setting. The experiences and insights gained on these occasions probably stay with the students long after memory work for a test has faded. Historical happenings may work particularly well in an integrated curriculum, giving the class one or two chances in the semester to get more fully into the spirit of the music and people being studied.

Integrated approaches to teaching music history, theory, and practice should help students understand the relationship of academic learning in music to their studies of musical performance. The current, loose relationship of the three separate areas of history, theory, and applied performance leaves students with little idea of how to carry over skills and knowledge from one area to the next. In an integrated curriculum, it should be more obvious to students that historical and theoretical knowledge of the music of any period is relevant to its performance because the relationship will be demonstrated repeatedly in practical exercises assigned in the academic classes. Accordingly, it should be possible to hold performance students accountable for remembering and applying historical and theoretical knowledge about the music they are performing and for learning to explain relevant facts and ideas to their audiences through program notes or discussion.

Integration could also have the positive effect of strengthening the connections of the subdisciplines of music history, theory, and performance to music education, lessening the isolation of that subdiscipline as well. Leaving issues of education to only one segment of a discipline, as currently practiced in music, is a bad policy. If scholars and practitioners in music and in humanities in general want to improve the public standing of their discipline, they must become more involved with education at all levels. The omission of music history and theory from precollege education in the past resulted in part from the lack of involvement by music theorists and musicologists in the design of that education. The recent emphasis in the Goals 2000 National Standards for the Arts[217] makes clear that music history and theory are necessary parts of a balanced musical education at every level, from K–12 through college study. In order to encourage implementation of those standards, music theorists and musicologists need to become involved in the design of precollege music curricula and of teacher training programs at the college level as well.

Integration of music history, theory, and practice of music in the college curriculum can do much to bring down the barriers of communication and training between music specialists and the general public. If music departments cover history, theory, and performance of contemporary popular and world musics as well as Western art music, the result will be an increase in public understanding about music of all kinds and a rise in the recognition of the importance of music in our lives and of music education in our schools. Education for music majors should improve as well as they are given the opportunity to learn practical skills and think critically about all kinds of music. There may be concerns that this approach will leave less time for the Western art tradition at a time when students have less background in that area than ever before. However, placing Western art music within the wider context of world music traditions may also increase students' motivation to learn about it, once they are encouraged to think critically about its relationship to themselves and the world.

# 8

# Towards Integrative, Interdisciplinary Education in the Arts and Aesthetics

In 1983, cultural critic Christopher Lasch opened his speech to a conference on "The Future of Musical Education in America" with the following remarks:

I accepted the invitation to address this distinguished gathering, I confess, in the hope that it would give me the chance to talk about a number of things I have decided opinions about: Beethoven's over-use of the diminished seventh; his addiction to chords in root position; the canard that Schumann couldn't orchestrate; the critical neglect of Ludwig Spohr; the Brahms-Wagner controversy (I believe the Wagnerites were dead wrong); the need for more compositions featuring prominent but easy parts for the viola.[218]

Lasch's remarks were tongue-in-cheek; he actually went on to address the need for music and humanities scholars to challenge the narrow consumeristic approach to education and life in late industrial America, instead of just participating in specialized professional debates. Unfortunately, Lasch's provocative suggestion was neglected in the discussions following his lecture.[219] In the context of a conference on music curriculum, it was easiest for the participants to focus on music alone rather than on the larger interdisciplinary challenge of rehumanizing American education and life.

The trouble is, under the single-disciplinary structure of American education today, there is almost no opportunity to consider interdisciplinary approaches or challenges in the arts, no matter how important they may be for improving that education. As discussed in Part I, the arts exist in our educational institutions as separate disciplines of art (visual arts), music, dance, and drama, in which concepts and competencies are defined and evaluated by single-disciplinary specialists. Single-disciplinary specialization in the arts has led to extraordinary levels of complexity and virtuosity in the areas of research and practice, but it has also had the effect of isolating the specialists who teach about the arts from each other and from contacts and influences from other academic disciplines.

The result of this isolation has been an ever-widening gap between arts specialists and the public that has in turn been devastating to public understanding and support for education in the arts.[220]

As previously discussed, there are many problems with the single-disciplinary structure of arts education. First, single-disciplinary arts education tends to neglect artistic developments outside the West, as well as the impact in general of social, political, and technological influences on artistic production and interpretation.[221] Second, single-disciplinary specialists and courses tend to neglect highly influential art forms that involve cross-disciplinary expression, such as song, drama, opera, and film. Third, in terms of career preparation, single-disciplinary degree programs provide inadequate preparation for students training for careers that involve knowledge of multiple art forms, including careers in arts management, business, law, journalism, and broadcasting. In terms of teacher training, single-disciplinary courses do little to help future K–12 teachers integrate the arts into their teaching of social studies, English, math, and science.

Perhaps most important, single-disciplinary teachers of music, art, drama, or dance are not as effective in explaining the importance of the arts and of arts education as they would be if they had some training in understanding and teaching the arts as a whole. Independently, none of the arts is seen as having comparable importance with history, English, math, or other subjects, so their representation in K–12 schools often depends on the presence of extra funding or on the perception of the discipline as providing a service to the school, as in the case of football marching bands or parent's night art exhibits. Representation of the arts is somewhat better at the college level. There, departments of the arts provide academic courses in the histories of the arts as well as instruction in practice and performance. Still, though, most college-level courses in the arts are designed entirely for students majoring in the disciplines; the few general courses are introductory surveys serving large numbers of anonymous students— courses unlikely to have lasting impact on their learning.

## THE IMPACT OF THE GOALS 2000 NATIONAL STANDARDS FOR ARTS EDUCATION

The omission of the arts in 1990 from Education 2000—the national program designed in the wake of the Carnegie Report in 1984—was a shock to arts educators that served to raise their awareness that the single-disciplinary approach to the arts was ineffective. As a result, a consortium of arts educators from music, visual arts, dance, and drama joined together in 1992 to prepare a set of national standards for teaching the arts at the precollege level. The consortium's work resulted in 1994 in the National Standards for Arts Education (NSAE), which in turn were incorporated into the final version of Education 2000, the Goals 2000: Educate America Act, passed into law by the United States Congress in 1995.[222] Since 1995, national and state budgets have made funds available for grants to help implement the standards, and arts organizations such as the Getty Education Institute for the Arts and the Music Educators National Conference have actively promoted their use.

At first glance, the new standards seem like an extraordinary step forward in arts education. The range of skills and knowledge called for goes far beyond the traditional emphasis on practical skills; in fact, the standards call for the teaching of artistic practices along with intellectual knowledge in the theory and history of the arts and their relationship to culture at all grade levels. The general goals stated at the beginning of the standards also give strong emphasis to the importance of interdisciplinary connections among the arts and other disciplines.

- *They should be able to communicate at a basic level in the four arts disciplines— dance, music, theater, and the visual arts.* This includes knowledge and skills in the use of the basic vocabularies, materials, tools, techniques, and intellectual methods of each arts discipline.

- *They should be able to communicate proficiently in at least one art form* including the ability to define and solve artistic problems with insight, reason, and technical proficiency.

- *They should be able to develop and present basic analyses of works of art* from structural, historical, and cultural perspectives, and from combinations of those perspectives. This includes the ability to understand and evaluate work in the various arts disciplines.

- *They should have an informed acquaintance with exemplary works of art from a variety of cultures and historical periods*, and a basic understanding of historical development in the arts disciplines, across the arts as a whole, and within cultures.

- *They should be able to relate various types of arts knowledge and skills within and across the arts disciplines.* This includes mixing and matching competencies and understandings in art making, history, and culture and analysis in any arts-related project.[223]

Unfortunately, despite the interdisciplinary nature of the general goals, the actual standards for content and achievement in the arts make no allowances for interdisciplinary implementation. Instead, they assign all responsibility for teaching the arts to single-disciplinary specialists in the various arts disciplines, as if schools commonly have specialists in all four disciplines, and as if students commonly take courses in each of those areas at every level—which, as discussed in chapter 1 is far from the case.

For example, consider the summary (given below) of the NSAE content standards for each of the four arts disciplines.

## MUSIC

1. Singing, alone and with others, a varied repertoire of music
2. Performing on instruments, alone and with others, a varied repertoire of music
3. Improvising melodies, variations, and accompaniments

4. Composing and arranging music within specified guidelines

5. Reading and notating music

6. Listening to, analyzing, and describing music

7. Evaluating music and music performances

8. Understanding relationships between music, the other arts, and disciplines outside the arts

9. Understanding music in relation to history and culture

## DANCE

1. Identifying and demonstrating movement elements and skills in performing dance

2. Understanding choreographic principles, processes, and structures

3. Understanding dance as a way to create and communicate meaning

4. Applying and demonstrating critical and creative thinking skills in dance

5. Demonstrating and understanding dance in various cultures and historical periods

6. Making connections between dance and healthful living

7. Making connections between dance and other disciplines

## THEATRE

1. Script writing by the creation of improvisations and scripted scenes based on personal experience and heritage, imagination, literature, and history

2. Acting by developing basic, acting skills to portray characters who interact in improvised and scripted scenes

3. Designing by developing environments for improvised and scripted scenes

4. Directing by organizing rehearsals for improvised and scripted scenes

5. Researching by using cultural and historical information to support improvised and scripted scenes

6. Comparing and incorporating art forms by analyzing methods of presentation and audience response for theater, dramatic media (such as film, television, and electronic media), and other art forms

7. Analyzing, evaluating, and constructing meanings from improvised and scripted scenes, and from theatre, film, television, and electronic media productions

8. Understanding context by analyzing the role of theater, film, television, and electronic media in the community and in other cultures

## VISUAL ARTS

1. Understanding and applying media, techniques, and processes

2. Using knowledge of structures and functions

3. Choosing and evaluating a range of subject matter, symbols, and ideas

4. Understanding the visual arts in relation to history and cultures

5. Reflecting upon and assessing the characteristics and merits of their work and the work of others

6. Making connections between visual arts and other disciplines[224]

In the breakdown of general goals to single-disciplinary standards, the interdisciplinary emphasis in the general goals is reduced to a single content standard among many, in each case one of the last standards mentioned and probably the one most easily forgotten. The problem is that very few schools exist that offer instruction in all four disciplines; there are often only one or two arts teachers present at a school, usually covering music and the visual arts. How, then, will students receive instruction in the content standards for drama ("theatre" in the NSAE standards), including script writing, acting, set design, research, comparison of dramatic media, and analysis of works and their cultural context? Leaving the standards to single-disciplinary specialists results in no instruction at all in the arts that are omitted.

Even in the arts that are usually covered, students are unlikely to be exposed to many of the standards. For instance, take the nine content standards for music including such activities as performing, improvising, composing, arranging, reading, notating, listening to, analyzing, and evaluating music, as well as understanding relationships among music, the other arts, other disciplines, history, and culture. Is the student who fills their high school arts requirement with band going to get instruction in all these areas? It isn't very likely. Chances are, this student's ensemble experience will cover only the second content standard: "performing on instruments, alone and with others, a varied repertoire of music." Even that is questionable given the frequent absence of solo opportunities and the varied repertoire mentioned in the standard. Think: this student will fulfill the high school arts requirement while achieving none of the standards for the visual arts, drama, and dance, and only part of one of the nine standards in music!

The detailed breakdown of student learning expectations for the content standards shows even more clearly the unlikelihood of their implementation under current conditions. Consider for example, student learning expectations for Content Standard 9: understanding music in relation to history and culture.

## GRADES K–4

1. Identify by genre or style aural examples of music from various historical periods and cultures

2. Describe in simple terms how elements of music are used in music examples from various cultures of the world

3. Identify various uses of music in their daily experiences (celebration of special occasions, background music for television, worship), and describe characteristics that make certain music suitable for each use

4. Identify and describe roles of musicians (orchestra conductor, folksinger, church organist) in various music settings and culture

5. Demonstrate audience behavior appropriate for the context and style of music performed

**GRADES 5–8**

6. Describe distinguishing characteristics of representative music genres and styles from a variety of cultures

7. Classify by genre and style (and, if applicable, by historical period, composer, and title) a varied body of exemplary (that is, high-quality and characteristic) musical works and explain the characteristics that cause each work to be considered exemplary

8. Compare, in several cultures of the world, functions music serves, roles of musicians (lead guitarist in a rock band, composer of jingles for commercials, singer in Peking opera), and conditions under which music is typically performed

**GRADES 9–12: PROFICIENT**

9. Classify by genre or style and by historical period or culture unfamiliar but representative aural examples of music and explain the reasoning behind their classifications

10. Identify sources of American music genres (swing, Broadway musical, blues), trace the evolution of those genres and cite well-known musicians associated with them

11. Identify various roles (entertainer, teacher, transmitter of cultural tradition) that musicians perform, cite representative individuals who have functioned in each role, and describe their activities and achievements

**GRADES 9–12: ADVANCED**

12. Identify and explain the stylistic features of a given musical work that serve to define its aesthetic tradition and its historical or cultural context

13. Identify and describe music genres or styles that show the influence of two or more cultural traditions, identify the cultural source of each influence, and trace the historical conditions that produced the synthesis of influences[225]

These expectations are unrealistically high in all respects. It is, for instance, completely unrealistic to imagine that all students in grades 5 through 8 will be able to "classify by genre and style (and, if applicable, by historical period, composer, and title) a varied body of exemplary (that is, high-quality and characteristic) musical works," even if music was a regular part of the curriculum—which is far from the case. For most students, their only exposure to musical education will have been occasional sessions with a music instructor in grades K–6 and a general music class or ensemble in grades 7 and 8. Given these limitations, general students rarely come away with an understanding of musical notation and fundamentals, let alone recognition of genres, styles, historical periods, composers, and works.

This is not to say that teaching recognition of styles to middle schoolers is inherently impossible, but it is unlikely under the current curriculum. The fact is, the pragmatic handling of secondary and middle-level musical education through large ensembles has led to a singular focus on learning repertoire reserved for those ensembles, often without consideration of historical and theoretical issues of that repertoire, let alone other genres and styles. The occasional teacher who goes beyond this model exists but is not likely to be encouraged.

Teachers who stick to a strict diet of rehearsal and performance, on the other hand, may expect regular administrative, parental, and student approval for their tangible results in terms of concert, contest, and athletic-event performances.

## BEYOND GOALS 2000: INTEGRATIVE, INTERDISCIPLINARY REFORMS IN THE DELIVERY SYSTEM

Because of their weaknesses, the Goals 2000 National Standards for Arts Education are unlikely to result in real improvement on their own. More likely, they will join the long list of other reform plans made over the last fifty years, as the situation has gone from bad to worse.[226] If real improvement in arts education is to take place, it will require more than the rhetoric of higher standards. Rather, it will require changes in the education delivery system: a modification of the single disciplinary structure of current arts education at the college level in order to allow for integrative interdisciplinary education in the arts for future K–12 teachers.[227]

In chapter 7 I discussed how integrative teaching of history, theory, and performance can improve musical understanding. In a fully interdisciplinary contest, integrative teaching can be even more powerful in reaching students with the power of artistic understanding and experience. Recent discoveries in cognitive science about the multiple modes of learning confirm the value of connecting experiential education with intellectual inquiry, in the arts and in general. The more connections students have with a concept, the better their chance is of accessing that concept and the knowledge about it from their long-term memories, when the need arises.[228]

The promotion of discipline-based art education (DBAE) by the Getty Education Institute has been a step in the direction of integrative arts education; unfortunately the Getty Institute has had little influence beyond the single discipline of the visual arts. In my view, what is needed is an interdisciplinary-based arts education (IBAE), wherein practice in each of the arts is related to aesthetic principles and cultural history. IBAE could begin in the earliest grades with discussion and interpretation about the meaning of artistic activities carried on in and out of class, including those of other historical times and cultures. Study and experience of the arts would include non-Western traditions, popular arts, and cross-disciplinary arts presently neglected in arts education and would link issues of style in art to understanding of the cultural and/or historical period in which they appeared. Such discussions would not have to exclude popular arts that are enjoyed by the general public, such as television shows and music videos. Rather, every experience that is staged for a perceptual effect would be potentially relevant to learning about the arts. Those artistic practices that have been particularly popular, such as Madonna's videos, or long-lasting (e.g., Shakespeare plays, Peking operas, and the folk songs of any number of cultures) would take on special interest, because of the depth and breadth of meaning they have for their own and other cultures. Instead of alienating students by ignoring or denigrating the artistic experiences that have had the most meaning for them, the teacher would draw on those very experiences to engage their interest in the arts of other times and cultures. Knowledge of the tremendous variety of ways in which humans express themselves artistically could lead students to a critical attitude toward the popular arts of their own culture and a critical understanding of how and why they function so successfully. Such critical attitudes and skills are crucial to the ability to function as a thinking human being in the age of electronic media. Perhaps more than any past culture, our society literally requires us to be, as former Labor Secretary Robert Reich has put it, "symbolic analysts,"[229] and the arts are the most appropriate place to teach students how to read and interpret the symbols of our complex world.

The integrative, interdisciplinary approach presents a difficult challenge for teachers trained in a single discipline, because they must learn how to integrate historical and theoretical issues with practice in a variety of art forms and cultures. In addition, general teachers of social studies, English, and even science and math need to learn how to incorporate relevant knowledge and experience of the arts into their courses. In the future it will be desirable to develop new courses to help teachers with this challenge, to be taught by new "interdisciplinary specialists." But even the most narrowly trained single-disciplinary specialist can move in the direction of integrative, interdisciplinary education by careful design of readings, assignments, tests, and class activities. For example, I have found the assignment of primary source readings to be more helpful than textbooks in promoting integrative learning because they make subject matter more immediate and more open to philosophical inquiry. Reading the text of a ninth-century lesson in music theory can bring alive the thoughts and worldviews of medieval thinkers in a integrative way that cannot happen with textbook readings, no matter how carefully written. Source readings may also invite students to imagine and even to recreate a historical artistic practice in a way that may be far more memorable than canonical learning through textbooks and lectures.

Integrative teaching methods can be used in a wide variety of courses at every level to improve student learning. In the single-disciplinary arts survey courses offered as core requirements or options at the college level, integrative teaching methods can be used to bring life to historical canons, helping students understand historical practices in an art form by actually experiencing or creating them and by asking philosophical questions about their significance to their creators and cultures. In drama classes, plays and scenes can serve as a basis for historical research, performance, and philosophical inquiry about issues of meaning and value therein. In music, students may be assigned to compose melodies, rhythms, or even short compositions as a way of understanding historical or theoretical concepts. History, experience, and philosophical inquiry can also be linked in visual arts and architecture surveys with assignments of simple design projects along with research on historical figures who used similar designs.

Obviously not all artistic practices and experiences lend themselves easily to instruction for nonspecialists. One cannot, for instance, ask an art survey student to read the letters of Vincent Van Gogh in *Dear Theo* and then paint like him. But with effort, one can find appropriate ways to integrate history, and philosophy, experience at many levels. In architecture, for example, one can assign nonspecialists a walking tour of local architectural sites, followed by reports and discussion of the architectural designs they saw and experienced. In the visual arts one can make experiential assignments in use of perspective, lighting, and composition that can do much to further students' understanding of the historical role and meaning of these elements to the visual art forms they study. Whatever the assignment, the result of integrative learning should be that students' sensual experience of the arts and the world in general is affected, as they learn to consciously engage their minds and their senses at the same time.

In my own teaching of general music courses, I aim to integrate lectures on historical issues with discussion of philosophical questions and with active experience of the music we are studying. Such fairly simple activities as singing chant, organum, polyphonic canons, and opera choruses or dancing to music in period styles can do much to make historical and philosophical concepts about music real to the students. In integrating history with philosophy and experience, it is often most effective and memorable to start with an experiential exercize and use it to lead into philosophical questions and historical data about the experience. For example, I use a humming exercise at the beginning of a music survey course (and in the music segment of an interdisciplinary arts course; see next chapter) to help students identify and understand the musical elements. Here is the version of this exercise that appears in my brief music survey text, *Music in the Western Tradition*:

While lying down on your back or sitting quietly in a chair, shut your eyes and hum for at least two minutes. Listen to yourself. If you are with others, listen to them and notice as much as you can about the experience. What sort of humming sounds do you make? How do they compare with the sounds your neighbors make? How long do your sounds tend to last? Be as specific as possible; these differences are the building blocks of music. Discuss the exercise with a partner and then with the class.[230]

In subsequent discussion about this exercise, classes not only identify the main elements of musical sound, including pitch, range, harmony, melody, and timbre; they also explore physical, emotional, and psychological aspects of these elements and their use in a way that makes the elements far more real than memorization for testing. For identification and discussion of the main elements of musical rhythm, I have students dance. In learning contrasting dances from different cultures and epochs, such as a Renaissance pavan versus a West African dance, students can sharpen their understanding of the relationship of rhythmic styles and features to culture in a very memorable way.

After all the musical elements have been introduced, I like to assign a short composition in which each student uses knowledge of the elements to design, or compose, a minute of their own music. Compositions may be presented and discussed in class, along with brief essays from composers analyzing their works. Later in the semester I may assign a Desert Island Project, in which students choose, present, and analyze a minute of their favorite piece of music.

## DEVELOPING INTERDISCIPLINARY COURSES AND PROGRAMS

In addition to integrative teaching methods, there is a need for interdisciplinary arts instruction at every level of education, as a complement to single-disciplinary instruction for specialists. With interdisciplinary instruction, all the arts could be represented in every school by the arts specialists and other teachers. Given the availability of interdisciplinary courses and programs, single-disciplinary specialists could begin to broaden their perspective and teach their discipline in a more connected manner, covering other art forms as well as their own when needed. Schools that can only afford to hire one or two specialists would not have to omit the coverage of the other arts and aesthetics, because those subjects would be more fully incorporated into other subjects that are covered.

Interdisciplinary college courses and programs in the arts can also be developed as the means by which future precollege teachers outside the arts and single-disciplinary arts majors learn to incorporate arts issues into their subject. If colleges of education collaborate with arts departments in curricular development, such courses can be required of preservice teachers, possibly in fulfillment of core university requirements for the arts and humanities. Interdisciplinary arts courses and programs should also be made available as core requirement options for college students in general, who may be more interested in an integrative, interdisciplinary approach to studying the arts than they are in traditional single-disciplinary lecture-surveys.

Interdisciplinary arts courses or minor degree programs can also act as a credential for teaching the high school "fine arts survey" courses now mandated in most states. Currently, the absence of interdisciplinary-trained teachers for these courses frequently results in their division between the art and music specialists—the specialists most often present in the schools—while drama, dance, and other art forms are simply not covered at all. Given interdisciplinary arts training, teachers of these courses would no longer be limited to coverage of only one or two art forms. Interdisciplinary-trained arts teachers could also serve as consultants in their schools for integrating the arts into all subjects and for encouraging special arts-oriented events such as festivals celebrating particular cultures and historical periods.

Some arts specialists may be uncomfortable with the idea of interdisciplinarity in arts education, fearing that they will function to "water down the arts and to lessen the energy of the individual art forms," as Libby Chiù put it during the debate over the National Standards for Arts Education.[231] On the other hand, single-disciplinary education in the arts is no guarantee of depth, especially when it results in the absence of any coverage at all for some art disciplines. Too, if interdisciplinary instruction includes integration of intellectual knowledge with and practice of the arts, students will have the opportunity to recognize the complexity and beauty of the practices about which they are learning more fully than is often achieved in single-disciplinary courses.

Single-disciplinary arts specialists also may fear that their jobs will be endangered by the interdisciplinary spread of knowledge and skills. This thinking is short-sighted, like the fear among computer programmers in the 1980s that widespread use of personal computers would put them out of business, instead of, as actually happened, making them even more central to the economy. Similarly, it is far more likely that interdisciplinary, integrative reforms in arts education will raise recognition of the need for arts specialists as the nature and importance of their disciplines are more widely understood. In fact, if the move to more soft-boundaried, interdisciplinary education in the arts is not made, arts educators may run the risk of having to refight the battle for inclusion of the arts in our curriculum on a regular basis. By contrast, integrative, interdisciplinary education in the arts could achieve a more permanent mainstreaming of the arts into our standard curriculum and thereby obviate the need for repeated political battles.

Considering the obvious need for interdisciplinary programs in the arts and aesthetics in American education, it is striking how few important programs have developed. The 1995 edition of the *College Blue Book* lists three degree programs in Interdisciplinary Studies in the Creative Arts; two programs in Art and Communication; and one each in Art and Music and Art and Music Education—none at large or otherwise distinguished institutions. Eighty-seven degree programs are listed under Arts but they are mostly associate degrees at small community colleges. By comparison the *College Blue Book* lists thousands of degree programs in the individual art disciplines, including programs at virtually all major universities.

Developing interdisciplinary courses, let alone programs, in this kind of vacuum is very difficult. Interdisciplinarity is regularly viewed with suspicion by single-disciplinary experts, and sometimes with good reason. Some interdisciplinary programs are developed primarily in order to secure funds from granting agencies that favor interdisciplinarity, such as the National Endowment for the Humanities. Some interdisciplinary research and teaching is superficial: a matter of two disciplinary experts comparing their wares for an interesting change of pace. As Hugh Petrie has pointed out, good interdisciplinary work requires scholars to be well-versed in their own discipline and to be competent to deal with the methodologies of the disciplines one brings together.[232] The challenges of interdisciplinary work should not be considered lightly. At the same time, the risks of failing to be sufficiently interdisciplinary—of approaching research and teaching in too hard-boundaried a manner—should be considered as well.

Even where interdisciplinary programs do exist, they may fall prey to decline if the participants are not careful. The current absence of interdisciplinary specialists (i.e., scholars with training in interdisciplinary research and teaching) means that interdisciplinary courses are generally team-taught by collaborating single-disciplinary specialists. Such team teaching can be exhilarating for instructors and students alike, but it also may lead away from true interdisciplinarity if the specialists become lazy and uninvolved in each others' teaching. Some interdisciplinary programs have faltered as their courses became more and more a matter of separate lectures from different specialists. Why continue the extra expense and effort of interdisciplinary teaching when one can just attend to one's own area? Careful planning and commitment to interdisciplinary values is necessary to avoid this result.

Where interdisciplinary courses do not exist, curricular reformers will likely need the support of the single-disciplinary specialists to enact the courses. Concerns that interdisciplinary treatment will water down a subject and that allowing core arts requirement credit for interdisciplinary courses will "drain" students away from the single-disciplinary courses may lead to strong opposition from existing arts departments. Involving as many single-disciplinary specialists as possible in the design of the new courses is one way to combat those fears. In the process of planning a new course, specialists can become genuinely excited about the possibilities of reaching general students with more imaginative approaches than are possible in single-disciplinary surveys. The specialists who become involved in the planning may later be helpful in addressing concerns of their departmental colleagues, voting for the new course or program, and guest lecturing or teaching in it. Administrators should also be involved, in order to get institutional support for interdisciplinary teaching. This may be the hardest challenge of all, because academic institutions have become so dependent on single-disciplinary structure and on the bottom line that funding for interdisciplinary courses and programs is more and more difficult to find.[233] On the other hand, creative administrators may recognize interdisciplinary programs as potential solutions to financial problems, particularly if one interdisciplinary course can be shown to serve multiple purposes more effectively than separate single-disciplinary courses.

At the University of Arkansas we have introduced an interdisciplinary course that includes the arts and aesthetics and that is available to all students in fulfillment of core fine arts and humanities requirements. In our approach, aesthetics provides a foundation for understanding issues of form, content, style, and meaning in each of the main art disciplines. The use of aesthetics rather than history as the structural foundation of the course allows for consideration of arts from all cultures and periods. (By contrast, using history as a foundation leads to a dominant emphasis on Western art, because the art-historical periods of Ancient, Medieval, Renaissance, Baroque, Classical, Romantic, and Modern have been designed in accordance with Western history.) Aesthetic grounding also encourages philosophical discussion of issues of art and aesthetics in contemporary culture, about which students will likely be most interested and aware. One can then extend the excitement of considering contemporary issues to the understanding of other art cultures of the past. The course structure also calls for some single-disciplinary consideration of art forms, so that complex issues of media and style are not ignored. Experiential exercises are used to enhance the understanding of each major art form, giving students the opportunity to relate historical and theoretical concepts to artistic creativity and experience. The course plan involves three major units.

## UNIT I. Introduction and the Dramatic Arts

Week 1. Introduction to Aesthetic Terms and Issues

What is meant by art, the arts, and aesthetics, and why are they (or aren't they) important to us?

Common classifications of media, disciplines, and forms in the arts.

Sampling and discussion of aesthetic views from Confucius, Plato, Aristotle, and Kant.

Week 2. Style, Culture, and Meaning in the Arts

Slide show and discussion on style and stylistic changes in Western versus Eastern art traditions; "high" versus "low" art forms; media and style in the pictorial arts.

Art and the museum. Discuss "museum culture" and its effect on aesthetic theory and learning.

*Experiential Exercise 1. Museum project. Bring a photograph or other representation of an artwork that you admire for display in class, along with a written statement of what you find meaningful about the work, to display alongside the work. Class members will tour and discuss exhibit, including comparison of the aesthetic tastes and perspectives represented.*

Week 3. Introduction to the Dramatic Arts

Roots of drama from religious ritual to Greek drama; Plato versus Aristotle on imitation and catharsis.

Dramatic crafts: lighting, scene design, direction, acting, music.

*Experiential Exercise 2. Class rehearsal and performance of scene from Greek drama.*

Week 4. Drama Continued

Lecture on Asian dramatic styles, with emphasis on Japanese Kabuki theater.

*Experiential Exercise 3. Eastern versus Western acting techniques.*

Week 5. Dance Principles and techniques of dance;
cross-cultural comparisons African dance and culture.

*Experiential Exercise 4: Learning African dance movements and techniques.*

**UNIT II. Visual, Musical, and Environmental Arts**

Week 6. Visual Arts

Design as the common aesthetic principle in the visual arts.

Media and style; individual style and creative vision.

Guest lecture, slide show, and discussion with visiting artist.

Week 7. Visual Arts Continued

Western tradition of painting from ca. 1400–1700: from early Renaissance perspective to late Baroque oil painting and trompe-l'oeil techniques.

Guest lecture, slide show, and discussion with visiting artist.

*Experiential Exercise 5. Create and be prepared to discuss a small sketch or other work of visual art representing something in your environment. (The medium may be anything, including collage, sculpture, installation work, etc.)*

Week 8. Musical Arts

Experiential introduction to the musical elements and their use through humming and dance exercises.

Sampling and discussion of musical styles, social function, and expression around the world—chant, blues, raga, fugue.

Week 9. Musical Arts Continued

Music in the concert hall—sonata form and motivic manipulation.

Music and culture in the twentieth century: jazz, rock, world beat, MTV, Cage and the avant-garde, serialism, minimalism, etc.

*Experiential Exercise 6. Desert Island musical excerpts. Present and discuss a 1-minute excerpt of your favorite musical work with an analysis of its stylistic and expressive content and the relationship of its style to its social function.*

Week 10. Environmental Arts

How aesthetics applies to architecture and environmental arts—designing and understanding the physical environment of a culture.

Issues of media, technology, geography, and style in the early history of architecture. Egypt, Greece, Rome, China, Islamic, Gothic, Renaissance, and Baroque.

Week 11. Environmental Arts Continued

Landscape architecture: designing nature. Versailles versus English gardens, Chinese and Japanese gardens, Frederick Law Olmstead and New York Central Park.

Architecture since 1750: neo-Classicism, neo-Gothic, Modernism, Postmodernism; personal visions of Frank Lloyd Wright and Gaudi.

*Experiential Exercise 7. Take an architectural tour of assigned sites in your town: comment on the different styles, materials, and histories of the buildings do you see, and when do they do they say about the lives and attitudes of the architects and inhabitants within?*

## UNIT III. The Arts in the Twentieth Century

### Week 12. Photography and Film
Is photography an art? What effect has its development had on twentieth-century culture?

History and technology of photography and film.

*Experiential Exercise 8. Designing lighting for a photograph or film scene. The visual side of drama involves staging, scenery, and in film, lighting for emotional effect. In this exercise students will place lights to create various effects for a brief movie scene and discuss their intentions and results.*

### Week 13. Other New Art Forms
Installation, Performance, and Feminist Art: Judy Chicago's *Dinner Party*.

Computer art and virtual reality; aesthetic experience in the future.

### Weeks 14–15. Shapes of the Present and Future
*Experiential Exercise 9. Group or individual reports on twentieth-century avant-garde movements with cross-disciplinary illustrations: may include cubism, dada, surrealism, Der Stijl, expressionism, abstract expressionism, magic realism, pop art, postmodernism, feminist art, anti-colonialist art.*[234]

Following an opening unit on the arts and aesthetics in general, the course examines the main traditional art forms individually in Unit II. The single-disciplinary examination begins with the art of drama, mainly because of drama's potential for immediate engagement of students in integrative study of history, philosophy, and practice and because drama is itself an interdisciplinary art form. (In contrast, most interdisciplinary arts and humanities courses begin with the visual arts, perhaps because of the relative ease of teaching visual-interpretive skills.) In the course of studying the main elements, genres, forms, and historical works and figures in drama, scenes from selected dramas may be preformed and discussed in terms of their historical context and the philosophical questions they raise. Prior introduction to the aesthetic theories of Plato and Aristotle allows discussion to go fairly deep and to include issues of artistic expression and morality in contemporary dramas, including popular movies and TV shows. Following the focus on drama, later discussions of music, visual arts, dance, and architecture include references to their use in drama and other multidisciplinary art forms. A final focus on architecture allows all the arts to be considered in the historical context of the structures in which they took place. The closing unit on the arts in modern times allows students the opportunity to study major twentieth-century movements such as expressionism, surrealism, and postmodernism in an interdisciplinary context, including the many cross-disciplinary influences and genres that have developed. Throughout each of the units, exercises in acting, singing, dancing, designing, and just looking, listening, and feeling give students the opportunity to connect historical and philosophical concepts in the arts with the experience of those concepts.

Courses like this have less emphasis on canonical facts, but they are not watered down. The limited time for canonical facts may even be a value, since it forces instructors to look beyond the traditional academic treatment of the arts—which is not working—to create a new structure. Some terms and canonical figures have to go, but that may be better than having them stay without being questioned. At the same time, the breadth of the course allows for more consideration of issues of value and meaning in the arts than is possible in single-disciplinary courses. The fact that all this can be achieved with only one three-credit course leaves room in most students' schedules for choosing an additional single-disciplinary course, a choice that can be better made after the interdisciplinary introduction. The course may also help future teachers of fine arts survey courses and all general subjects to incorporate interdisciplinary arts and aesthetics issues into their teaching.

Another way to spread interdisciplinary education in the arts and aesthetics is to offer workshops or regular courses for in-service teachers of general subjects on how to integrate arts teaching into their lesson plans in science, math, language arts, history, and social studies. Arts specialists with interdisciplinary training can offer these workshops and can also act as consultants in their schools, helping their colleagues to understand and use arts resources and plan interdisciplinary programs including the arts and aesthetics.[235]

These ideas are ambitious and modest at the same time. They are ambitious because they call for increased coverage of the arts and aesthetics at every level of our educational system. They are modest because they require very little in the way of new courses and instructors; such programs can be taught by available specialists with some interdisciplinary training, in some cases more economically than under the status quo (given the possibility of covering multiple arts with one or two specialists). Once introductory interdisciplinary courses have been created, additional courses and minor degree programs may be pursued, perhaps as a means for credentialling social studies and English teachers for teaching fine arts survey courses. Interdisciplinary minors should be relatively cheap and simple too; along with the introductory course and a choice of three or four single-disciplinary arts courses, the addition to the curriculum of a single advanced interdisciplinary colloquium should suffice to complete the program. Interdisciplinary majors are also desirable, especially since they solve the problem of finding funds to pay for interdisciplinary teachers and courses.

Individual states and schools can be laboratories in which we try out various interdisciplinary improvements to education in the arts and aesthetics. If through this process of curricular reform we can soften the disciplinary boundaries of the arts and aesthetics, we may be able to help students and the public better understand the complex sensory experiences of our world and prepare to understand the even more challenging virtual realities of our future.

# 9

# Virtual Reality and Aesthetic Competence in the Twenty-First Century

"Waco Standoff Already TV Movie." That was the front-page headline in *USA Today* on 26 March 1993.[236] The column went on to explain that the mother of cult leader David Koresh had already—while the siege was still going on—sold the rights to her son's story to NBC for the making of a television movie. At the time of the sale, nobody knew that the siege would end with an FBI invasion of the compound, followed by Koresh's suicidal response of setting the site and the people within it on fire. It was simply assumed that, whatever the outcome, it would be commercially profitable to tell the story.

To me, this was a singularly troubling headline. Although the commercial sale of news for entertainment has become fairly common in our consumer culture, the sale of Koresh's siege before it ended in flames went beyond common commercialism in my mind. It seemed emblematic of a rather recent state of affairs in our culture wherein events and the stories about them—reality and representation—are increasingly difficult to distinguish from each other. By selling Koresh's story before it was over, Koresh's mother entered into a real sequence of events as if it were merely a story. Her entry may not have affected the outcome of the case, but it could have—just as the coverage of the infamous O. J. Simpson trial clearly affected the outcome there.

Such mixtures of reality and representation are not entirely new. In fact, realism—the use of techniques that create realistic effects in the arts—has been a mainstay of many artistic styles and media throughout history. With the rise of computer and other electronic media in late twentieth-century America, however the technology for representing actual life experience has become far more realistic—more plausibly lifelike—than ever before. We are now on the threshold of an age of interactive sensually immersive technologies, in which the boundaries between reality and representation are regularly blurred. Indeed, the very concept of reality has changed in our time. Reality itself is now commonly recognized in postmodern theory as a stage: a sensory representation of a world that we can never fully enter or know. As suggested in the 1998 movie *The Truman Show*, it may soon be possible to make an artificial world indistinguishable from reality and vice versa.

The treatment of actors in our culture is a striking reflection of our increasing confusion of reality and representation. Since the rise of the representational media of film and television—by which theatrical dramas can be captured and repeated an infinite number of times—Americans have become increasingly infatuated with the actors and other celebrities that they encounter repeatedly through those media. This is especially true for television actors, who reportedly enter our living rooms and bedrooms at the rate of over seven hours a day for the average American, usually far more often than we let our real-life friends and relatives in. By virtue of their apparently intimate access to us and vice versa, these actors become our closest companions, with whom we wish to share everything. Intellectually we may know that they are strangers who happen to make their living by pretending to be the dramatic characters they represent. Nonetheless, we consistently confuses actors with the characters or roles they play. When we like an actor, we will take advice from them about any number of things, from what products to buy to what life decisions to make.

Of course, the more we love the faces on the screen, the less time we have to relate to the real human beings in our lives. This process feeds on itself, as new magazines and television channels are established to profit from the public's interest in actors and to publish and broadcast every possible detail about their professional and personal lives. As a result of their constant representation in the media, actors (and some other prominent media-star celebrities) have in effect entered the realm of our mythos. *People* magazine, the E! channel, the Planet Hollywood restaurants are all in the business of offering millions of consumers contact with the relics of the mythos in a postmodern version of the medieval pilgrimage.

In my view, the mixture of reality and fantasy created by our new immersive, interactive media carries serious implications for education. The power and uses of these new media cannot be studied or understood under our current hardboundaried system of education in the arts and aesthetics because they so clearly transcend the boundaries of that system. In effect, the mass reproducibility of experience by electronic media has brought us to a new stage in the relationship of society and the arts. In this stage, inadequate education in the arts and aesthetics will likely have more serious consequences than ever before. The question is: shall we be passive subjects to the new electronic media, or shall we develop the skills to understand the exploitation of our senses and emotions in this consumer culture? The answer to that question lies in our ability to soften boundaries and improve education in the arts and aesthetics.

## VIRTUAL REALITY

The most striking example of a new medium that blurs the lines between reality and representation is "virtual reality," defined as "an immersive, interactive experience generated by a computer."[237] Virtual reality is a recent development, based mainly on the advances of computer technology since the 1980s. Current technology for virtual reality involves erasing the computer screen (in effect, the computer's proscenium) and entering the illusion of another reality. Various designs of headsets allow a sense of immersion into the sights and sounds of other worlds; gloves add the illusion of touch to the fantasy. Current virtual reality experiences barely touch the surface of what is possible. Obviously, the senses of taste and smell may also be harnessed in the creation of fantasy worlds in virtual reality, just as the current simulations of sight, sound, and touch can be improved to offer effects of greater sensory immersion.

While the purpose of virtual reality may be to increase our sense of immediacy, there are signs that the actual result may be the opposite. As sensory experience increasingly reaches out to surround us, we seem to react with increasing passivity and decreasing imagination and intellect. Indeed, experience with virtual reality and other computer technologies may dull our minds and sensitivities, to the point where we lose touch with the meaning of what we are experiencing.

Virtual reality has a past, a relationship to earlier technology for the simulation or heightening of experience, including the development of photography and motion pictures. Cinerama and other new video technologies of the 1950s were an attempt to make the movies far more realistic than the newly competitive medium of television could be. Holography—the use of laser beams to produce highly realistic three-dimensional images, was invented in 1948 by Dennis Gabor, later winner of the Nobel Prize in physics.

But it is the combination of video and computer technologies together that has made the blurring of reality and fantasy most possible. One of the first uses of this combined technology was the flight simulator, first used widely in World War II to train pilots without the actual experience of flying. More recently, interactive computer games have been designed to create increasingly powerful immersive experiences for the player with complex video and aural effects. Amusement parks have also started using computer technology to create heightened experiences in their rides. At Universal Studios, the combination of computer simulation and traditional roller coaster technology has created a new type of ride that immerses groups of twenty at a time into adventures far more exciting than Disneyland's Matterhorn or Pirates of the Caribbean even though the riders seem to onlookers to stay in the same place. In the musical arena, CD and CD-player technology allows the consumer to program the musical worlds they will visit with greater specificity and immediacy than ever before. The computer system in Bill Gates's house even programs rooms to know what visual and aural stimuli their owner or other occupants wish to have. Rooms that can transform themselves into Honolulu, Paris, or New Orleans may soon be a part of the middle-class future as well. The next step will probably be the holodeck: a sensory simulation machine featured on *Star Trek, Wild Palms*, and other science fiction shows that allows viewers to enter into the realities of their choice.

The historical context in which interactive, immersive computer technologies have developed should raise serious concerns about their potential misuse. Since the rise of advertising in the 1950s, visual and aural experience has become the major engine of our consumer culture, creating the desire and influencing the purchase of all kinds of products. At about the same time, the rising influence of electronic media in American life has brought the public unprecedented access to artistic and aesthetic experience. Today, our most influential artistic media—TV, sound recordings, and film—are financed largely through consumer advertising. In the case of TV shows and sound recordings, consumer ads literally pay for the cost of production. In the case of blockbuster films, merchandising of the film's name, characters, and plot details, often makes more money than the movie itself. When we go to McDonald's to get hamburgers and action figures from the latest blockbuster movie, we are deeply implicated in the functioning of that consumer culture. We are, in effect, engaging in a powerful rite of that culture.

Since the onset of our late industrial consumer culture in the 1950s, businesses have commonly used music to affect workers and customers without their knowledge and consent. Developments in virtual reality will likely give businesses and perhaps governments even more psychological control over their communities. It will be hard for those in authority not to abuse such intimate control over the sensory experience and emotional responses of the public; in fact, those alarmed over the potential of genetic technology to interfere with human freedom would be well-advised to consider the power and potential of the technology for virtual reality. We should also be concerned about the possibility of decreasing sensitivity to sensory experience in the face of increasing stimulation. The progression of the "body count" and other indices of "excitement" in motion pictures of the last twenty years suggests that increasing stimulation has a numbing effect on art consumers that some say translate into insensitivity to violence and suffering in real life. Similarly, the emphasis on killing or being killed in interactive video games is a dangerous lesson to teach the children that buy and use them.

The greatest danger of the new sensually immersive technologies may be that people—especially children—will become addicted to them, as many have become addicted to computer games. Even without the new technologies addiction has become a major problem in American society. Indeed, mind-altering drugs appear to serve a very desirable function, that of breaking through our sense of isolation from community and meaning, although usually with very harmful side effects. There can be no doubt that drug addiction is dangerous to our ability to think and make choices in our lives, but perhaps not as dangerous as the future immersion of children in more and more powerful technologies of virtual reality will be to their ability to grow up. MIT sociologist Sherry Turkle disagrees with concerns about addiction in her recent book, *Life on the Screen: Identity in the Age of the Internet*; in her view labeling intense involvement with computers as addictive keeps us from learning more about the positive role that new interactive media can play in our lives. In fact, she says, "many people who seem 'addicted' to computers are in fact using them to work through personal issues in very constructive ways."[238] On the other hand, as long as we provide little or no education on the aesthetic power of new media and technologies, it is hard to be unconcerned about their potential effects on the young.

## MIMESIS IN THE AGE OF REPETITION

In the age of interactive, sensually immersive technologies, mimesis—the human tendency and desire to imitate the actions of others—remains a central human activity, just as Aristotle defined it in his *Poetics*. In fact, mimesis has taken on increased importance in the twentieth century as electronic technology has made possible the mass reproduction of representations of sights and sounds through audio and video recordings.[239] With such sensually reproductive technologies human have gained the mimetic power, not only to make images from objects, but the far more godlike power of making objects—like audio- and videotapes—from images, through the use of aural, video, and perhaps other types of sensual image molds.

Jacques Attali suggests that the "repetition culture" created by the image-making mass media of the twentieth century has produced a regression among human consumers to a tribal/ritual experience of the arts, in which individuals are immersed in sensory experience without awareness or exercise of critical judgment.[240] Unlike early humans, however, contemporary and future consumers have the power and freedom to choose to have private, simulated experiences based on computerized re-creations of activities and environments, rather than having to cooperate with other human beings and share the experiences of their communities.

To Americans, the value of the freedom to choose has been axiomatic since our revolution. But freedom to choose among experiences in which one engages with other human beings is different from the freedom to choose recorded simulations of such experiences. Having the latter freedom makes us more like solitary gods than humans. The question is, when we have godlike power to create and transform our reality at will, will we still learn to communicate and cooperate with the realities of other human beings? Or, to pose a more sensationalistic version of this question, will human beings still learn to love and communicate with each other when they can rent a virtual reality love video instead? Will we, in short, continue to be thinking, feeling human beings in communication and community with each other, or will we become the ultimate couch potatoes, creating individual experiential worlds of our choosing with the mere touch of a remote control? In my view, education in artistic and aesthetic experience holds the most hopeful answer to this important question, but again, only if that education transcends the hard, single-disciplinary boundaries of our current educational system.

Besides discouraging human communication and interaction, the new immersive, interactive technologies may also discourage or channel thinking in ways that may be more harmful than we yet realize. Has experience with computers led us to view life as a series of multiple-choice menus, without recognition of messier realities and choices? Philosopher Hilde Hein recognized this problem by watching her granddaughter.

A twinge of pain overcame me as I noted recently that my once wierdly articulate, six year old grandaughter (now seven), having just begun first grade, was seeing the world in terms of multiple–"fill in the blank" options! They've got her, I thought. She has acquiesced to the principle that freedom is menu-driven choice (rather than self-determination). I feel similarly despondent when I hear my students wail with anxiety about placement interviews and "finding a job," rather than thinking about what they want to do with their lives. They too are preparing to fill slots, to satisfy ready-made alternatives. Since when, I want to ask, has freedom consisted of choosing between a pre-existent A or B or C?[241]

Of course, Hein is aware of Foucault's analysis that all technologies, not just the postmodern kind, contribute to the way we construe thinking and knowledge. It is the particular kind of epistemological pollution represented by computer menus that she finds troubling and literally dangerous to our ability to think and choose freely. "User-friendly" computer programming obscures this danger and the corollary need for education by making entry and choices within cyberspace seem easy, but just because we can do something does not mean that we understand it. A similar concern is raised by our use of remote control technology. We may love our remote controls and channel surfing, but what are we learning from them? The power to turn experiences on and off without moving from one's chair increases passivity and isolation to the point where necessary human skills of communication and interpretation may lie unused or undeveloped.

## NEW ROLES FOR ART AND ARTISTS

It is interesting to speculate on the role future artists will play in blurring the boundaries between fantasy and reality as virtual reality technologies continue to emerge. Will artists use the new media to challenge us, or will they use it to serve the wishes of government or wealthy patrons? Or will there literally be an end to art, as computer technology disenfranchises artists and art objects?[242] In that scenario, everyone would become their own artist, using the new technologies to explore and develop their own creative impulses without the necessity of extended study of traditional skills. Jim Griffin, director of technology at Geffen Records, finds the latter prediction unlikely; he believes that the relatively small market for computer games and interactive music CD-ROMS suggests that claims of the dawning of a new creative age are wrong; that we seem to prefer "laying back and being catered to, being entertained . . . I'm afraid our greatest level of interaction is the remote control."[243]

Perhaps future artists will find ways to explore or expand our understanding of the meanings of reality and fantasy, as twentieth-century artists René Magritte, Andy Warhol, and Cindy Sherman have done. Magritte's *The Treason of Images* famously used a photo-realistic painting of a pipe on top of the words *"Ceci n'est pas une pipe"* ("This is not a pipe") to challenge the meaning of images of reality, at a time when photographic representations were emerging as a constant part of daily life. Andy Warhol's multiple reproductions of iconic images of Marilyn Monroe, Elvis Presley, the Mona Lisa, and Campbell's soup cans were similarly challenging at a time when mass reproduction and advertising had become dominant. Cindy Sherman's photographs have shown the artist herself in iconic poses from every historical period: an artist literally in the act of making and questioning identity in the age of easy images. More than any philosophers or writers, these artists have posed the question of how we can keep the reality and fantasy straight in an era when images are so easily reproducible. In the age of virtual reality, when images become even more immediate to the senses, the boundaries of fantasy and reality will blur even more.

Comic film directors such as Woody Allen have frequently played with the boundaries of fantasy and reality in their movies, for example, in Allen's *Mighty Aphrodite* (1996) and *The Purple Rose of Cairo* (1985). My own favorite bit of reality/fantasy confusion comes in Mel Brooks's *Spaceballs* (1987), when Brooks's character forgets his next line and has to get the video of his own movie—already on sale along with other *Spaceballs* merchandise—to find out what happens next. As he winds the movie to the place he is at, Brooks realizes that the movie is waiting for him to act next before it can convert it into film, and we in the audience realize that we are caught in the loop as well. In *The Truman Show*, the hero finds a way out of the fantasy world that his TV producer has created for him since his birth by sneaking out of view of the camera and sailing to the end of the world (i.e., the studio where his world is being filmed). Truman's final disappearance to the television audience is a happy ending because it signals the beginning of his real life. But that's Hollywood: the way out of virtual reality for the average Joe may be more difficult than Truman's escape.

Assuming there is no "end of art," there will probably be an increased use of computers in its production and distribution. In *Hamlet on the Holodeck: Music after Modernism* (1997) Janet H. Murray predicts that future fiction writers will be "half hacker, half bard." In Murray's words, "The spirit of the hacker is one of the great creative wellsprings of our time, causing the inanimate circuits to sing with ever more individualized and quirky voices; the spirit of the bard is eternal and irreplaceable, telling us what we are doing here and what we mean to one another."[244]

The images brought forth by "half hacker, half bard" are not those of Homer, Dante, Shakespeare, and Goethe, but Murray is probably right that future artists will need to engage imaginatively with the possibilities created by new computer resources. Perhaps if Goethe had been a computer hacker as well as a bard, he might have linked the text of *Faust* to all kinds of web sites with appropriate musical and visual imagery, sufficient to bring the immense imaginative conceptions of that work "to life." On the other hand, it is likely that the hacker-bards of the future will bear more resemblance to Larry Flynt than to Goethe and that the artistic products of the half-bard, half-hacker artists of the future will likely be more notable for sensationalism than quality. Indeed, if art appears on the web, how would anyone know, and who would be present with whom to appreciate it? Such speculations remind us how important it is to share the experience of art with human beings with whose faces and minds we have tangible contact. The more we rely on computer technology to create art, the more human contact we may give up.

In the future computers may even make art by themselves, without human involvement. There is already a strand of artificial intelligence research, that of "computational phenomenology," that focuses on ways of artificially reproducing the aesthetic faculty of common sense that Kant said was engendered by sensory experience.[245] If computers can develop taste, they can make art and judge it too. On the positive side, computers may be able to make and distribute art in a more democratic way than has been possible under capitalism or feudalism. On the negative side, what will art mean for human beings when it is produced and distributed by computers?

## CONCLUSION

Although some implications of the new sensually immersive technologies are troubling, I am not comfortable with doomsday predictions of the end of art, or "the vicious spiral of reflexivity"[246] in the postmodern era. Historical changes have always brought with them the development of new artistic styles and genres, and teachers have always had the challenge of dealing with them. Murray's optimistic view that "every medium allows us to capture human experience with a new power," may turn out to be justified.[247] As for fears of a computer–controlled future, the computer age has its regimented side, but computers have also been a democratizing force, capable of setting free the creative abilities of a wider range of the public than ever before.

Still, the changes in society and the arts that we face on the threshold of the twenty-first century are different in more than kind from the changes of the past. In the future, the ability of humans to function intelligently in the aesthetic realm—to literally make sense of sensory experience—will become a greater challenge than ever, at least as great as the challenges of understanding modern science and mathematics. Without softening the boundaries of the disciplines of the arts and aesthetics we cannot meet that challenge. Only with teachers and students trained to value and pursue relationships among the arts, aesthetics, and our lives will we be prepared to navigate the deep waters of twenty-first-century experience.

And so the question is, how can we as educators help people prepare to engage intelligently with the new media of virtual reality? Plato would likely have advised censorship, if not a complete ban, on the new technologies. In America, though, the censorship that Plato recommended for the arts in a more innocent time is, of course, impossible; the consumer culture would never permit it, even if the First Amendment did.

Failing censorship, it should be clear that we will need full development and use of our intellectual and emotional resources as well as our senses for understanding the arts and aesthetic experience in the coming century and that those of us in education must do a better job in helping students and the public reestablish access to them. Hard boundaries will fail even more in the future as interactive, sensually immersive art forms overflow the boundaries of the disciplines. If we do not reform education in the arts and aesthetics, there will be no place in the schools for consideration of the power, influence, and meaning of the new forms of art and experience. Only a softening of the boundaries of our current disciplines and concepts will allow for full education about the meaning and power of art and aesthetic experience in our lives. Without that education we may literally lose the ability to think or communicate about our experiences and, with it, our understanding of what it is to be human.

# Notes

1. As I will further discuss in chapters 1 and 3, "aesthetics" is a highly contested term with many different meanings and associations. Standard dictionary definitions tie aesthetics to the study of "beauty," which was the focus of the first inquiries in aesthetics in the eighteenth century. Since then, however, the practice of aesthetics has widened to include inquiries into sensory perception in general, with emphasis on perception in the arts. In this book I have suggested the definition "the practice of making sense of sensory experience." It is short, simple, and somewhat poetic, as I think a definition of aesthetics should be.

2. Neil Postman, *The End of Education: Redefining the Value of School* (New York: Knopf, 1995), pp. 19–36, especially p. 31.

3. Howard Gardner has made this point repeatedly in his work. See, for example, his *Multiple Intelligences: The Theory in Practice* (New York: Basic Books, 1993), p. 16, where he defines and describes seven types of intelligence that should be engaged in education, including musical intelligence, bodily kinestethic intelligence, logical-mathematical intelligence, spatial intelligence, interpersonal intelligence, and intrapersonal intelligence.

4. Philosopher Mara Miller made this point in a panel on "Mainstreaming Aesthetic Education" at the 1997 Santa Fe, N.M., meeting of the American Society for Aesthetics. Also see Charles Fowler, *Strong Arts, Strong Schools* (New York: Oxford University Press, 1996), pp. 112–18; and David Elliott, *Music Matters* (New York: Oxford University Press, 1996), pp. 207–12 and 291–94. Incidentally the term "American" in this book is shorthand for "pertaining to the United States of America," while perhaps more multi-culturally correct, is too awkward for regular use here.

5. Ernest Gellner, *Plough, Sword, and Book: The Structure of Human History* (Chicago: University of Chicago Press, 1989), pp. 44–45.

6. Charles Van Doren, *A History of Knowledge: Past, Present, and Future* (New York: Ballantine Books, 1991), p. 141.

7. See R. Freeman Butts, *A Cultural History of Education: Reassessing Our Educational Tradition* (New York: McGraw-Hill, 1947), pp. 460–525, for further discussion

of the development of curriculum in secondary and higher education in the nineteenth century.

8. Bruce Wilshire, *The Moral Collapse of the University* (Albany: State University of New York Press, 1990), pp. 55–56.

9. From National Cultural Alliance, *The Importance of the Arts and Humanities to American Society* (Washington, D.C.: National Cultural Alliance, 1993), p. 13; cited by Fowler, *Strong Arts, Strong Schools*, p. 157.

10. Erich Kahler, *Out of the Labyrinth: Essays in Clarification* (New York: Braziller, 1966), pp. 34–35; Kahler refers to the structuring of the sciences as "vertical" and the structuring of the humanities as "horizontal."

11. Elliott Eisner discussed this problem, along with his concern about lax standards in much of the research on the effect of the arts on intelligence, in his address to the 1999 Charles Fowler Colloquium on Arts Education, May 19, in College Park, Maryland.

12. See Fowler, *Strong Arts, Strong Schools*, pp. 187–90, for a breakdown of high school arts requirements for individual states.

13. See Howard Gardner, *Art Education and Human Development* (Los Angeles: The Getty Institute for Art Education, [1990]); Gardner, *Art, Mind, and Brain: A Cognitive Approach to Creativity* (New York: Basic Books, 1982); Gardner, *Frames of Mind: The Theory of Multiple Intelligence* (New York: Basic Books, 1983); Gardner, *The Unschooled Mind: How Children Think and How Schools Should Teach* (New York: Basic Books, 1991); Gardner, *Multiple Intelligences*.

14. Fowler, *Strong Arts, Strong Schools*, pp. 57–66.

15. Ibid., p. 106. Fowler's focus on the arts in this book includes aesthetic education.

16. See the *National Standards for Arts Education* (Reston, Va.: Music Educators National Conference, 1994). Also see Gordon Cawelti and Milton Goldberg, "To the Reader," in *Priorities for Arts Education Research* (Washington, D.C.: Goals 2000 Arts Education Partnership, 1996), who remark that the "renewed interest in arts education has been stimulated in large measure by public concern over the quality of American schools." Cawelti was executive director of the Association for Supervision and Curriculum Development from 1973 to 1992; Goldberg was executive director of the National Commission on Excellence in Education that issued the Carnegie report, *A Nation at Risk: The Imperative for Educational Reform* (Washington, D.C.: National Commission on Excellence in Education, 1983). The National Standards will be more fully discussed in chapter 8, "Towards Integrative Interdisciplinary Education in the Arts and Aesthetics."

17. The arts of architecture and film are less regularly represented in college-level education. For example, architecture may be covered in "art" departments or in separated departments or schools of architecture; whereas film may be covered in English, communication, or "art" departments.

18. This problem was also noted by Fowler, *Strong Arts, Strong Schools*, pp. 128–37.

19. Even among aesthetics specialists, there is recognition that the concerns of the discipline have been insular and uninviting. See for example Anita Silvers, "Aesthetics for Art's Sake, Not for Philosophy's!" 141–50, and Joseph Margolis, "Exorcising the Dreariness of Aesthetics," *Journal of Aesthetics and Art Criticism* 51 (1993): 133–40. On the other hand, there are many aestheticians who fear that making aesthetics more clearly applicable and accessible to the arts and the public is dangerous to its scholarly rigor. See, for example, Peter Kivy, "Differences," *Journal of Aesthetics and Art Criti-*

*cism* 51 (1993): 123–32, who says that aesthetic theories and principles apply to the arts in different rather than general ways. In my view, Kivy's insistence on the complexity of aesthetics leads inevitably and unfortunately to less rather than more coverage of aesthetic issues in general education. Moreover, as I will further discuss in chapters 2 and 3, it is ahistorical and misleading to understand the arts as separate from one another when they have so often been joined in practice.

20. Alexander Baumgarten, *Reflections on Poetry* (1735); discussed in *The Encyclopedia Britannica* (rev. 1990), s.v. "Aesthetics."

21. Although cognitive science has promoted a softer-boundaried view of cognition as connected to intellectual, emotional, and physical experience, scholarly disagreement still exists as to how connected or disconnected cognition, or mind, is from the physical and emotional experience of the body. The long-dominant Cartesian tradition of philosophy recognized a sharp distinction between mind and body, but that distinction was lessened in Kant's philosophy and has been even more strongly challenged by feminist philosophy and by brain research that suggests that, not only is the mind in the body, but the body is in the mind. See, for example, George Lakoff and Mark Johnson, *The Metaphors We Live By* (Chicago: University of Chicago Press, 1980).

22. Friedrich Schiller, *Letters on the Aesthetic Education of Man*, trans. Reginald Snell (London: Routledge, 1954), p. 110. I have taken the liberty of substituting the more inclusive "human beings" for "man" in Snell's translation of this passage, although not in Schiller's title. Incidentally, Schiller's connection of aesthetics to morality means that he does not hold with the Kantian concept of pure disinterestedness. Actually, even Kant breaks the disinterested nold by suggesting that experiences of the sublime may have moral significance. See Kant, *Critique of Judgment*, pp. 128–37.

23. Author Schopenhauer, *The World as Will and Representation*, trans. E.F.J. Payne (New York: Dover, 1969), Book 3, esp. pp. 178–81; also see G.W.F. Hegel, *On Art, Religion, Philosophy: Introductory Lectures to the Realm of Absolute Spirit*, ed. J. Glenn Gray (New York: Harper and Row, 1970), who categorized the arts and aesthetic experience along with religion and philosophy as one of the three ways by which human beings could transcend material existence to the deified level of pure thought.

24. The idea of "emotional judgment" may strike traditionalists as oxymoronic, but on the other hand, reference to "intellectual judgment" alone is inexact and potentially misleading, if one assumes that it excludes emotion. Current research in cognitive science suggests a more soft-boundaried interpretation of the relationship of intellect and emotions.

25. Harry S. Broudy, *The Uses of Schooling* (New York: Routledge, 1988), p. 61.

26. See R. Freeman Butts, *Cultural History of Education*, pp. 460–62.

27. Quoted in Lydia Goehr, "The Institutionalization of a Discipline: A Retrospective of *The Journal of Aesthetics and Art Criticism* and the American Society for Aesthetics, 1939–1992," *Journal of Aesthetics and Art Criticism* 51 (1993): 100.

28. See Mary Deveraux, "The Status of Aesthetics as a Discipline," *ASA Newsletter* 18, no. 1 (Spring 1998): 1–3; Deveraux's remarks are from a panel discussion of the same title held at the annual 1997 meeting of the American Society for Aesthetics in Santa Fe, N.M., which also marked the founding of the committee.

29. For example, the following Getty publications argue for an approach called "discipline-based arts education," according to which practice in each art form is connected to the aesthetic principles of the form: *Beyond Creating: The Place for Art in America's Schools* (Los Angeles: Getty Center, [1985]); *Inheriting the Theory: New*

*Voices and Multiple Perspectives on DBAE* (Los Angeles: Getty Center [1990]; Kay Alexander and Michael Day, eds., *Discipline-Based Art Education: A Curriculum Sampler* (Los Angeles: Getty Center [1991]); Gardner, *Art Education and Human Development*; and Stephen S. Kaagan, *Aesthetic Persuasion: Pressing the Cause of Arts Education in American Schools* (Los Angeles: Getty Center [1990]).

Reimer's works include *A Philosophy of Music Education* (Englewood Cliffs, N.J.: Prentice-Hall, 1970, 1989); *Developing the Experience of Music*, 2nd ed. (Englewood Cliffs, N.J.: Prentice-Hall, 1985); Reimer and Jeffrey E. Wright, eds., *On the Nature of Musical Experience* (Niwot, Colo.: University Press of Colorado, 1992); and Reimer, Elizabeth Crook, and David Walker, *Silver Burdett Music* (Morristown, N.J.: Silver-Burdett, 1974, 1978, 1981, 1985).

30. Elliott, *Music Matters*, pp. 41–42.

31. See, for instance, Bennett Reimer and Edward G. Evans, Jr., *The Experience of Music* (Englewood Cliffs, N.J.: Prentice-Hall, 1972), where "aesthetics" is defined formalistically as "self-contained expressiveness . . . [apart from] practical, scientific, religious, political, or other meanings," p. 3.

32. See Elliot, *Music Matters*, pp. 34–35; also see pp. 291–93.

33. Elliott, Bowman, and Regelski expressed this view in a discussion of Elliott's *Music Matters* at the June 18 Dallas, Texas meeting of the Mayday Group, an international organization dedicated to curricular reform in music education.

34. For example, recent volumes of the most prestigious journal in aesthetics, the *Journal of Aesthetics and Art Criticism*, contain many issues devoted in part or in full to this research. See, for example, vol. 48, no. 4 (Winter 1990), *Feminism and Traditional Aesthetics*, a special issue; and vol. 56, no. 2 (Spring 1998); *Environmental Aesthetics*, a special issue. Also see Richard Shusterman *Pragmatist Aesthetics: Living Beauty, Rethinking Art* (Oxford: Blackwell, 1992), who discusses the recent revival of pragmatist aesthetics as an alternative to the analytic model.

35. Elliott prefers a variety of more creative practices for his curriculum of music making (pp. 285–91); unfortunately, pragmatic school administrators are unlikely to make room for them in their programs. They like the economy of the large ensemble as the main unit for music instruction as well as the prestige that comes to large ensembles and their schools as a result of performances and competitions.

36. From James Mursell, *Music in American Schools* (New York: Silver Burdett, 1943), as quoted in *Source Readings in Music Education History*, ed. Michael L. Mark (New York: Schirmer Books, 1982), p. 210.

37. Also see Fowler, *Strong Arts, Strong Schools,* chapter 13, "Cultivating the Arts in High School"; pp. 128–37; Fowler finds an overemphasis of performance specialties in music and visual arts education.

38. See, for example, Egon Kraus, ed., *The Present State of Music Education in the World* (Cologne: International Society for Music Education, [1960]) for comparative articles on developments in Australia, Chili, India, Israel, and Europe; and Charles Plummeridge, *Music Education in Theory and Practice* (London: Falmer Press, 1991).

39. Indeed the term "aesthetics" is intimidating to many people, and unfortunately, there is no adequate synonym. To confuse matters more, the term sometimes appears with the spelling "esthetics," perhaps to avoid the foreign-looking diphthong, ae. Common definitions of aesthetics do little to clear up confusion: some emphasize the connection of aesthetics to beauty, some to the arts, and some to sensual experience in general.

40. Plato, *The Laws*, trans. by Trevor J. Saunders (New York: Penguin Books, 1970), pp. 87–88.

41. This is a rough transcription of an advising conference I had with a student in 1994, when I was acting as a freshman adviser. It is also a composite of many such conferences, both in my experience and in that of colleagues in the arts. It is, I am claiming, pretty typical.

42. Walter Kauffman, *Tragedy and Philosophy* (Princeton, N.J.: Princeton University Press, 1968), Part I, "Plato: The Rival as Critic," pp. 1–29, suggests that Plato's great attention and hostility to the arts in his writings may be partly due to the fact that the arts were better represented and honored in Greek education than was philosophy. This is not the place for criticism of Plato's position on the arts, but the fact that he is among the least generous of philosophers in his attitude towards them should indicate that I am not prejudicing my comparison of past and present with an unfairly idyllic picture of the past. Moreover, despite Plato's frequent criticism of artists, his writings show that he not only assumed the arts were crucial to education, but that he put them there himself in his dialogues.

43. The Nielsen survey of television watching for 1996–1997 showed an average of 7 hours and 15 minutes of watching time per day per household, over an hour a day increase from 1976–1977.

44. Joseph Margolis, ed., *Philosophy Looks at the Arts: Contemporary Readings in Aesthetics*, 3rd ed. (Philadelphia: Temple University Press, 1987), pp. 8–9.

45. Margolis seems to recognize the failure of *Philosophy Looks at the Arts* to communicate much understanding of the arts in his preface, where he concludes, "I should very much like to see a companion volume that, in the spirit of this edition, addresses the actual arts in an ample and detailed way." And in fact, authors of some recent textbooks in aesthetics have attempted to choose articles that are more clearly relevant and accessible to general students, but still the emphasis in even the more accessible textbooks remains on promoting analytical thinking about definitions.

46. The narrowness of the musical canon has been recognized in recent years, thanks in part to the following work: Rose Rosengaard Subotnick, *Developing Variations: Style and Ideology in Western Music* (Minneapolis: University of Minnesota Press, 1991); Katherine Bergeron and Philip V. Bohlman, eds., *Disciplining Music: Musicology and Its Canons* (Chicago: University of Chicago Press, 1992); and Marcia J. Citron, *Gender and the Musical Canon* (Cambridge: Cambridge University Press, 1993).

47. See the *National Standards for Arts Education*, and *Summary Statement: Education Reform, Standards, and the Arts* (Reston, Va.: Music Educators National Conference, 1994).

48. In fact, there are already signs that despite the inclusion of the arts in Goals 2000 they still occupy a secondary position in curricular reform, behind skills such as mathematics and reading, which have received additional national attention and programs since the passage of Goals 2000.

49. See Thomas Leddy, "The Socratic Quest in Art and Philosophy," *Journal of Aesthetics and Art Criticism* 51, special issue, *Philosophy and the Histories of the Arts* (1993): 399–410; also see Jacob Needleman, *The Heart of Philosophy* (New York: Alfred A. Knopf, 1982), who similarly defines philosophy as a questioning process that serves to put human beings in touch with their inner lives.

50. One thinks particularly of the historicizing influence of Thomas Kühn, *The Struc-*

*ture of Scientific Revolutions* (Chicago: University of Chicago Press, 1970); and the works of Michel Foucault.

51. See Arthur Danto, *Narration and Knowledge: Including the Integral Text of Analytical Philosophy of History.* (New York: Columbia University Press, 1985), pp. ix–xii.

52. For example, Peter Kivy's books on music, especially the historically oriented *Osmin's Rage: Philosophical Reflections on Opera, Drama, and Text* (Princeton, N.J.: Princeton University Press, 1988).

53. Anita Silvers, "The Story of Art Is the Test of Time," *Journal of Aesthetics and Art Criticism* 48 (1990): 212.

54. Kenneth Clark, *Civilisation: A Personal View* (New York: Harper and Row, 1970), p. 220, refers aptly to the way in which the light of experience narrowed its beam after the initial stages of the scientific revolution.

55. Philip Gossett, "History and Works That Have No History: Reviving Rossini's Neapolitan Operas," in Bergeron and Bohlman, eds., *Disciplining Music*, pp. 96.

56. In this case, I am inclined to agree with Peter Kivy that the language of music theory is "as mysterious as the Kabala, and about as interesting as a treatise on sewage disposal." *Sound Sentiment: An Essay on the Musical Emotions* (Philadelphia: Temple University Press, 1989), p. 3. See chapter 6, "Soft Boundaries, Aesthetics, and Music Theory," for more discussion of the hard boundaries of current practice in music theory.

57. *New World Dictionary of the American Language*, 2nd coll. ed. (New York: World Publishing Co., 1970), s.v. "canon."

58. Erich Kahler, *The Meaning of History*, p. 27.

59. See Emile Durkheim, *The Elementary Forms of Religious Life*, trans. J. W. Swain (1915; London 1976); René Girard, *Violence and the Sacred*, trans. Patrick Gregory (Baltimore, Md.: Johns Hopkins University Press, 1977), pp. 89–118; and Ellen Dissanayake, *Homo Aestheticus: Where Art Comes From and Why* (New York: Free Press, 1992), pp. 46–48, who views art and ritual as socially organized containers and molders of human feelings.

60. Many scholars have emphasized the central significance of the emergence of writing to human evolution. In the context of writing's significance for artistic evolution, see Dissanayake, *Homo Aestheticus*, pp. 206–7.

61. See Lynne V. Cheney, "Telling the Truth," *Humanities* 13, no. 5 (September 1992); and a response by Betty Jean Craige in "Point of View," *Chronicle of Higher Education* 39, no. 18 (6 January 1993): A56.

62. Music histories have often dated the end of the Classical period and the beginning of the Romantic period at 1827, with the death of Beethoven. See Reinhard Pauly, *Music in the Classic Period*, 3rd ed. Prentice Hall History of Music Series (Englewood Cliffs, N.J.: Prentice-Hall, 1988). See pp. 8–9 for further discussion.

63. I recognized the problem of isolated dance canons in conversation with dance historian Sally Banes during her presentations at the 1991 NEH Institute on Philosophy and the Histories of the Arts. Also see Lincoln Kirstein, *A Short History of Classic Theatrical Dancing* (New York: Putnam's Sons, 1935), and Janet Adshead and June Layson, eds., *Dance History: A Methodology of Study* (London: Dance Books, 1983). Neither of these texts deals with the relationship of classical dance to opera.

64. Donald Grout's *A Short History of Opera*, 3rd ed. (New York: Columbia University Press, 1988) has been the standard text, and it is completely canonical and music oriented. Grout's avoidance of the literary issues left room for a canon of operatic li-

brettos, Patrick Smith's *The Tenth Muse: A Historical Study of the Opera Libretto* (New York: Alfred A. Knopf, 1970).

65. Sir Joshua Reynolds, *Discourses on Art*, ed. Robert R. Wark (New Haven, Conn.: Yale University Press, 1975); these are Reynolds's lectures to the Royal Academy between 1769 and 1790.

66. See John Berger, *Ways of Seeing* (London: BBC, 1972); and Philip Fisher, *Making and Effacing Art: Modern American Art in a Culture of Museums* (New York and Oxford: Oxford University Press, 1991) for recent critiques on the effect of the "museum culture" on public understanding of the arts.

67. See, for example, Frederick Hartt, *History of Italian Renaissance Art: Painting, Sculpture, Architecture*, 2nd ed. (Englewood Cliffs, N.J.: Prentice-Hall, 1979), colorplate 78 on p. 583, adjacent to Titian's *Portrait of a Bearded Man* and *Sacred and Profane Love*, on pp. 582 and 584. Hartt's discussion on pp. 599–600 focuses on the painting's place in the evolution of Titian's style, specifically on whether there was a direct Roman influence.

68. See, for example, Robert von Hallberg, ed., *Canons* (Chicago: University of Chicago Press, 1984), containing articles from *Critical Inquiry*; and Bergeron and Bohlman, eds., *Disciplining Music*, both anthologies of articles primarily by historians and other specialists of the arts.

69. "Strict constructionism" is the popular term; scholars of jurisprudence, such as Ronald Dworkin, use different, somewhat conflicting terminology; see Dworkin, *Law's Empire* (Cambridge, Mass.: Harvard University Press-Belknap, 1986), pp. 49–53, where he distinguishes between "conversational interpretation" (comparable to the common usage of "strict constructionism") and "creative" or "constructive" interpretation, wherein allowance is made for the complexities of communication and intentionality. Later, however, Dworkin discusses "strict" interpretation in accordance with the common understanding of strict constructionism (pp. 358–59).

70. "Enhanced formalism" is Philip Alperson's term for Kivy's theory. See Alperson, "The Arts of Music," *Journal of Aesthetics and Art Criticism* 50 (1992): 217–30. The major works in which Kivy's theory is expounded are *The Corded Shell*, republished in expanded form as *Sound Sentiment: An Essay on the Musical Emotions* (Philadelphia: Temple University Press, 1989); *Sound and Semblance: Reflections on Musical Representation* (Princeton, N.J.: Princeton University Press, 1984); and *Music Alone: Philosophical Reflections on the Purely Musical Experience* (Ithaca, N.Y.: Cornell University Press, 1990).

71. Kivy, *Music Alone*, pp. 158–63. Also see Kivy, "Is Music an Art?" *Journal of Philosophy* 88 (1991): 544–554, where he applies eighteenth-century conceptions of the fine arts in order to question whether untexted instrumental music should be generally classified as an art. Also see Anthony Savile, *The Test of Time: An Essay in Philosophical Aesthetics* (Oxford: Clarendon Press, 1982) who recognizes historicism mainly in an effort to contain it.

72. See Kivy, "On the Concept of the 'Historically Authentic' Performance," *Monist* 71 (1988): 278–90. Also see Kivy, "What Was Hanslick Denying?" *Journal of Musicology* 8 (1990): 13, where he distinguishes most succinctly between issues of music as sound and music "qua music, qua art, qua aesthetical object."

73. On the other hand, some critics of early music performance practice have complained that their creativity is being stifled by research into historically informed performance. This is a debate peculiar to the art of music, where the predominant focus by

twentieth-century performers on old music requires them to be more scholarly or cura-
torial in their approach than they would need to be if they were performing mainly
contemporary works. Unfortunately, the hard boundaries of music training make such a
distinction between performance and academic study that performers often get the idea
that study of the music they perform and of music in general is not very relevant to the
practice of their skills. This will be discussed further in chapter 4.

74. Jerrold Levinson, *Music, Art, and Metaphysics: Essays in Philosophical Aesthetics*
(Ithaca, N.Y.: Cornell University Press, 1990), p. 12.

75. Also see foundationalist Nöel Carroll's historicist approach to defining art in "Art,
Practice, and Narrative," *Monist* 71 (1988): 140–56. Carroll avoids Levinson's emphasis
on works, but his reliance on historical narration to determine whether or not a practice
is art has a similar effect of reinforcing the canon.

76. David Carrier, *Artwriting* (Amherst: University of Massachusetts Press, 1987); and
Carrier, *Principles of Art History Writing* (University Park: Pennsylvania State University
Press, 1987).

77. See Lydia Goehr, "Being True to the Work," *Journal of Aesthetics and Art Criticism* 47 (1989): 55–67. Also see her *Imaginary Museum of Musical Works* (London:
Oxford University Press, 1991). Goehr dates the influence of the concept "musical work"
at ca. 1800, but my own view is that 1800 is a bit late, since the rise of the concert
culture in the eighteenth century lays the groundwork for the concept and the concept
becomes influential by the latter eighteenth century.

78. Silvers, "The Story of Art Is the Test of Time," 211–24. Also see Silvers,
"Has Her(oine's) Time Now Come?" *Journal of Aesthetics and Art Criticism* 48 (1990):
365–79.

79. Since first drafting this chapter in 1993, I have come to favor adding an experiential, practical component to philosophical history to create a fully integrated, interdisciplinary approach to studying the arts and aesthetics; this addition aspect will
be discussed in chapter 8, "Integrative, Interdisciplinary Education in the Arts and Aesthetics."

80. Dissanayake, *Homo Aestheticus*. Dissanayake's work is related to the new field of
material culture studies, in which art works are viewed through an interdisciplinary lens
as artifacts whose meaning is always related to the culture of origin.

81. Danto, "The End of Art" (pp. 81–115) and "Art, Evolution, and the Consciousness
of History" (pp. 187–210) in *The Philosophical Disenfranchisement of Art* (New York:
Columbia University Press, 1986).

82. Richard Wollheim, *Painting as an Art* (Princeton, N.J.: Princeton University
Press), p. 20, presents a psychoanalytic, intention-based view of the evolution of painting
as progressive "thematization." George Kübler, *The Shape of Time: Remarks on the
History of Things* (New Haven, Conn.: Yale University Press, 1962), analyzes the internal
structure of the evolution of things, including artworks. There is also a philosophicohistorical approach in some social histories, such as Arnold Hauser, *The Social History
of Art*, 4 vols., trans. Standley Godman (New York: Vintage Books, 1951); and in Marxist
criticism, e.g., Jacques Attali, *Noise: The Political Economy of Music*, trans. Brian Massumi (Minneapolis: University of Minnesota Press, 1985).

83. Danto, "The End of Art," pp. 81–115.

84. Gellner, *Plough, Sword, and Book.*

85. Harry S. Broudy, *The Uses of Schooling*, p. 61, makes a similar suggestion when
he says that "What art education needs is a method of perceiving and analyzing aesthetic

properties that can be taught to children in the elementary grades by the classroom teacher. . . . Until this becomes possible the arts will remain nice but not necessary."

86. Printed on the inside cover of each issue of the *Journal of Aesthetics and Art Criticism*.

87. Anita Silvers, "The Story of Art Is the Test of Time," 212.

88. The distinction between realist and relativist historicism is derived from Thomas Leddy's "The Socratic Quest in Art and Philosophy," *Journal of Aesthetics and Art Criticism* 51 (1993): 399–410, but he uses the term "pragmatist" instead of "relativist." Another term used for "realist" historicism, suggested to me by Anita Silvers, is "foundationalist"; it avoids confusion with the meaning of realism in other contexts.

89. See Danto, "The Artworld," *Journal of Philosophy* 61 (1964): 571–84; and *The Transfiguration of the Commonplace: A Philosophy of Art* (Cambridge, Mass.: Harvard University Press, 1981) for his theory of interpretation. Also see "The End of Art" (pp. 81–115) and "Art, Evolution, and the Consciousness of History" (pp. 187–210) in *The Philosophical Disenfranchisement of Art* for his views on the "end of art."

90. Danto, *Narration and Knowledge*, p. 149.

91. Danto, "Narrative and Style,"*Journal of Aesthetics and Art Criticism* 49 (1991): 205.

92. Danto, *Philosophical Disenfranchisement of Art*, pp. ix–xvi.

93. See Jerrold Levinson, *Music, Art and Metaphysics*, a collection of his essays from 1979–1989 includes the initial essay on "Defining Art Historically" (pp. 3–25), the later essay "Refining Art Historically" (pp. 37–59), and some essays on music, including "What a Musical Work Is" (pp. 63–88), "What a Musical Work Is, Again" (pp. 215–30), and "The Concept of Music" (pp. 267–78).

94. Discussed in Margolis, ed., *Philosophy Looks at the Arts*, pp. 137–42, introduction to "Part II: The Definition of Art." Morris Weitz's article "The Role of Theory in Aesthetics," which originally appeared in the *Journal of Aesthetics and Art Criticism* 15 (1956): 27–35.

95. Levinson's later article, "Refining Art Historically," parenthetically allows for "item, object, entity" as interpretations of "thing"; see *Music, Art and Metaphysics*, p. 38.

96. Levinson, "Defining Music Historically," in *Music, Art and Metaphysics*, pp. 10–11. See Lydia Goehr, "Being True to the Work," pp. 55–67, for a discussion of the historical relativity of the concept "musical work," applicable mainly to European music after 1800; also see Goehr, *The Imaginary Museum of Musical Works*. Levinson acknowledges Goehr's work and sees no conflict with his own because, he says, "I am confining my inquiry to that paradigm of a musical work." "What a Musical Work Is," in *Music, Art and Metaphysics*, p. 64. Nonetheless, he frequently makes reference to music before 1800, to the "Western fine art" tradition in general.

97. Wollheim, *Painting as an Art*; and Savile, *The Test of Time*, pp. 60–64, where he argues for a combination of the artists's intentions and the best available contemporary reading to "fix" the meaning of historical art works.

98. Levinson, "What a Musical Work Is, Again," in *Music, Art, and Metaphysics*, p. 261. This definition represents a slight shift from Levinson's earlier definition of a musical work as a dually indicated "sound/performing means structure"; see "What a Musical Work Is," in *Music, Art and Metaphysics*, pp. 63–88.

99. Ibid., pp. 66–67.

100. Levinson, "Defining Art Historically," in *Music, Art, and Metaphysics*, pp. 23–25.

101. In "Extending Art Historically," in the special issue on *Philosophy and the His-*

*tories of the Arts* of the *Journal of Aesthetics and Art Criticism* 51 (1993): 411–23, Levinson suggests solving this problem by establishing a special status for "ur-arts" as nonarts on which the first arts are then based. Such a solution assumes the problem of evolving cultural-artistic practices to be limited to the "very earliest stages of the story of art"; however, the example of Gregorian chant given above shows that the problem may extend considerably farther than that.

102. Levinson, "The Concept of Music," in *Music, Art, and Metaphysics*, p. 270. Presumably Levinson would not admit Gregorian chant to the category of musical work, but he does explicitly include it as music, which he defines as "sounds temporally organized by a person for the purpose of enriching or intensifying experience through active engagement (e.g., listening, dancing, performing) with the sounds regarded primarily, or in significant measure, as sounds." Note that although this definition is intended to extend to musical practices of all cultures and practices, it still would seem to exclude Gregorian chant and a great many other musical practices, because of its l'art pour l'art emphasis on engagement with sound for sound's sake.

103. Carroll, "Art, Practice, and Narrative," pp. 140–56.

104. Ibid., pp. 151–54.

105. See for example Hayden White, *The Content of the Form: Narrative Discourse and Historical Representation* (Baltimore, Md.: Johns Hopkins University Press, 1987); and Jay Clayton, "Narrative and Theories of Desire," *Critical Inquiry* 16 (1989): 33–53. In fact, Carroll explicitly intends the use of narrative to "reveal unities within the practice of art, its coherence, so to say." Carroll, "Art, Practice, and Narrative," p. 151.

106. See, for example, Linda Nochlin, *Women, Art, and Power, and Other Essays* (New York: Harper and Row, 1988). Also see Susan McClary, *Feminine Endings: Music, Gender, and Sexuality* (Minneapolis: University of Minnesota Press, 1991).

107. See Silvers, "The Story of Art Is the Test of Time," pp. 211–24.

108. Ibid., p. 218.

109. Ibid., p. 223.

110. Silvers, "Has Her(oine's) Time Now Come?" pp. 365–79.

111. Margolis, "Works of Art as Physically Embodied and Culturally Emergent Entities," *British Journal of Aesthetics* 14 (1974): 187–96.

112. Margolis, "Reconciling Analytic and Feminist Philosophy and Aesthetics," *Journal of Aesthetics and Art Criticism* 48 (1990): 328.

113. See Goehr, "Being True to the Work," pp. 55–67; and *The Imaginary Museum of Musical Works*.

114. Wilshire, *The Moral Collapse of the University*, pp. 55–56.

115. By comparison, the discipline of "art" (i.e., the visual arts) has two main disciplines for its members, the College Art Association and the College Art Educators.

116. Michael L. Mark and Charles Gary, *A History of American Music Education* (New York: Schirmer Books, 1992), pp. 141–53.

117. Discussed in Joseph Kerman, *Contemplating Music: Challenges to Musicology* (Cambridge, Mass.: Harvard University Press, 1985).

118. Quoted in Mark and Gary, *History*, p. 270.

119. There are, of course, many liberal arts colleges with little emphasis on football, where athletic money plays no role in the determination of majors. The majority of music majors, however, are trained at large state schools where athletic programs and money are a fact of life and an enormous influence on the functioning of music departments.

120. I first heard this expression in a paper of Robert Cutietta responding to David

Elliott's *Music Matters* at the June 1998 meeting of the Mayday Group; it perfectly expresses the fact that American musical education has created a peculiar musical culture that is unconscious to its own peculiar emphases and failures and to its dissimilarity to musical practices outside the educational system. Wayne Bowman also suggested the term in this context in his comments on a late draft of this book.

121. The *Journal of the American Musicological Society* is the most prestigious musicology journal. This list of articles is typical for the 1960s through the 1980s, when positivism dominated the discipline.

122. See Charles Hamm, *Putting Popular Music in Its Place*, pp. 1–40 and 55–97. For further discussion of the insular nature of modern musicology.

123. This issue was chosen as an example because, like the issues of other music journals whose contents also serve as examples in this chapter, it was the most recent available at the time I wrote this chapter.

124. Donald Grout and Claude Palisca, *A History of Western Music*, 6th ed. (New York: Norton, 1996); "the Grout" has been the main textbook in music history for decades.

125. Recent meetings of the American Musicological Society show a new concern with issues of teaching, probably as a result of the influence of culturally oriented "new musicologists."

126. Renée Lorraine, "Musicology and Theory: Where They've Been, Where They're Going," *Journal of Aesthetics and Art Criticism* 51 (1993): 235–44.

127. *Music Theory Spectrum* 19/2 (Fall 1997).

128. Joseph Kerman has made this point about the comparative absence of music criticism repeatedly. See, for example, "How We Got into Analysis and How to Get Out of It."

129. Issues of education in music theory are the focus of the *Journal of Music Theory Education*, founded by Michael Rogers in 1985.

130. Pieter Van den Toorn, *Music, Politics, and the Academy* (Berkeley and Los Angeles: University of California Press, 1995), argues vigorously against the idea, which he attributes to the influence of McClary, Treitler, and Kerman, that music theory's approach is limiting: "As evidence of a consuming interest in music, why should we trust a facility with words, poetic expression, or sociopolitical moment rather than the methods of music theory and analysis, methods presumably more germane to the matter at hand?" (p. 1).

131. These are well-known, influential methods for teaching children music through special instruments and musical ideas developed especially for simplicity and ease of understanding.

132. See Elliott, *Music Matters*, pp. 27–28.

133. Elliott, Regelski, Bowman, and others (including myself) have joined together in an organization for curricular reform in music known as the Mayday Group, founded by Terry Gates and Thomas Regelski in 1993. The Mayday Group meets one or two times a year to share papers and discussion on aspects of reform needed. Although the Mayday Group began as an organization of college-level music educators in the United States and Canada, it now has an international membership with representation from musicology, music theory, and performance.

134. The difference between the "scholarship" of music performers and that of traditional academic scholars is still preserved in their terminal degree: Doctor of Musical

Arts (D.M.A.), not Doctor of Philosophy. Some universities now grant Ph.D.s to performers, but the D.M.A. remains by far the more common terminal degree.

135. See Ronda Mains, "Group Learning Techniques in the Private Studio," *Segue: The Journal of the Arkansas Music Educator*, 18/3 (Fall 1997): 5–7, for an imaginative variety of group learning techniques for private studio use.

136. From an address given by Willis—then general superintendent of schools in Chicago, at the 1954 MENC Biennial Convention in Chicago. Excerpted in Mark, *Source Readings in Music Education History*, p. 187. Willis went on to urge ensemble directors to "keep foremost in your mind the *importance* of maintaining the integrity of your total profession—music education—and the relative *unimportance* of overemphasizing compartmentalization *within your own field*," a message that is just as necessary today.

137. Martin Heidegger, *Basic Writings*, ed. David Farrell Krell (New York: Harper and Row, 1977), in chapter 8, "Building Dwelling Thinking," p. 332.

138. Jerome Klinkowitz, *Rosenberg, Barthes, Hassan: The Postmodern Habit of Thought* (Athens: University of Georgia Press, 1988), p. 8.

139. See Heidegger, *Basic Writings*. See also John Dewey, *Art as Experience* (New York: Minto, Balch and Co., 1934), whose focus on experience is becoming influential again in aesthetic circles; see, for example, Arnold Berleant's recent *Art and Engagement* (Philadelphia: Temple University Press, 1991); and Marcia Eaton's *Aesthetics and the Good Life* (London and Toronto: Associated University Presses, 1989).

140. See Jacques Derrida, "Structure, Sign and Play in the Discourse of the Social Sciences," in *The Structuralist Controversy: The Languages of Criticism and the Sciences of Man*, ed. Richard Macksey and Eugenio Donato (Baltimore, Md.: Johns Hopkins University Press, 1971), pp. 247–65, for the definitive poststructuralist attack on Western logocentrism. Also see Jane Flax, *Thinking Fragments: Psychoanalysis, Feminism and Postmodernism in the Contemporary West* (Berkeley, Los Angeles, and Oxford: University of California Press, 1990), pp. 187–221, for an insightful general discussion of the postmodern epistemologies of Derrida, Foucault, Jean-François Lyotard, and Richard Rorty.

141. Jean-François Lyotard, *The Postmodern Condition: A Report on Knowledge*, trans. Geoff Bennington and Brian Massumi (Minneapolis: University of Minnesota Press, 1984), 81.

142. See, most notably Carol Gilligan, *In a Different Voice: Psychological Theory and Women's Development* (Cambridge, Mass.: Harvard University Press, 1981); and Nancy Chodorow, *The Reproduction of Mothering: Psychoanalysis and the Sociology of Gender* (Berkeley and Los Angeles: University of California Press, 1978).

143. See, for instance, Jane Gallop, *Thinking Through the Body* (New York: Columbia University Press, 1988); and Heide Göttner-Abendroth "Nine Principles of a Matriarchal Aesthetic," in *Feminist Aesthetics*, ed. Gisela Ecker, trans. Harriet Anderson (Boston: Beacon Press, 1985), pp. 81–94. Also see Hilde Hein, "The Role of Feminist Aesthetics in Feminist Theory," *Journal of Aesthetics and Art Criticism* 48, no. 4 (1990): 281–91. Hein finds both feminist theory and feminist aesthetics to be grounded in the notion of experience (288–89). In addition, the implicit pluralism of the paradigm has ties to feminist theory in that many feminists, like postmodernists, view traditional logocentric thinking as inherently monistic, hierarchic, and marginalistic because of its habitual binary divisions and the tendency to privilege one member of the binary pair over the other (as in the structuralist dyads of culture/nature, cooked/raw, and masculine/feminine). Such an observation is feminist, not just postmodern, because as biological and

cultural mothers women have the role and consequent hardships of our society's primary Other, and they are thus best positioned to recognize and theorize on the functioning and ramifications of marginalization in general. See Dorothy Dinnerstein, *The Mermaid and the Minotaur: Sexual Arrangements and Human Malaise* (New York: Harper Colophon Books, 1976). Also note the feminist essentialist position of Luce Irigaray, *This Sex Which Is Not One*, trans. Catherine Porter (Ithaca, N.Y: Cornell University Press, 1985), who makes a biological-sexual connection of monism to the male body (thus the term "phallocentric") and pluralism to the female. But see Judith Butler, *Gender Trouble: Feminism and the Subversion of Identity* (New York: Routledge, 1990), who warns against the use of all such binary distinctions; see especially chapter 1, "Subjects of Sex/Gender/Desire," pp. 1–34.

144. Susan Bordo, "The Cartesian Masculinization of Thought," *Signs* 11 (1986): 439–56, especially 448–55. Also see Arthur C. Danto, *The Philosophic Disenfranchisement of Art*, for a nonfeminist perspective on the tendency of philosophy to disenfranchise art.

145. Terry Eagleton, *The Ideology of the Aesthetic* (Cambridge, Mass.: Basil Blackwell, 1990), p. 93.

146. Catherine Clément, *Opera, or the Undoing of Women* (Minneapolis: University of Minnesota Press, 1988), p. 9. Also see John Shepherd, "Music and Male Hegemony," in Richard Leppert and Susan McClary *Music and Society: The Politics of Composition Performance and Reception*, ed. (Cambridge: Cambridge University Press, 1987), pp. 151–72. Shepherd says the power and physical relatedness of musical sound "reminds men of the fragile and atrophied nature of their control over the world" (p. 158).

147. Eduard Hanslick, *On the Musically Beautiful*, trans. Geoffrey Payzant (Indianapolis: Hackett Publishing Co., 1986), p. 29 and throughout. I use the term "formalist" instead of the more frequently encountered "cognitivist," in order to avoid confusion with the sense of "cognitivist" found in experimental psychology, where it comprises physical, emotional, and formalistic mental functions.

148. Leonard B. Meyer, "Some Remarks on Value and Greatness in Music," in *Music, the Arts, and Ideas: Patterns and Predictions in Twentieth-Century Culture* (Chicago: University of Chicago Press, 1967), p. 36. Meyer's writings, in which he posits universal formalist criteria for musical meaning and value, remain in print and influential. His more recent work, however, shows an increased recognition of the relatedness of musical meaning and value to cultural context. See, for example, "Exploiting Limits: Creation, Archetypes, and Style Change," in *Contemplating Music: Source Readings in the Aesthetics of Music*, ed. Ruth Katz and Carl Dahlhaus, Aesthetics in Music 5 (New York: Pendragon Press, 1987), vol. 2, pp. 678–717.

149. Peter Kivy, *Osmin's Rage*, p. 184. Kivy's notion that all art requires theory assigns his own activity of theorizing the proudest place in the art-making process. It thereby illustrates Eagleton's suspicions about the aesthetic ideology being used to obscure the critics' own agendas.

150. Ibid., p. 261.

151. Kivy, "What Was Hanslick Denying?" p. 13. Kivy denies the relationship of music to what he insistently refers to as the "garden variety" emotions (i.e., love, hope, fear, joy, and sorrow).

152. From the *Saturday Night Live* sketch of the Coneheads with Frank Zappa, rebroadcast on *The Best of Saturday Night Live*, 28 February 1991.

153. See Bram Dijkstra, *Idols of Perversity: Fantasies of Feminine Evil in Fin-de-*

*Siècle Culture* (New York: Oxford University Press, 1986), pp. 372–76; and Lawrence Kramer, "Culture and Musical Hermeneutics: The Salome Complex" *Cambridge Opera Journal* 2 (1990): 269–94.

154. Jacques Attali, *Noise*, pp. 65–72. Attali gives a Marxist analysis of nineteenth-century concert culture in general, especially the orchestra and the "genealogy of the star." See also Ann E. Kaplan, "Gender Address and Gaze in MTV," in her *Rocking Around the Clock: Music TV, Postmodernism, and Consumer Culture* (New York: Routledge, 1987), pp. 89–142, for an analysis of the psychological relationship between star and fans in contemporary rock music.

155. Steve Reich's music and writings demonstrate this; see his *Writings About Music* (Halifax: Press of Nova Scotia College of Art and Design; New York: New York University Press, 1974), especially pp. 9–11.

156. See essays in Ellen Koskoff, ed., *Women and Music in Cross-cultural Perspective*, Contributions in Women's Studies 79 (Westport, Conn.: Greenwood Press, 1987); and Marcia Herndon and Suzanne Ziegler, eds., *Music, Gender and Culture*, Intercultural Music Studies 1 (Wilhelmshaven, Germany: Florian Noetzel Verlag, 1990).

157. For a clear and concise discussion of these issues, including their particular application to music, see Roland Barthes, "From Work to Text," in Margolis, ed., *Philosophy Looks at the Arts*, pp. 518–24.

158. The article on "notation" is one of the longest in the standard reference work for music, *The New Grove Dictionary of Music and Musicians*, ed. Stanley Sadie (London: Macmillan, 1980), with eighty-seven pages and four authors (Ian D. Bent, David Hiley, Margaret Bent, and Geoffrey Chew). Given the complexity of the issues around musical notation and the score, the effort among analytic aestheticians such as Nelson Goodman to define the composer's intentions and the musical work by reference to it would seem to be an example of the wrong, hard-boundaried paradigm at work.

159. Roland Barthes seems to have originated the postmodern trope "death of the author"; see Barthes, "The Death of the Author," in *Image-Music-Text*, trans. Stephen Heath (New York: Hill and Wang, 1977), pp. 142–48.

160. See John Cage, *Silence: Lectures and Writings by John Cage* (Middletown, Conn.: Wesleyan University Press, 1939); and *John Cage at Seventy-Five*, a special issue of *Bucknell Review* 32, no. 2 (1989), ed. Richard Fleming and William Duckworth.

161. Quoted and discussed further in Robert P. Morgan, *Twentieth-Century Music: History of Musical Style in Modern Europe and America* (New York and London: Norton, 1991), p. 454.

162. Elizabeth Tolbert, "Magico-Religious Power and Gender in the Karelian Lament," in *Music, Gender and Culture*, pp. 41–53.

163. Carol Robertson, "Singing Social Boundaries into Place: The Dynamics of Gender and Performance in Two Cultures," *Sonus* 10, no. 1 (Fall 1989): 59–71; and 10, no. 2 (Spring 1990): 1–13.

164. The academic evasion of music's cultural relatedness is further discussed in Susan McClary, "Terminal Prestige: The Case of Avant-Garde Music Composition," *Cultural Critique* 12 (1989): 57–81. Also see Judith Becker, "Is Western Art Music Superior?" *Musical Quarterly* 72 (1986): 341–59, for more discussion of the Eurocentrism of musicologists.

165. *The Music of Man* videos accompany K. Marie Stolba's *The Development of Western Music: A History* (Dubuque, Iowa: Brown, 1990), ironically the first major history textbook to prominently include material on women in music.

166. See, for example, Heinrich Schenker, *Free Composition*, trans. Ernst Oster (New York: Longman, 1979), in which analytical diagrams overlook prominent intended phrase and sectional endings in order to emphasize organic continuity, his universal value. Schenkerian method is a foundation of the current music theory profession, and it is often applied to repertories across cultural periods, regardless of relevance.

167. See Berger's influential analysis of seventeenth- to nineteenth-century European oil painting, *Ways of Seeing*, pp. 83–112.

168. Immanuel Kant, *Critique of Judgment*, trans. Werner S. Pluhar (1790; reprint, Indianapolis: Hackett Publishing Co., 1987), pp. 176–78.

169. Susan McClary's book *Feminine Endings* refers in its title to the common gender associations in music-theoretical language; see especially chapter 1.

170. There is no time to develop this point adequately here, but resistance to authority is apparent in the composer's relationship to his father and in the attitudes to musical and social conventions expressed in his letters, as for instance when he makes fun of the French "First Stroke of the Bow" in a letter of 12 June 1778. W. A. Bauer and O. E. Deutsch, eds., *Mozart: Briefe und Aufzeichnungen*, vol. 2 (Kassel: Barenreiter, 1962), pp. 378–79.

171. See Rudolphe Angemüller, *New Grove Dictionary of Music and Musicians* s.v. "Maria Anna Mozart" on her retirement from public musical achievement. Also see Eva Rieger, "Dolce Semplice? On the Changing Role of Women in Music," in *Feminist Aesthetics*, ed. Gisela Ecker, trans. Harriet Anderson (Boston: Beacon Press, 1988), pp. 135–49, for a discussion of the psychological effect of the "cultural muting" of musical women such as Anna Maria Mozart, Clara Wieck Schumann, Cosima Liszt Wagner, and Alma Schindler Mahler on their creativity, pp. 147–48.

172. See, for example, Peter Schickele's combination of Baroque and country Western idioms in *Oedipus Tex and other Choral Calamities* (Telarc CD-80239, 1990).

173. See McClary, *Feminine Endings*, pp. 132–66, for further discussion of Laurie Anderson and of the popular musician Madonna as examples of women finding their creative musical voices through new feminist-minded discursive strategies.

174. McClary, *Feminine Endings*, 112–31.

175. Ibid., p. 112.

176. Ibid.

177. For example, see Remi Clignét, *The Structure of Artistic Revolutions* (Philadelphia: University of Pennsylvania Press, 1985), who applies to art the analysis of paradigms in science of Thomas Kühn, *The Structure of Scientific Revolutions*. For discussion of the idea of a feminist aesthetic paradigm for the arts, see Nochlin, *Women, Art, and Power and Other Essays*, p. 146; and Mary Deveraux, "Oppressive Texts, Resisting Readers, and the Gendered Spectator: The *New* Aesthetics," *Journal of Aesthetics and Art Criticism* 48/4 (Fall 1990), special issue, *Feminism and Traditional Aesthetics*, 337–48, especially 339 and 344–46.

178. Exemplified in Kant, *Critique of Judgment*. Also see Eagleton, *Ideology of the Aesthetic*; and Janet Wolff, *Aesthetics and the Sociology of Art* (London: Allen and Unwin, 1983), for Marxist critiques of the underlying agenda of aesthetics.

179. For example, see Sherry Ortner, "Is Female to Male as Nature Is to Culture?" in *Woman, Culture, and Society*, ed. Michelle Rosaldo and Louise Lamphere, (Stanford, Calif.: Stanford University Press, 1974), who showed early in the development of feminist theory that the identification of woman with devalorized aspects of nature is universal (this would include culture in the nonvalorized sense of tribe or group). Also see

Helene Cixous and Catherine Clément, *The Newly Born Woman*, trans. Betsy Wing (1975; Minneapolis: University of Minnesota Press, 1987), who initially wrote of the connection between logocentrism's binary oppositions, such as "Head/Heart," and the original couple, man/woman, pp. 63–64. For other discussions see Susan Bordo, "The Cartesian Masculinization of Thought," especially pp. 448–55; Bordo and Alison M. Jaggar, *Gender/Body/Knowledge: Feminist Reconstructions of Being and Knowing* (New Brunswick, N.J.: Rutgers University Press 1989); and Sandra Harding, *Whose Science? Whose Knowledge? Thinking for Women's Lives* (Ithaca, N.Y.: Cornell University Press, 1991).

180. See Clive Bell, *Art* (1911; New York: Capricorn Books, 1958), pp. 25–27; and Eduard Hanslick, *On the Musically Beautiful*, especially p. 29. Since World War I, autonomist/formalism has been most evident in the New Criticism, whereby works of art are judged without reference to historical context or authorial intention.

181. See Fisher, *Making and Effacing Art*, especially Part I, "The Work of Art, The Museum Culture, and the Future's Past," pp. 3–140. Also see Goehr, *The Imaginary Museum of Musical Works*, 1991), who argues that the rise of the musical museum of the concert hall in the eighteenth and nineteenth centuries has promoted the concept of the musical work and the (in my terms) autonomist-formalist aesthetic concepts for judging its value. On the other hand, many recent art forms—for example, public art and performance art—are not part of the museum culture and do not lend themselves well to autonomist-formalist judgments.

182. This sign was exhibited with a nineteenth-century piano in a July 1991 display at the San Francisco Museum of Art. For further discussion of the "institutional theory," see Danto, "The Artworld," pp. 571–84; and George Dickie, *Art and the Aesthetic: An Institutional Analysis* (Ithaca, N.Y.: Cornell University Press, 1974).

183. Also see Rose Rosengaard Subotnick, "Individualism in Western Art Music and Its Cultural Costs," in her *Developing Variations*, pp. 239–64, who discusses the role of modern concepts of private property and individualism in disenfranchising people other than composers from music.

184. Barbara Ehrenreich and Deirdre English, *For Their Own Good: 150 Years of the Experts' Advice to Women* (New York: Doubleday, 1978), especially pp. 15–20. Also see Linda Nochlin, "Why Have There Been No Great Women Artists?" in *Art and Sexual Politics*, ed. Thomas Hess and Elizabeth Baker (New York: Collier, 1971), pp. 1–39, for a classic discussion of institutional exclusion of women from painting in the nineteenth century. For a discussion of institutional exclusion in nineteenth-century music, see Nancy B. Reich, "European Composers and Musicians, 1800–1890," in *Women and Music: A History*, ed. Karin Pendle (Bloomington: Indiana University Press, 1991), pp. 97–122; and Eva Rieger, "Dolce Semplice? On the Changing Role of Women in Music," in *Feminist Aesthetics*, ed. Gisela Ecker, trans. Harriet Anderson (Boston: Beacon Press, 1985), pp. 135–49. Also see Norma Broude and Mary Garrard, eds., *Feminism and Art History: Questioning the Litany* (New York: Harper and Row, 1982); and Marcia J. Citron, "Gender, Professionalism, and the Musical Canon," *Journal of Musicology* 8 (1990): 102–17, for further analyses of the institutional exclusion of women from the visual and musical arts. Women in the literary arts were less affected, since writing skills were widely shared and since exercising those skills takes little more than a room of one's own.

185. See Kerman's *Contemplating Music* for discussion of how the excessive isolation and positivism on the part of music theorists and musicologists has prevented the de-

velopment of a serious music criticism, able to engage with the "latest chariots (or band-wagons) of intellectual life," including poststructuralism, deconstruction, and feminist theory (p. 17). Also see Kerman, "How We Got into Analysis, and How to Get Out," p. 311–31; and Lawrence Ferrara, *Philosophy and the Analysis of Music: Bridges to Musical Sound, Form and Reference* (New York: Excelsior Music Publishing Co., 1991), especially p. 44, for critiques of the attitudes and approaches of standard music theory and analysis. Recent research among some music theorists into the semiotics of music illustrates a departure from the autonomist/formalist position, but that research is highly complex and has yet to influence the general teaching and practice of music theory.

186. Renee Lorraine has argued that Greek theoretical writing on music had as a hidden agenda the subjugation of some of the gynocentric musicocultural practices the Greek tribes had encountered in their conquest of the Aegean region and the advancement of musical practices that were considered more masculine. The Greek agenda of mas-culinizing music is reflected in Aristotle's preference for the "manly character" of the Dorian mode (associated with the Greek Dorian mode tribe) over the Phrygian mode that was associated with the gynocentric Phrygians they had conquered). Aristotle also den-igrates musical performers, who were still largely female at the time, in consequence of music's long-term use in female ceremonies of goddess worship. See Renee Cox, "A History of Music," *Journal of Aesthetics and Art Criticism* 48 (1990): 395–409, who describes the Phrygian musical culture that the Greeks supplanted and to which Plato and Aristotle later referred (395–98).

187. Ibid., pp. 398–400. Also see Julius Portnoy, *The Philosopher and Music: A Historical Outline* (New York: Humanities Press, 1954), who views the history of music philosophy as frequently opposed to cultural practices.

188. See John Hollander, *The Untuning of the Sky: Ideas of Music in English Poetry, 1500–1700* (New York: Princeton University Press, 1961: Norton, 1970), for further examination of the more practical theoretical view of music starting in the late Renais-sance.

189. See, for example, Rameau, *Treatise on Harmony*, ed. and trans. Phillip Gossett (1722; New York: Dover, 1971); two sections of the treatise are devoted to speculative and two sections to the practical issues of composition and accompaniment. Rameau's famous innovative concept of the fundamental bass—an imaginary bass line of chord roots, preferably 5th-related, was both speculative and practical.

190. Carl Dahlhaus, *Nineteenth-Century Music*, trans. J. Bradford Robinson (Berkeley and Los Angeles: University of California Press, 1989), pp. 27–28.

191. See Matthew Brown and Douglas Dempster, "The Scientific Image of Music Theory," *Journal of Music Theory* 33 (1989): 65–106, for a critique of music theory's identification with science from a philosophical standpoint; see McClary, "Terminal Pres-tige," for a musicological critique. Also see Bruce Wilshire, *The Moral Collapse of the University*, for a more general discussion of the underlying causes and the effects of academic professionalism, positivism, and specialization.

192. David Kraehenbühl, "Foreword," *Journal of Music Theory* 1 (1958): 1. Also see Kerman, *Contemplating Music*, chapter 3: "Analysis, Theory, and New Music," pp. 60–112, for more institutional history on the societies and other journals the new theorists formed.

193. See, for example, Allen Forte, "Schenker's Conception of Musical Struc-ture,"*Journal of Music Theory* X (1967); "A Theory of Set Complexes for Music," *Journal of Music Theory* 8 (1968): 136–83; and *The Structure of Atonal Music* (New

Haven and London: Yale University Press, 1973); and "New Approaches to the Linear Analysis of Music," *Journal of the American Musicological Society* 41 (1988): 315–48.

194. See Richmond Browne, "The Inception of the Society for Music Theory," *Music Theory Spectrum* 1 (1979): 2–5. Leonard Meyer, who has been involved with explorations of style and interdisciplinary theoretical models from psychology and linguistics, was the only theorist to express concern about the fragmentation from musicology, although he later joined the board of the organization. In his keynote address to the eleventh Society for Music Theory meeting in 1988, Meyer warned that "the time has come, this Walrus thinks, for music theorists and psychologists to consider seriously the claims of culture, and of history." (Meyer, "A Pride of Prejudices: Or, Delight in Diversity," *Music Theory Spectrum* 13 (1991): 241–51. But most theorists have found the separation exhilarating. See Allen Forte, "Banquet Address: SMT, Rochester, 1989," in *Music Theory Spectrum* 11 (1989): 95–99, who makes an analogy to Schenkerian layers and finds musicology in the background, practical music in the foreground, and music theory in the middleground, "where all the action is" (p. 99).

195. See Milton Babbitt, "The Structure and Function of Musical Theory," in *Perspectives on Contemporary Music Theory*, ed. Benjamin Boretz and Edward Cone (New York: Norton, 1972), pp. 10–21.

196. Babbitt, "Three Essays on Schoenberg: *Moses und Aron*," in *Perspectives on Schoenberg and Stravinsky*, ed. Benjamin Boretz and Edward Cone, rev. ed. (New York: Norton, 1972), pp. 53–60. There is an extraordinary distance between Babbitt's formalistic analysis and the literary-critical analysis of George Steiner, "Schoenberg's *Moses and Aron*" in *George Steiner: A Reader* (New York: Oxford University Press, 1984), who discusses the opera's unique position in "the history of modern theater, of modern theology, of the relationship between Judaism and the European crisis" (p. 234). Babbitt's approach would seem to indicate that following verifiability to extremes can lead to meanings not worth communicating.

197. John Rahn, *Basic Atonal Theory* (New York and London: Longman, 1980), chapter 1, pp. 4–18. Rahn, "Notes on Methodology in Music Theory," *Journal of Music Theory* 33 (1989): 143–54. Rahn also includes nonformalistic approaches to analysis in "Aspects of Musical Explanation," *Perspectives of New Music* 17 (1979): 204–24; but they are all stated in the form of binary dyads, which invite the reader to marginalize the second, less-scientific half of the dyad.

198. See Babbitt, "The Structure and Function of Musical Theory," p. 11: "I like to believe that a not insignificant consequence of the proper theory of music is to assure that a composer who asserts something such as 'I don't compose by system, but by ear,' thereby convicts himself of, at least, an argumentum ad populum by equating ignorance with freedom, that is, by equating ignorance of the constraints under which he creates with freedom from constraints." It follows, of course, that music of such composers does not merit analysis.

199. See Robert Gauldin and Mary Wennerstrom, "Pedagogy," *Music Theory Spectrum* 11 (1989): 66–73, who find that, notwithstanding the wide range of research activity during the first ten years of the Society for Music Theory, the pedagogy of theory has hardened, moving away from comprehensive, chronological, experimental and integrated curricula, towards maximal simplification and clarification, separate courses for each subject and skill, and a more limited repertoire of common-practice music. Also see Gunther Schuller, "The Compleat Musician in the Compleat Conservatory," *Musings: The Musical Worlds of Gunther Schuller* (New York: Oxford University Press, 1986),

pp. 237–46, for more discussion of the narrowness of musical education in colleges and conservatories.

200. Allen Forte, *Tonal Harmony in Concept and Practice*, 3rd ed. (New York: Holt, Rinehart and Winston, 1979), p. 1. Also note the first sentence of the first article, first issue, and first journal of the Society for Music Theory, by David Beach: "The discovery, description, and codification of principles of pitch structure in music are and always have been of primary concern to music theorists." See Beach, "Pitch Structure and the Analytical Process in Atonal Music: An Interpretation of the Theory of Sets," *Music Theory Spectrum* 1 (1979): 7.

201. See Pieter van den Toorn, "What Price Analysis?" *Journal of Music Theory* 33 (1989): 167, who criticizes the "claustrophobic" approach with particular reference to the theory and analysis of twentieth-century music. Also see Gauldin and Wennerstrom, "Pedagogy," who mention falling cultural literacy in music and in general as a problem exacerbated by the fragmented pedagogy of current music theory.

202. Goehr, *The Imaginary Museum*; and her "Being True to the Work."

203. See Nicholas Cook, "Music Theory and 'Good Comparison': A Viennese Perspective," *Journal of Music Theory* 33 (1989): 121.

204. Van den Toorn, "What Price Analysis?" pp. 167–68; and Richard Taruskin, "Review of Forte, *The Harmonic Structure of the 'Rite of Spring,'* " *Current Musicology* 28 (1979): 119, who explains that circularity is readily broken by external corroboration of details in the composition, performance, and transmission of musical works.

205. See, for example, Nicholas Cook, *A Guide to Musical Analysis* (New York: George Braziller, 1987), for a demonstration of his more pragmatic, less formalistic approach; traditional, Schenkerian, psychological, formalistic, and semiotic approaches to analysis are all explored, each with reference to the historical context in which they arose. Also see Richmond Browne, "Report: The 1988 Oxford Music Analysis Conference,"*Journal of Music Theory* 33 (1989): 228–36, who reports a turn to sociological factors in current music theory research; and Mary Louise Serafine and Wayne Slawson, "Interdisciplinary Directions in Music Theory," *Music Theory Spectrum* 11 (1989): 74–83.

206. Since film music frequently uses the Wagnerian technique of leitmotivic restatement and transformation, the comparison here is most apt. And while it's true that some film music is mentioned—for example, Bernard Hermann's music for Alfred Hitchcock films—such mentions rarely extend beyond the name of the composer and a brief characterization of overall style into the more significant issue of the symbolism of musical forms and motifs.

207. Becker, "Is Western Art Music Superior?" p. 359. Discussion of a paradigm shift is found in Joseph Kerman, "American Musicology in the 1990s," *Journal of Musicology* 9 (1991): 131–44, where he suggests the current presence of a paradigm shift (p. 142), in part because of the rise of feminist scholarship in musicology. Also see Rahn, "New Research Paradigms," *Music Theory Spectrum* 11 (1989): 84–94.

208. See Leo Treitler, "The History of Music Writing in the West,"*Journal of the American Musicological Society* 35 (1982): 243–44.

209. McClary, *Feminine Endings*, chapters 1–3.

210. Grosvenor Cooper and Leonard B. Meyer, *The Rhythmic Structure of Music* (Chicago: University of Chicago Press, 1960). But nonformalistic theoretical studies of rhythm are now on the rise, perhaps as part of the suggested paradigm shift; see especially Jonathan Kramer, *The Time of Music* (New York: Schirmer, 1988); and Lawrence Ferrara,

*Philosophy and the Analysis of Music*, who emphasizes phenomenology and time in his "eclectic" approach to music analysis.

211. Walter Abell, "Toward a Unified Field in Aesthetics," in *Aesthetics Today*, ed. Morris Philipson (New York: World Publishing Co., 1961), pp. 432–65. Literary critic Lawrence Kramer demonstrates this approach, commonly found in criticism of the literary and visual arts, in his "Culture and Musical Hermeneutics: The Salome Complex," *Cambridge Opera Journal* 2 (1990): 269–94.

212. For example, this was a focus of Robert Glidden's plenary address, "Preparing for Pride and Performance in the Professoriate," and a panel session on "New Paradigms in College Music Teaching" at the 1997 annual meeting of the College Music Society, and also Leon Botstein's 1995 plenary address. Also see Gunther Schuller, "The Compleat Musician in the Compleat Conservatory," in his *Musings*, I also wish to thank Elliott Schwarz of Bowdoin College, Fred Maus of the University of Virginia, Roger O. Johnson of Ramapo College, and members of the Mayday Group for the information and insights I have gained on curricular reform at their institutions through discussion and correspondence.

213. Kivy, *Sound Sentiment*, p. 3.

214. See, for example, David Perkins, *Smart Schools: Better Thinking and Learning for Every Child* (New York: Free Press, 1992), pp. 73–98, for further application of learning theory to pedagogy; Perkins is co-director with Howard Gardner of Harvard Project Zero, the foremost research center on childhood learning. Also see Thomas Regelski, *Teaching General Music: Action Learning for Middle and Secondary Schools* (New York: Schirmer Books, 1981).

215. Jerome Bruner, *The Culture of Education* (Cambridge, Mass.: Harvard University Press, 1996), especially pp. 80–85.

216. Regelski, *Teaching General Music*, was ahead of his time in applying learning theory to music, recommending many participatory, group learning techniques, pp. 282–306. But little has been done up to now to apply these techniques to college-level teaching of music history and theory, probably because, as discussed in chapter 4, of the separation of these subdisciplines from music education.

217. See *National Standards for Arts Education*.

218. Christopher Lasch, "The Degradation of Work and the Apotheosis of Art," in *The Future of Musical Education in America: Proceedings of the July 1983 Conference*, ed. Donald J. Shetler (Rochester, N.Y.: Eastman School of Music Press, 1983), p. 11.

219. According to the "Summary of Group Discussions," ibid., p. 20. Issues that were discussed, according to the summary, included the nature of play and the neglect of improvisation, orchestral performance, computer-assisted music instruction, music as a science and an art, and the importance of education in music aesthetics. Also see Charles Fowler, *Strong Arts, Strong Schools* (Oxford University Press, 1996), who argues for a more general, comprehensive approach to teaching the arts as a means of improving education in general.

220. For more discussion of the decline of arts education see Fowler, *Strong Arts, Strong Schools*.

221. Such neglect arises from the tendency of the traditional historical surveys to use categories, including historical periods, designed only for study of Western traditions before the influence of late twentieth-century multiculturalism on the curriculum.

222. *National Standards for Arts Education*.

223. See Ibid.

224. Ibid., pp. 23–35.

225. Drawn from *National Standards for Arts Education*, charts on pp. 29, 45, and 63.

226. See, for example, the description of the 1963 Yale Curriculum Development Project in Kenneth A. Wendrich, ed., *Essays on Music in American Education and Society* (Washington, D.C.: University Press of America, 1982), pp. 71–80; in many respects the project recommended an integrated approach similar to that recommended here, but without the analysis of the structural forces acting against its implementation. Also see Mark, *Source Readings in Music Education History*, for excerpts of panel discussions and other meetings on music and arts education throughout the century. Particularly over the last fifty years, laments about the state of that education and statements of more appropriate goals for that education are quite similar to those in this book, but apparently without positive effect.

227. "Integrative" is a common term among arts educators, however seldom it is found in practice. See, for example, Fowler, *Strong Arts, Strong Schools*, p. 165. The Getty Education Institute for the Arts uses the term "inquiry-based learning" for the same concept.

228. See David Perkins, *Smart Schools*, pp. 73–98, for further applications of learning theory to pedagogy; Perkins is co-director of the Harvard Project Zero center on childhood learning.

229. See Robert B. Reich, *The Work of Nations: Preparing Ourselves for 21st-Century Capitalism* (New York: Knopf, 1994).

230. Claire Detels, *Music in the Western Tradition* (Mountain View, Ca.: Mayfield, 1998), p. 7.

231. Libby Chiù, "Integration: The Arts and General Literacy," in John J. Mahlmann, project director, *The Vision for Arts Education in the 21st Century* (Reston, Va.: Music Educators National Conference, 1994), pp. 13–14; Chiù is director of institutional advancement at the Boston Conservatory.

232. See Hugh Petrie, "Do You See What I See? The Epistemology of Interdisciplinary Inquiry," *Journal of Aesthetic Education* 10 (1976): 29–43, for a general summary of the challenges of interdisciplinary research.

233. College faculty typically receive course load credit and pay only through their departments; interdisciplinary teaching may not count at all, much less reward the innovators. See Wilshire, *The Moral Collapse of the University*, pp. 330–34, for further discussion of administrative problems and solutions in interdisciplinary programs.

234. This course plan is based closely on the syllabus used by Professor Frank Scheide and myself for Humanities 1003 at the University of Arkansas starting in the fall of 1998. It is assumed that the course plan will vary each time the course is taught, depending on the backgrounds and interests of the teachers, the visiting artists, and the arts events available in the community.

235. Charles Fowler emphazies this approach in *Strong Arts, Strong Schools*, partly because he believes interdisciplinary curricular reforms are unlikely.

236. *USA Today*, 26 March 1993, A1.

237. Ken Pimentel and Kevin Teixeira, *Virtual Reality: Through the New Looking Glass* (New York: Intel Windcrest/McGraw Hill, 1993).

238. Quoted in Vic Sussman, "Computers Taking Art Forms into a New Dimension," *USA Today*, 4 November 1997, p. 8D.

239. See Erich Harth, *The Creative Loop: How the Brain Makes a Mind* (New York: Addison-Wesley, 1993), pp. xxiii, 168.

240. See Attali, *Noise*, pp. 87–132.

241. Hilde Hein, "Epistemological Pollution," keynote address to the Eastern chapter meeting of the American Society for Aesthetics, March 1997, in Worcester, Massachusetts, p. 8. I am grateful to Professor Hein for providing me with a copy of her address.

242. See Danto, "The End of Art," pp. 81–115. Danto's literal prediction is that philosophy is disenfranchising art, but by extrapolation this could include making art so self-conscious and transparent that technology could replace it.

243. Quoted in Vic Sussman, "Computers Taking Art Forms into a New Dimension *USA Today*, 4 November 1997," p. 8D.

244. Janet H. Murray, *Hamlet on the Holodeck: The Future of Narrative in Cyberspace* (New York: Free Press, 1997), quoted in Sussman, "Computers Taking Art Forms into a New Dimension."

245. Warren Sack, "Artificial Intelligence and Aesthetics," in *The Encyclopedia of Aesthetics*, ed. Michael Kelly (New York: Oxford University Press, 1997).

246. Erich Harth, *The Creative Loop*, p. 169, quoting R. Kearney, *The Wake of Imagination* (University of Minnesota Press, 1988), p. 360.

247. Murray, quoted in Sussman, "Computers Taking Art Forms into a New Dimension." Also see Michael L. Mark, *Source Readings in Music Education History*, for excerpts of essays about the changing curriculum by various education authorities in the nineteenth and twentieth centuries, including Horace Mann and John Dewey.

# Selected Bibliography

Abell, Walter. "Toward a Unified Field in Aesthetics." In *Aesthetics Today*, ed. Morris Philipson. New York: World Publishing Co., 1961.

Aiello, Rita. *Musical Perceptions*. New York: Oxford University Press, 1994.

Alexander, Kay, and Michael Day, eds. *Discipline-Based Art Education: A Curriculum Sampler*. Los Angeles: Getty Institute for Art Education, 1991.

Alperson, Philip, ed. *What Is Music?* New York: Haven Press, 1987.

Attali, Jacques. *Noise: The Political Economy of Music*. Trans. Brian Massumi. Minneapolis: University of Minnesota Press, 1985.

Babbitt, Milton. "The Structure and Function of Musical Theory." In *Perspectives on Contemporary Music Theory*, ed. Benjamin Boretz and Edward Cone. New York: Norton, 1972.

Barthes, Roland. *Image-Music-Text*. Trans. Stephen Heath. New York: Hill and Wang, 1977.

Becker, Judith. "Is Western Art Music Superior?" *Musical Quarterly* 72 (1986): 341–59.

Bell, Clive. *Art*. 1911; New York: Capricorn Books, 1958.

Berger, John. *Ways of Seeing*. London: BBC, 1972.

Bergeron, Katherine, and Philip V. Bohlman, eds. *Disciplining Music: Musicology and Its Canons*. Chicago: University of Chicago Press, 1992.

Berléant, Arnold. *Art and Engagement*. Philadelphia: Temple University Press, 1991.

———. "The Historicity of Aesthetics: Parts I and II." *British Journal of Aesthetics* 26 (1986): 101–11; 195–203.

Bérubé, Michael, and Cary Nelson, eds. *Higher Education under Fire: Politics, Economics, and the Crisis of the Humanities*. New York: Routledge, 1995.

Bordo, Susan. "The Cartesian Masculinization of Thought." *Signs* 11 (1986): 439–56.

Bordo, Susan, and Alison M. Jaggar. *Gender/Body/Knowledge: Feminist Reconstructions of Being and Knowing*. New Brunswick, N.J.: Rutgers University Press, 1989.

Bowers, C. A. "Implications of Gregory Bateson's Ideas for a Semiotic of Art Education." *Studies in Art Education: A Journal of Issues and Research* 31 (1989): 69–77.

Bowman, Wayne. *Philosophical Perspectives on Music*. New York: Oxford University Press, 1998.

Broude, Norma, and Mary Garrard, eds. *Feminism and Art History: Questioning the Litany*. New York: Harper and Row, 1982.

Broudy, Harry S. *The Uses of Schooling*. New York: Routledge, 1988.

Broudy, Harry S., B. Othanel Smith, and Joe R. Burnett. *Democracy and Excellence in American Secondary Education: A Study in Curriculum Theory*. Chicago: Rand McNally, 1964.

Brown, Matthew, and Douglas Dempster. "The Scientific Image of Music Theory." *Journal of Music Theory* 33 (1989): 65–106.

Bruner, Jerome. *The Culture of Education*. Cambridge, Mass.: Harvard University Press, 1996.

Burrows, David L. *Sound, Speech, and Music*. Amherst: University of Massachusetts Press, 1990.

Butts, R. Freeman. *A Cultural History of Education: Reassessing our Educational Traditions*. New York: McGraw-Hill, 1947.

Carrier, David. *Artwriting*. Amherst: University of Massachusetts Press, 1987.

———. *Principles of Art History Writing*. University Park: Pennsylvania State University Press, 1987.

———. "Why Art History Has a History." *Journal of Aesthetics and Art Criticism* 51 (1993): 299–312.

Carroll, Nöel. "Art, Practice, and Narrative," *Monist* 71 (1988): 140–56.

———. "Historical Narratives and the Philosophy of Art." *Journal of Aesthetics and Art Criticism* 51 (1993): 313–26.

Citron, Marcia J. *Gender and the Musical Canon*. Cambridge: Cambridge University Press, 1993.

Clignet, Remi. *The Structure of Artistic Revolutions*. Philadelphia: University of Pennsylvania Press, 1985.

Cobb, Nina, ed. *The Future of Education: Perspectives on National Standards in America*. New York: College Entrance Examination Board, 1994.

Collins, G., and R. Sandell. *Women, Art, and Education*. Reston, Va: National Art Education Association, 1984.

Cook, Nicholas. *Music, Imagination, and Culture*. Oxford: Clarendon Press, 1990.

———. "Music Theory and 'Good Comparison': A Viennese Perspective." *Journal of Music Theory* 33 (1989): 117–41.

Cook, Susan, and Judy S. Tsou, eds. *Cecilia Reclaimed: Feminist Perspectives on Gender and Music*. Urbana: University of Illinois Press, 1994.

Danto, Arthur. "The Artworld." *Journal of Philosophy* 61 (1964): 571–84.

———. "A Future for Aesthetics." *Journal of Aesthetics and Art Criticism* 51 (1993): 271–77.

———. *Narration and Knowledge: Including the Integral Text of Analytical Philosophy of History*. New York: Columbia University Press, 1985.

———. "Narrative and Style." *Journal of Aesthetics and Art Criticism* 49 (1991): 201–9.

———. *The Transfiguration of the Commonplace: A Philosophy of Art*. Cambridge, Mass.: Harvard University Press, 1981.

———. *The Philosophical Disenfranchisement of Art*. New York: Columbia University Press, 1986.

Dewey, John. *Art as Experience*. New York: Minto, Balch and Co., 1934.

Dissanayake, Ellen. *Homo Aestheticus: Where Art Comes From and Why*, New York: Free Press, 1992.

———. *What Is Art For?* Seattle: University of Washington Press, 1988.

Dziemok, Bohdan. "Artistic Formalism: Its Achievements and Weaknesses." *Journal of Aesthetics and Art Criticism* 51 (1993): 185–93.

Eagleton, Terry. *The Ideology of the Aesthetic*. Cambridge, Mass.: Basil Blackwell, 1990.

Eaton, Marcia. *Aesthetics and the Good Life*. London and Toronto: Associated University Presses, 1989.

Ecker, Gisela, ed. *Feminist Aesthetics*. Trans. Harriet Anderson. Boston: Beacon Press, 1985.

Elliott, David. *Music Matters*. New York: Oxford University Press, 1996.

Ernst, Karl D., and Charles L. Gary, eds. *Music in General Education*. Washington, D.C.: Music Educators National Conference, 1965.

Ferrara, Lawrence. *Philosophy and the Analysis of Music: Bridges to Musical Sound, Form and Reference*. New York: Excelsior Music Publishing Co., 1991.

Fisher, Philip. *Making and Effacing Art: Modern American Art in a Culture of Museums*. New York and Oxford: Oxford University Press, 1991.

Fowler, Charles. *Strong Arts, Strong Schools: The Promising Potential and Shortsighted Disregard of the Arts in American Schooling*. New York: Oxford University Press, 1996.

Gablik, Suzi. *Has Modernism Failed?* New York: Thames and Hudson, 1984.

Gallop, Jane. *Thinking Through the Body*. New York: Columbia University Press, 1988.

Gardner, Howard. *Art Education and Human Development*. Los Angeles: The Getty Institute for Art Education [1990].

———. *Art, Mind, and Brain: A Cognitive Approach to Creativity*. New York: Basic Books, 1982.

———. *Multiple Intelligences: The Theory in Practice*. New York: Basic Books, 1993.

Gauldin, Robert, and Mary Wennerstrom. "Pedagogy." *Music Theory Spectrum* 11 (1989): 66–73.

Gellner, Ernest. *Plough, Sword, and Book: The Structure of Human History*. Chicago: University of Chicago Press, 1989.

Goehr, Lydia. "Being True to the Work." *Journal of Aesthetics and Art Criticism* 47 (1989): 55–67.

———. *The Imaginary Museum of Musical Works*. London: Oxford University Press, 1991.

———. "The Institutionalization of a Discipline: A Retrospective of *The Journal of Aesthetics and Art Criticism* and the American Society for Aesthetics, 1939–1992." *Journal of Aesthetics and Art Criticism* 51 (1993): 99–121.

Hallberg, Robert von, ed. *Canons*. Chicago: University of Chicago Press, 1984.

Hanslick, Eduard. *On the Musically Beautiful*. Trans. Geoffrey Payzant. Indianapolis: Hackett Publishing Co., 1986.

Harth, Erich. *The Creative Loop: How the Brain Makes a Mind*. New York: Addison-Wesley, 1993.

Hauser, Arnold. *The Social History of Art*. 4 vols. Trans. Standley Godman. New York: Vintage Books, 1951.

Hausman, Jerome J., ed. *Arts and the Schools*. New York: McGraw-Hill, 1980.

Hegel, G. W. F. *On Art, Religion, Philosophy: Introductory Lectures to the Realm of Absolute Spirit*. Ed. J. Glenn Gray. New York: Harper and Row, 1970.

Heidegger, Martin. *Basic Writings*. Ed. David Farrell Krell. New York: Harper and Row, 1977.

Hein, Hilde, and Carolyn Korsmeyer. *Aesthetics in Feminist Perspective*. Bloomington: Indiana University Press, 1993.

Helm, E. Eugene. *The Canon and the Curricula: A Study of Musicology and Ethnomusicology Programs in America*. Stuyvesant, N.Y.: Pendragon Press, 1994.

Herndon, Marcia, and Suzanne Ziegler, eds. *Music, Gender and Culture*. Wilhelmshaven, Germany: Florian Noetzel Verlag, 1990.

Hess, Thomas, and Elizabeth Baker, eds. *Art and Sexual Politics*. New York: Collier, 1971.

*Journal of Aesthetics and Art Criticism* 51, special issue, *Philosophy and the Histories of the Arts* (1993).

Kaagan, Stephen S. *Aesthetic Persuasion: Pressing the Cause of Arts Education in American Schools*. Los Angeles: Getty Institute for Art Education, 1990.

Kahler, Erich. *The Meaning of History*. Cleveland, Ohio: World Publishing Co., 1964.

————. *Out of the Labyrinth: Essays in Clarification*. New York: Braziller, 1966.

Kant, Immanuel. *Critique of Judgment*. Trans. Werner S. Pluhar. 1790; reprint, Indianapolis: Hackett Publishing Co. 1987.

Kaplan, Ann E. *Rocking Around the Clock: Music TV, Postmodernism, and Consumer Culture*. New York: Routledge, 1987.

Kaufman, Irving. Art and Education in Contemporary Culture. New York: MacMillan, 1966.

Kauffman, Walter. *Tragedy and Philosophy*. Princeton, N.J.: Princeton University Press, 1968.

Kerman, Joseph. "American Musicology in the 1990s." *Journal of Musicology* 9 (1991): 131–44.

————. *Contemplating Music: Challenges to Musicology*. Cambridge, Mass.: Harvard University Press, 1985.

————. "How We Got into Analysis and How to Get Out of It." *Critical Inquiry* 7 (1980): 311–31.

Kivy, Peter. *The Corded Shell: Reflections on Musical Expression*. Princeton, N.J.: Princeton University Press, 1980; republished in expanded form as *Sound Sentiment: An Essay on the Musical Emotions*. Philadelphia: Temple University Press, 1989.

————. "Differences." *Journal of Aesthetics and Art Criticism* 51 (1993): 123–32.

————. *Music Alone: Philosophical Reflections on the Purely Musical Experience*. Ithaca, N.Y.: Cornell University Press, 1990.

————. "What Was Hanslick Denying?" *Journal of Musicology* 8 (1990): 13.

Klinkowitz, Jerome. *Rosenberg, Barthes, Hassan: The Postmodern Habit of Thought*. Athens: University of Georgia Press, 1988.

Korsmeyer, Carolyn. "Pleasure: Reflections on Aesthetics and Feminism." *Journal of Aesthetics and Art Criticism* 51 (1993): 99–206.

Kramer, Lawrence. *Classical Music and Postmodern Knowledge*. Berkeley and Los Angeles: University of California Press, 1995.

Kübler, George. *The Shape of Time: Remarks on the History of Things*. New Haven, Conn.: Yale University Press, 1962.

Kühn, Thomas. *The Structure of Scientific Revolutions*. Chicago: University of Chicago Press, 1970.

Lakoff, George, and Mark Johnson. *The Metaphors We Live By*. Chicago: University of Chicago Press, 1980.

Langer, Suzanne K. *Philosophy in a New Key: A Study in the Symbolism of Reason, Rite, and Art*. Cambridge, Mass.: Harvard University Press, 1942.

Leddy, Thomas. "The Socratic Quest in Art and Philosophy." *Journal of Aesthetics and Art Criticism* 51 (1993): 399–410.

Leonard, Charles, and Robert W. House. *Foundations and Principles of Music Education*. New York: McGraw-Hill, 1959.

Levinson, Jerrold. *Music, Art, and Metaphysics: Essays in Philosophical Aesthetics*. Ithaca, N.Y.: Cornell University Press, 1990.

Lorraine, Renée. "Musicology and Theory: Where They've Been, Where They're Going." *Journal of Aesthetics and Art Criticism* 51 (1993): 235–44.

Margolis, Joseph. "Exorcising the Dreariness of Aesthetics." *Journal of Aesthetics and Art Criticism* 51 (1993): 133–40.

————, ed. *Philosophy Looks at the Arts: Contemporary Readings in Aesthetics*. 3rd ed. Philadelphia: Temple University Press, 1987.

————. "Works of Art as Physically Embodied and Culturally Emergent Entities." *British Journal of Aesthetics* 14 (1974): 187–96.

Mark, Michael L., ed. *Source Readings in Music Education History*. New York: Schirmer Books, 1982.

Marsh, David. *1999 ASCD Yearbook: Preparing Our Schools for the Twenty-first Century*. Alexandria, Va.: Association for Supervision and Curriculum Development, 1999.

McClary, Susan. *Feminine Endings: Music, Gender, and Sexuality*. Minneapolis: University of Minnesota Press, 1991.

————. "Terminal Prestige: The Case of Avant-Garde Music Composition." *Cultural Critique* 12 (1989): 57–81.

McLaughlin, John T. *Toward a New Era in Arts Education: Interlochen Symposium*. New York: American Council for the Arts, 1988.

Meyer, Leonard. "A Pride of Prejudices: Or, Delight in Diversity." *Music Theory Spectrum* 13 (1991): 241–51.

————. "The Dilemma of Choosing: Speculations about Contemporary Culture." In *Value and Values in Evolution*, ed. E. A. Marziarz, pp. 117–41. New York: Gordon and Breech, 1979.

————. "Exploiting Limits: Creation, Archetypes, and Style Change." In *Contemplating Music: Source Readings in the Aesthetics of Music*, ed. Ruth Katz and Carl Dahlhaus. New York: Pendragon Press, 1987.

————. *Music, the Arts, and Ideas: Patterns and Predictions in Twentieth-Century Culture*. Chicago: University of Chicago Press, 1967.

Miller, Simon, ed. *The Last Post: Music after Modernism*. Manchester: Manchester University Press, 1993.

Murray, Janet H. *Hamlet on the Holodeck: The Future of Narrative in Cyberspace*. New York: Free Press, 1997.

Mursell, James. *Music in American Schools*. New York: Silver Burdett, 1943.

*Music in the Undergraduate Curriculum: A Reassessment*. Boulder, Colo.: College Music Society, 1989.

National Cultural Alliance. *The Importance of the Arts and Humanities to American Society*. Washington, D.C.: National Cultural Alliance, 1993.

*National Standards for Arts Education.* Reston, Va.: Music Educators National Conference, 1994.

Needleman, Jacob. *The Heart of Philosophy.* New York: Alfred A. Knopf, 1982.

Nochlin, Linda. *Women, Art, and Power and Other Essays.* New York: Harper and Row, 1988.

*Papers from the Dearborn Conference on Music in General Studies.* Boulder, Colo.: College Music Society; and Reston, Va.: National Association of Schools of Music, 1984.

Pendle, Karin, ed. *Women and Music: A History.* Bloomington: Indiana University Press, 1991.

Perkins, David. *Smart Schools: Better Thinking and Learning for Every Child.* New York: Free Press, 1992.

Petrie, Hugh. "Do You See What I See? The Epistemology of Interdisciplinary Inquiry." *Journal of Aesthetic Education* 10 (1976): 29–43.

Pimentel, Ken, and Kevin Teixeira. *Virtual Reality: Through the New Looking Glass.* New York: Intel Windcrest/McGraw Hill, 1993.

Plummeridge, Charles. *Music Education in Theory and Practice.* London: Falmer Press, 1991.

Portnoy, Julius. *The Philosopher and Music: A Historical Outline.* New York: Humanities Press, 1954.

Postman, Neil. *The End of Education: Redefining the Value of School.* New York: Random House, 1995.

*Priorities for Arts Education Research.* Washington, D.C.: Goals 2000 Arts Education Partnership, 1996.

Rahn, John. "Aspects of Musical Explanation." *Perspectives of New Music* 17 (1979): 204–24.

———. *Basic Atonal Theory.* New York and London: Longman, 1980.

———. "New Research Paradigms." *Music Theory Spectrum* 11 (1989): 84–94.

———. "Notes on Methodology in Music Theory." *Journal of Music Theory* 33 (1989): 143–54.

Rameau, Jean Phillipe. *Treatise on Harmony.* Ed. and trans. Phillip Gossett. 1722; New York: Dover, 1971.

Regelski, Thomas. *Teaching General Music: Action Learning for Middle and Secondary Schools.* New York: Schirmer Books, 1981.

Reimer, Bennett. *A Philosophy of Music Education.* Englewood Cliffs, N.J.: Prentice-Hall, 1970, 1989.

———, and Jeffrey E. Wright, eds. *On the Nature of Musical Experience.* Niwot, Colo.: University Press of Colorado, 1992.

Reynolds, Joshua. *Discourses on Art.* Ed. Robert R. Wark. New Haven, Conn.: Yale University Press, 1975.

Robertson, Carol. "Singing Social Boundaries into Place: The Dynamics of Gender and Performance in Two Cultures." *Sonus* 10, no. 1 (Fall 1989): 59–71; and 10, no. 2 (Spring 1990): 1–13.

Rogers, E. Turner, and Richard E. Brogdon. "A Survey of the NAEA Curriculum Standards in Art Teacher Preparation Programs." *Studies in Art Education: A Journal of Issues and Research in Art Education* 31 (1989): 168–73.

Savile, Anthony. *The Test of Time: An Essay in Philosophical Aesthetics.* Oxford: Clarendon Press, 1982.

Schenker, Heinrich. *Free Composition*. Trans. Ernst Oster. New York: Longman, 1979.

Schiller, Friedrich. *Letters on the Aesthetic Education of Man*. Trans. Reginald Snell. London: Routledge, 1954.

Schopenhauer, Arthur. *The World as Will and Representation*. Trans. by E. F. J. Payne. New York: Dover, 1969.

Schuller, Gunther. *Musings: The Musical Worlds of Gunther Schuller*. New York: Oxford University Press, 1986.

Serafine, Mary Louise, and Wayne Slawson. "Interdisciplinary Directions in Music Theory." *Music Theory Spectrum* 11 (1989): 74–83.

Shetler, Donald J., ed. *The Future of Musical Education in America: Proceedings of the July 1983 Conference*. Rochester, N.Y.: Eastman School of Music Press, 1984.

Shusterman, Richard. *Pragmatist Aesthetics: Living Beauty, Rethinking Art*. Oxford: Blackwell, 1992.

Silvers, Anita. "Aesthetics for Art's Sake, Not for Philosophy's!" *Journal of Aesthetics and Art Criticism* 51 (1993): 141–50.

———. "The Story of Art Is the Test of Time." *Journal of Aesthetics and Art Criticism* 48 (1990): 211–24.

Small, Christopher. *Music and Society: The Politics of Composition, Performance and Reception*. Cambridge: Cambridge University Press, 1987.

Solie, Ruth A., ed. *Musicology and Difference: Gender and Sexuality in Music Scholarship*. Berkeley and Los Angeles: University of California Press, 1993.

Subotnick, Rose Rosengaard. *Developing Variations: Style and Ideology in Western Music*. Minneapolis: University of Minnesota Press, 1991.

Swanwick, Keith. *Musical Knowledge: Intuition, Analysis, and Music Education*. London: Routledge, 1994.

Tait, Malcolm, and Paul Haack. *Principles and Processes of Music Education: New Perspectives*. New York: Columbia University Teachers College Press, 1984.

Treitler, Leo. *Music and the Historical Imagination*. Cambridge, Mass.: Harvard University Press, 1989.

Van Doren, Charles. *A History of Knowledge: Past, Present, and Future*. New York: Ballantine Books, 1991.

Van den Toorn, Pieter. *Music, Politics, and the Academy*. Berkeley and Los Angeles: University of California Press, 1995.

———. "What Price Analysis." *Journal of Music Theory* 33 (1989): 160–69.

*The Vision for Arts Education in the Twenty-first Century*. Reston, Va.: Music Educators National Conference, 1994.

Volk, Terese M. *Music, Education, and Multiculturalism: Foundations and Principles*. New York: Oxford University Press, 1998.

Wager, Willis, and Earl J. McGrath. *Liberal Education and Music*. New York: Columbia University Teachers College Bureau of Publications, 1962.

Wendrich, Kenneth A., ed. *Essays on Music in American Education and Society*. Washington, D.C.: University Press of America, 1982.

White, Hayden. *The Content of the Form: Narrative Discourse and Historical Representation*. Baltimore, Md.: Johns Hopkins University Press, 1987.

Wilshire, Bruce. *The Moral Collapse of the University*. Albany: State University of New York Press, 1990.

Wollheim, Richard. *Painting as an Art*. Princeton, N.J.: Princeton University Press, 1988.

# Index

**About the Author**

CLAIRE DETELS is Professor of Music, University of Arkansas, Fayetteville.

ISBN 0-89789-666-1